ANNE GEDDES

AN AUTOBIOGRAPHY

A Labor
of Love

**Andrews McMeel
Publishing, LLC**

Kansas City

for my sisters
Susan, Kaye, Sally, and Helen

Contents

Stephanie, Port Douglas, 1999

Twenty-five years ago, when I first picked up a camera, I could never have dreamt that my life would change so completely. In my heart, there was no other option than to photograph babies. And yet I don't remember it being a conscious decision at all. I was just so naturally drawn to them and fell in love with them, even before being fortunate enough to have two beautiful babies of my own. Certainly I had no notion then of the path my photographic life would take, and once it started, there was no turning back. Had anyone suggested at the time that I would be writing my life story now, I would never have believed it were possible.

prologue

The aim of this book is to give you not just an insight into my work, my photographic images, but to have you feel as if you know more about the person behind those images and to share with you some of the experiences of my life. Photographing babies exclusively, although extremely rewarding, has in many ways also been challenging, and at this stage in my life and career, I feel the need to share with you the motivation for my life's work.

I suppose we all have preconceived notions about people who find themselves in the public eye. My experience has been that often when I meet people they say, "I didn't think you would look like you do" or "I imagined someone totally different." I have often wondered what they really expected.

Babies are for me an incredibly emotive subject matter and naturally my work is intensely personal, but I feel that it also expresses passionate and deeply held universal human values. Probably, as a result of this, everyone comes to my images from their own sense of judgment and perspective.

From a photographer's viewpoint, actually writing a book has been an interesting and yet somewhat daunting experience. Naturally, I am more accustomed to speaking through my imagery, which is where I feel most comfortable. What has been surprising is that the writing process has taught me a lot about myself as I have revisited many of the different stages of my life.

Working on *A Labor of Love* has also allowed me much pleasurable time to reflect on what has been an extraordinary journey through my twenty-five years of photography, a journey that I am very proud and honored to have taken and shared with many talented and dedicated people. I'm so fortunate to have had the opportunity to follow my own dreams and passions, and my true hope is that, through the process, I have created a body of images that will have a profoundly positive effect far into the future.

Reviewing over two thousand of my images was both nostalgic and emotional, as I was able to clearly see myself growing in both skill and confidence as a photographer, and my work maturing and changing as a result. It also gave me a poignant sense of time passing. Some of the babies I photographed during my formative portraiture years are now in their twenties and are parents themselves. It was far too easy to linger over some of the images, as vivid memories flooded back, memories I thought had drifted into the back of my mind forever.

As I sifted through those years and on to the creation of my very first calendar images in the early 1990s, I discovered that I remembered, with surprising clarity, names, faces, and stories about each shoot, as if it had all happened yesterday. At times, I couldn't stop laughing, as I recalled humorous little moments with babies; and there were, occasionally, tears over emotional events that had taken place. Indeed, babies reach out to people on all levels, emotional, physical, and spiritual. Because of this, my photographic life has not only been rich and rewarding, but I have had the great privilege of having close personal contact with so many delightful babies. Babies, particularly newborns, have such a life-giving, affirming and magical essence, and my working life has been hugely enriched by their continuous presence.

previous page: me holding baby Lucas, 2 weeks old. Lucas is the newborn son of one of my team members. The rocking chair we're both relaxing in has been used in my studio for many years, rocking literally hundreds of newborns, and occasionally me, to sleep.

The images I have chosen for inclusion in *A Labor of Love* are not only some of my personal favorites, but I also feel that they are a fairly accurate representation of my photographic journey over the past twenty-five years. The selection process was definitely not an easy task because there are many images that I wasn't able to include purely because of space restrictions.

Some of these images will be instantly recognizable; others have never been published before. My hope is that *A Labor of Love* will give you an understanding of the love and, sometimes, gentle humor behind my work; to bring you an intimate look "behind the scenes" and give you a sense of what is involved in the creation of my imagery, from the planning stage through to the completed photograph.

Most importantly, I hope you will feel as if you know more about the way I think and feel. Media interviews often have a time span of three to four minutes (at most), and because I communicate more naturally via imagery, the interview process often leaves me feeling not just inadequate, but frustrated at not being able to say more. Therefore, in the past, it has often been difficult to adequately describe why I do what I do with such passion and commitment, or even to answer in detail many of the practical questions I am frequently asked, such as: "Where do you find the babies?" "Do you hold auditions?" "How do you get the babies to sleep so well?" "How old is the youngest baby you've ever photographed?" Finally, I have the uninterrupted opportunity to do so!

Understandably, everybody seems to have a preconceived idea of what the environment is like in my studio during a photo shoot. They assume, for instance, that it must be noisy and chaotic, or perhaps not an ideal environment for young babies. In fact, people who have been there often tell me that it is a totally different experience than expected. Parents, especially, often write to me afterward to say how much they enjoyed not just having their baby photographed but being made, themselves, to feel valued and special.

Throughout *A Labor of Love* is a collection of personal images from my early childhood and many photographs of myself and my team at work in the studio. As well, photographs of family, friends, and colleagues—people who have helped me on my way and supported me through my photographic life and beyond.

This story is not just about me. Over the years I have come to realize that newborn babies are very powerful little people. The Chilean poet Pablo Neruda once said, "They can cut all the flowers, but they can't stop the spring," and this is what newborn babies represent to me . . . our eternal chance at new beginnings.

These tiny babies have carried my work to where it is today; they are the true stars of the show—as they should be. They are our future—so pure, so perfect, so innocent, and with so much promise. They should, each and every one of them, be protected, nurtured, loved, and encouraged. Photographing them, and being around them, is exactly where I want to be for the rest of my life. It's really very simple—I couldn't imagine doing anything else.

my childhood

I have very few photographs of myself as a baby, and those that I do have do not show great detail. Certainly I have no images at all of myself as a newborn, which is why I often gaze at the minute detail in some of my images of babies and think how wonderful it will be for these children, as they grow into adults, to have a record of themselves when they were so brand-new and so perfect.

It has taken me almost a year to write *A Labor of Love*, a rich, rewarding, and sometimes difficult time. My words, particularly in relation to my childhood, have often felt very painful and, as is frequently the case in writing about a life, a small number of those pages took the majority of the year to complete. My reward has been that the book has brought many people together who might otherwise not have had the opportunity to do so. There is an old saying: "It's OK to look back on the past, but don't stare." I agree, to a point. Although sometimes it can be very fulfilling and healing to look back for a while and quietly reflect.

opposite page: me (approximately seven months), 1957
above left: me (approximately seven months), 1957
above right: (L–R) Kaye, me, Susan, 1957

I come from a family of five girls and was raised on a beef cattle property in North Queensland, Australia. I was the middle daughter, with two older and two younger sisters. Even though I have spent most of my adult life living in large cities, in my heart I'll remain attached to the wide open spaces and the solitude of the country.

Perhaps my love for the beauty and peace of an isolated environment was an escape from difficulties in my childhood home. It is hard for me to paint an entirely rosy picture of my childhood, although the few actual photographs I have look like snapshots of anyone else's country upbringing. As a family we were fairly well off financially, so it wasn't that my sisters and I lacked for anything in a material sense, but an emotionally barren environment, which is virtually invisible and almost impossible to define, can have a quietly insidious effect on a child for a lifetime. Perhaps I need to go back to my parents first, because they were instrumental in forming the color and the shape of my memories.

There are no photographs from my father and mother's wedding in early 1952. Apparently the circumstances under which they married were extremely difficult. My mother's parents, and in particular her father, were devout Catholics, and in those days my mother's marriage to my father, who was Church of England, was religiously unacceptable and a social scandal. Consequently, my mother's parents and her siblings did not attend the wedding. The only guests were my father's immediate family. For the ceremony in St. James Cathedral, in Townsville, I have been told that my mother wore a beautiful white suit in heavy self-coin-spot silk and a little hat with a tiny veil.

My mother never pretended that leaving the Catholic faith was difficult for her, but her family's public rejection could not have been easy for her to forget. In this case, worse was to come, because apparently after my eldest sister, Susan, was born, one of the clergy called on my mother at home to remind her that Susan must be christened in the Catholic Church—or else she would be doomed to hellfire, and my mother with her, no doubt. After a repeat visit, my father went to speak with the priest and he called no more.

Not long after their wedding, my parents moved to the property where I was to grow up. Apparently, this move was not necessarily their own choice, but more a result of pressure from my father's own wealthy and very dominating father, who had long fancied being in the cattle business and wanted his son to run the property. My father, who in his youth was evidently very handsome and more than a little charming, had his own heart set on building a real estate business in the city. He was supposedly good at selling and would probably have done very well, but unfortunately it wasn't to be. There can't have been a more perfect recipe for two unhappy and frustrated lives.

I don't suppose it was easy for my mother, as a city girl, to adjust to life on a cattle property and, eventually, the added responsibility of raising five daughters. She initially found herself very isolated, with no next-door companionship and a limited social life. I always had the sense that she wanted something more and knew that she certainly hoped that life would be different for her own girls. As a young woman in the 1940s and 1950s she wouldn't have had many personal choices available to her and, with the natural intuition of a child, I could feel her frustration and sense of unhappiness with her role in life. Eventually, she just seemed to disappear into herself. Even though she was my mother, I never felt as if I really knew her well at all. I often wish now that I'd had the opportunity to speak honestly with her and hear her story told in her own words.

I suppose she was trying to keep the lid of social acceptability firmly on top of her frustrations and her own hopes for a different and possibly more glamorous life. She was never a country girl at heart.

opposite page: my mother in the late 1940s
above: me at age two (center) with my two older sisters, Susan and Kaye, 1959

An old photograph (overleaf), taken around the time she was married, shows her horse-riding with my father, which is unusual, because I never saw her ride a horse during my childhood. She told me once that she was very lonely for many years after she and my father first moved to the property. She said that small-town communities can be very closed and it was hard for her to break into any sort of social circle and develop her own friendships. She used to say, jokingly, that it took her ten years to be considered a local. None of this could have been easy for her, especially when she was already estranged from her own family.

My mother loved clothes and I remember her always being smartly dressed. In old photographs, there are my sisters and me, typical country kids, and there is my mother, looking impeccable. I guess she would have loved seeing us off to Sunday school each week, dressed like regular little girls for a change. Today, looking back at old photographs of her, I wonder what her thoughts were during the days when we were all at school and she was at home alone. For some reason, whenever I think about this, I remember coming home from school on the days when she had polished the wooden floor in our dining room to a brilliant shine and her proudly asking us what we thought of her efforts. It all seemed a bit pointless.

right: my parents, circa 1952
above top: (L–R) my sister Sally, me, my mother, circa 1968
above: (L–R) Susan, me, Sally, going to Sunday school, circa 1963

I remember the last time I saw her, shortly before she died. She was in her late sixties, very ill at this stage and quite frail. Now, I am tall, at five foot ten and my mother was small, around five foot two. All of her five daughters ended up dwarfing her as we grew up. As I was leaving, I wasn't quite sure what to do, but I took her in my arms and she felt so tiny and brittle. The gap between the thought and the action seemed huge, such a long way to jump, and if I hadn't instigated this gesture, I don't think she would have done it herself. The moment felt very awkward. I said to her, "I love you," which was a huge thing for me to say, the words felt very wooden, and in return she said that she loved me too. It was the first time I'd heard her say that, even though I think that in her own way, she did love us all.

afraid. I always believed he felt disappointed that he had never had a son, and on a subconscious level that was what I wanted to be for him. I was always trying to impress him, which wasn't an easy task, perhaps to attract some sort of positive reinforcement; to know I was important to him. It was hard to know where we stood with him, as his domineering behavior could be very erratic. I realize now that this was possibly out of a sense of frustration and disappointment with his own life. Perhaps he also believed that his authoritarian approach to raising children was correct and, to a certain extent, he was a product of the way he himself was raised. However, there is no excuse for this type of behavior toward children at any time.

Naturally enough, my parents had a huge impact on my early life, and as much as we all try to shake off or ignore any negative influences, much of our inner character is shaped by circumstances and attitudes we adopt as children. Today, the wisdom and understanding which comes from maturity has enabled me to accept that my less than perfect upbringing was instrumental in forming one of my most deeply held values, the responsibility of us all to protect, nurture, and love babies and children. At least by opposition, my childhood experiences provided the inspiration for my future work.

To this day, every time I say the words, "I love you," I am very conscious of them—it's almost as if I have to squeeze them out. Their importance to me is so deeply felt, the words seem to be very heavy. I am gradually getting better at this, through sheer persistence. I tell my husband and daughters that I love them all the time, and whenever we part we always reaffirm our love for each other. So in their case, I feel proud that I have managed to break the cycle, and as a mother, in this regard certainly, my past has made me a better parent.

I'm unsure whether I said those words for me, or for her. I felt more sorry for her than loving toward her.

I remember thinking as we were both standing there together, "How could such a physically small human being have had such a huge impact on our lives? And how could she have got it so wrong?"

My memory of my relationship with my father was that it was always very strained. He was often demeaning and never gave us a sense that he was proud of us for who we were. As a result, my sisters and I grew up with no real sense of our self-worth. There was often an element of tension at home. I was wary of him and, at times,

Since becoming a mother myself, I have been acutely aware of the importance of doing the best job I know how. That is, to strive to be an excellent parent, not a perfect one; perfection is an impossible standard. My feelings of success, in this regard, are judged by my children's sense of their own self-worth and, I like to think, the unwavering belief that they are very much loved.

My earliest memory is of standing next to my father and holding tightly to his leg, begging him to take me with my two older sisters to examine the level of flooding in one of our front paddocks. My head came up to his knee, so I must have been no more than two years of age.

"there is always one moment
in childhood when the door
opens and lets the future in . . ."

left: me, front row 2nd from right (in apron), as a "Tweenie,"
prior to becoming a fully fledged "Brownie," circa 1965
below: me sitting on our horse Patches, circa 1958

was a similar-sized cattle station owned by my father's brother and his family. My sisters and I were true country kids; our feet were so tough we were even undeterred by prickle patches—we would simply walk through them on our heels. In fact, for most of our primary school years, the only time we wore shoes to school was when it was compulsory—on the one day in the year the school inspector came to visit.

In a lot of ways, it was a typical country childhood: baking cakes on Saturday mornings, going to Brownies and Girl Guides on Saturday afternoons, and afterward having sixpence to spend on a little paper bag of assorted sweets at the local milk bar. I would always buy long dark liqorice sticks, raspberry-flavored false teeth, and a packet of candy cigarettes—which I pretended to smoke, languidly, in the back of the car on the long drive home, trying to be like those glamorous women I used to stare at on the covers of records that my mother owned. We would have meat pies for dinner every Saturday night while we all lay in a row on the floor in front of the television and watched *The Wonderful World of Disney* at 6:30 p.m., a highlight of our week.

From a very young age, I was always aware of some sort of calling in my life, a constant sense that the future held something more for me. I always felt very comfortable and confident about this notion, although I had no idea what form it would take. I once read, "There is always one moment in childhood when the door opens and lets the future in," and this is exactly what happened for me.

I have a distinct memory of standing in our front garden with my mother when I was around seven or eight years of age and telling her that there was something I needed to do, but I didn't quite know what it was. It was a sunny day, very hot, and she was hanging the laundry on our clothesline. I remember exactly where I was standing. At the time she must have assumed I meant some activity that was about to happen on that particular day, because she casually replied that I should run off and play, but I said, "That's not what I mean," and she looked at me strangely. As confusing as it seemed for her, it was a moment of absolute clarity for me. I've often read since then of successful people, in many and varied fields, who have experienced similar premonitions as children.

Our cattle property bordered the fringes of a vast sugarcane farming district. There were ten and a half thousand hectares (twenty-six thousand acres) in all, consisting mainly of open grassland, edged to the inland by a chain of low hills. On the other side of the hills

opposite page: swimming in the flooded dam in the wet season
(L–R) me, Sally, Kaye, circa 1969

left: Helen (2 years) in flooded creek bed, circa 1966
below left: Helen and my father, with our family dog, Jill, flooded dam, circa 1967
below: A visit from Grandma—me, Susan (standing), Sally, Kaye (seated), circa 1964
opposite page: Sally as "Cousin It" at Osborne School Fancy Dress Ball, circa 1968

Her house was in the middle of town, right on the busy main road, and she had the most beautifully manicured front lawn. To me, the grass always seemed to be a vivid green, soft underfoot and so perfect, a total contrast to our much more rustic garden at home. We would all run around madly in her front yard, rolling on the grass, excited by the thought of being in the city, with the novelty of other houses all around us, and the strange sounds of the constantly passing traffic. Living out on the property, where it was so isolated and quiet, we could hear a car approaching when it was still miles away.

Often, these Saturday nights would be spent at my grandmother's home, in Townsville, just over an hour's drive from our property. We all adored Grandma; she was very kind to us and every visit to her was eagerly anticipated. The Saturday afternoon horse-racing was a big social event, which my parents loved to attend, leaving us girls at Grandma's. Grandma and her ladies committee would have spent all of Saturday morning in her kitchen, making hundreds of sandwiches and various cakes for the Members Club at the racecourse, and when we all arrived, around midday, and piled out of the car, she would be there with fresh sandwiches and lamingtons laid out. If you aren't Australian, or don't know what a lamington is, you don't know what you're missing!

As is often the case in country childhoods, your siblings are your world and we were no exception. My sisters and I were each other's friends, confidantes, and playmates, especially in the early years. Susan and Kaye were both older than me and Sally and Helen younger. For most of our early years, we slept in a row of beds lined up on our enclosed verandah, with mosquito nets suspended from the ceiling over each bed. At night, the nets were tightly tucked into the mattress all around each bed, not just to keep out the mosquitoes, but the odd snake as well. Of course, in the tropics the summers were always very humid and hot, but it was more the winters that I recall, because in the country it was so cold—Mum would warm our pajamas in the wooden stove before we put them on.

We roamed at will in those days, spending hours down on the creek beds fishing, building dams and all manner of small imaginary structures. We had no television when I was very young. Television didn't come to Australia until 1956, the year I was born, and our own black-and-white television didn't arrive until I was six years old. I remember it sitting there, gleaming at the end of the living room. What a momentous day that was! Shortly after this, in 1963, John F. Kennedy was assassinated and I sat on our sofa, amazed that we were able to watch the coverage on television.

There was a small local primary school, about 10 kilometers (6 miles) from our home on the property, which was attended by virtually every child within a 40-kilometer (25-mile) radius. It was a typical Australian country schoolhouse, consisting of only two classrooms and two teachers to cater for everybody from Year One until Year Seven. All of my childhood friends were from sugarcane farming families. In my first year of school, when I was five, there were about fifteen children in my class—an unusually large intake and almost unheard of. Most classes were much smaller, some consisting of just one or two pupils.

My life at primary school was largely happy and I have fond memories of hotly contested games of marbles in the dirt under the shade of the huge tamarind tree in the front schoolyard and some not-so-fond memories of sitting in class in the stifling tropical heat of summer, next to young country boys who loved to slowly suffocate flies in small tins on the hot sunny window ledge. I can vouch that it can take a couple of days for a sturdy fly to finally expire.

We spent our lunch periods swinging perilously back and forth on the huge tractor tire swing hanging from a branch at the back of the school, with as many kids as possible crammed around the tire.

The social highlight of the school year was the annual fancy dress ball. One of the local fathers could play the bagpipes and, for weeks beforehand, we would practice our marches and dancing in preparation for the big night. Of course there was fierce competition among us for the best costumes. I remember one year dressing as a pineapple and winning first prize. Unfortunately, no photograph remains of this

momentous event, but here is my little sister Sally (below), around the same time, dressed as Cousin It from the television series *The Addams Family.* She won first prize. When I asked her permission to use this photograph in the book, she laughingly said OK, but that it was severely testing our relationship!

The freestanding old hall next to the school was also used each Sunday for Sunday school, which we were made to attend on a regular basis. I hated Sunday school—I found it tedious and boring and our Sunday school dresses prickly and uncomfortable, particularly in the summer. Besides, we even had to wear shoes and socks. On Sundays, after Sunday school was over, my father would often kill a few chickens for our family meals and we would watch (horrified and thrilled at the same time) their heads being chopped off and them running around headless for a few minutes. Then they would be placed in a large copper boiler to soften their feathers and we would help with the plucking. In the fridge, there was always a big bucket of milk, fresh from our cows and, as it cooled, a thick layer of cream would form on the top. We were so used to drinking this milk that the pasteurized product we would be made to drink at school made me feel ill. I guess country kids are always more in touch with the origins of the food on their table.

dry season

A lot of my childhood memories are very sensory and seem closely connected to nature and the changing of seasons. In the tropical north of Australia, especially to those who make their living from the land, there are only two seasons each year, "the wet" and "the dry." It's as simple as that. At the end of the dry season, when the clouds started to build, we could smell the rain approaching, days before it arrived. I still love the smell of rain, which to me as a child meant muddy puddles to jump in, mudpies, flooding creeks and dams, and having to be quick enough to catch worms popping up out of the ground. There would invariably be a line of buckets on our tank stand, full of tadpoles in various stages of development into toads or frogs.

The rain also often meant that the unsealed dirt road leading out of our property would become impassable and we couldn't attend school for days on end, which we girls thought was fantastic. I have vivid memories from the wet season of sitting terrified in the back of our old canvas-topped four-wheel drive, being eaten alive by mosquitoes and thrown back and forth as my father negotiated boggy and flooded roads in a sometimes abortive attempt to get us to school.

I have always loved the scent of freshly cut grass; to me it's very sweet and satisfying. Somebody tried to bottle that unique fragrance once and I thought they came close, because I felt compelled to buy some (and then tried to figure what on earth to do with it). My daughters took one sniff and looked at me oddly, but the smell of cut grass instantly takes me back to my childhood when my father would mow our back lawn and I would sit on the back step and inhale deeply.

My sisters and I have always been animal lovers and we always had pets as children. In old photos over the years the various beloved family dogs invariably make an appearance. As a child, I was also an avid horse rider and for many years had a horse called Queenie. She and I had many adventures together. Not surprisingly, I had quite a few topples from horses over the years, most notably (and

wet season

embarrassingly) when I was around ten years old and Queenie and I momentarily parted company when she pulled up suddenly, dumping me into a pile of fresh cow manure, right in front of a crowd of onlookers—very humiliating, as you can imagine.

I loved to go out mustering cattle and generally taking part in any activities around the property. I particularly liked to be out by myself horse-riding, probably because it was an opportunity not just to be alone, but to be in my own headspace and to daydream, which I think is essential in every childhood; certainly I did quite a lot of daydreaming. I also loved to read and at a very young age I discovered the Gumnut Babies, who were created in 1916 by the well-known Australian children's author and illustrator May Gibbs. Through her unique imagination, May Gibbs introduced a love of flora, fauna, and all things mysterious and magical to generations of Australian children, and I was no exception. She really helped me to open my imagination and realize that there were so many different and individual ways of seeing things. I would lie in bed at night and stare at her illustrations; I was captivated by them. Even today, I have a Gumnut Babies illustration on the noticeboard in my office, as a constant reminder to try to see through the eyes of a small child. Children have the clearest and most remarkable way of seeing and interpreting life in general—they never cease to amaze me.

I learned to drive through necessity when I was very young, as a lot of country kids do, in order to help out on the land. At around eleven or twelve years of age, I remember driving the Land Rover slowly through parched paddocks in the dry season, with my sisters standing on the back, dropping hay for the cattle.

My sisters and I, with this newfound freedom of being able to drive, loved to pack a picnic and drive out to an old hut on the property, which was attached to cattle yards about 15 kilometers (10 miles) from the house. We would enjoy our picnic on the verandah of the hut, way out in the middle of nowhere. I wonder what we all talked about? I have absolutely no recollection.

In the summer, when we were mustering, and cattle were gathered in these same yards, we would eat our packed lunches (invariably corned beef sandwiches) during the midday heat with the team who worked as stockmen, and then doze in the shade of the old veranda until it cooled down slightly and everybody went back to work. My Uncle Humphrey, of whom we were very fond, would boil a big billy of tea over a fire next to the hut, and thrill us with his method of swinging the boiling billy in a circle over his head. He claimed this was to make the tea draw better, but I think he just loved his audience of delighted little girls! Those big tin cups of strong, sweet black tea were delicious. We would spend all afternoon in the stockyards and come home at night covered head to toe in dust. We looked like chimney sweeps. My mother always pretended to be mortified when we climbed out of the back of the Land Rover with big smiles on our faces, after those long days.

Every dry season, there would be a new batch of poddy calves to care for. Poddy calves were orphans whose mothers had perished in the drought. We would have to feed them by hand and every morning and night, like clockwork, they would be all lined up at the fence outside our laundry, noisily demanding to be fed. Eventually, we acquired a machine—a new invention called a "calf-a-teria"—a huge steel milk urn with a circle of teats around the top, which made the feeding process far quicker and so much easier. It was difficult not to become attached to some of these orphans and I grew very fond of a skinny little calf, whom I named Wesley. In no time at all, Wesley morphed into a fully grown bull, far bigger than me, but he still demanded his bottle on a regular basis. At the fence each night, he would loom out of the dark and bellow for me. I'd try to avoid him, but he'd always be there, watching the laundry door . . .

For many years, we had a pink and grey galah (cockatoo) called Henry, who lived in his large birdcage by the laundry door. (As you may have guessed by now, our laundry was a bit of a social hub!) He was a real character, quite vocal and intelligent, and would squawk all of our names in an exact imitation of my mother's voice whenever she stood near his cage and called us loudly from wherever we were at the time. Often we were miles away and would come running all the way in from whatever we were doing, only to find that it wasn't Mum calling us at all, but Henry. He would regard us with a baleful eye when we looked at him accusingly.

A bowerbird who lived in our back garden was an expert thief. As is typical of bowerbirds, he was obsessed with shiny objects,

particularly blue ones. He would conduct secret raids through our open kitchen window and furtively remove stray pieces of cutlery, aluminium foil, anything he could find whenever he had the opportunity. My mother finally discovered his bower—two rows of interwoven sticks forming a display area—under a bush in the paddock nearby; of course, with all of the missing items proudly intertwined as sparkling treasures in his magnificent home.

I was quite wild and adventurous as a child, probably a little too much so, to be honest. I used to practice cracking a whip for hours on end and became quite good at it. (I wonder if I could still do it now?) In fact, I've since learned that nobody was more surprised than my mother that I actually survived my childhood at all. I broke or sprained most of my limbs during the primary school years, either falling off horses, out of trees or, in one instance, when I broke my arm, climbing up the underside of a slippery slide while upside down and facing backward. My mother once told me that at the beginning of each year she used to wonder to herself about whether I would survive the next twelve months. Today, as a mother myself, I can only breathe a sigh of relief that my own daughters did not put me through the same degree of stress when they were small.

I presume that my mother's annual sense of foreboding began when I was bitten by a snake in our front garden when I was only two years old. I have no recollection of this, but the story, as related to me by my sisters, is that the family cat had apparently carried the snake in from a nearby paddock and I thought I'd join in the fun. I was extremely lucky that the snake was non-poisonous. I still have a scar on the back of my knee from that little incident, making for a great tale in later life.

My altercation with the snake took place at a very inconvenient time, particularly for my mother (although I don't suppose there is any *convenient* time to be bitten by a snake). Once a week she would treat herself to a long, hot bath instead of the brief shower she was generally afforded, having to look after three young children at the time. On bath day it was an unwritten rule in our household that under no circumstances was she to be disturbed. Unfortunately, it was bath day when the snake and I met.

My two sisters hotly debated as to who was going to knock on the bathroom door to tell Mum. When one of them finally plucked up enough courage and knocked, she was promptly told to go away. My sister raced back to the garden only to see me sobbing on the lawn. She wisely thought a second knock was in order, but received the same response. Finally she found the courage to quietly say, "Anne's been bitten by a snake, Mum." There was a brief pause then out came my mother, bathrobe flying, water dripping; she grabbed me and drove 17 kilometers (10.5 miles) to the nearest doctor. A few hours later, I arrived back home with my leg bandaged and, in my hands, clutching a brand-new teddy bear. There were jealous stares from my sisters.

Now when I come back to spend more time in Australia, after having lived in New Zealand for many years, where snakes are non-existent, I am reminded that snakes seem to be a continuing theme throughout my childhood. I remember one day proudly taking a jam jar of wriggling (and probably quite poisonous) baby black snakes to school for "show and tell," and the night I discovered a rather large carpet snake curled up under my pillow when I reached underneath to retrieve one of my many comic books that were stored there. My father was absolutely livid when he discovered one day that we had been hiding baby king brown snakes in the hay shed.

Every now and then, a snake would become trapped in our henhouse in the middle of the night, which created huge excitement for us as children. We would be awakened by the screeching of chickens and would all run down there in the dark, in our pajamas, and climb to the top of the chicken wire, shining our torches and watching while our father located the snake, who had generally managed to slither in through the chicken wire quite easily, but had found that once a chicken had been swallowed whole, it wasn't so easy to escape. It was all so thrilling!

There was an old and very large carpet snake that used to dwell in the rafters of an old iron shed on our property. To a small child, he looked extremely threatening and he was definitely huge, but he was allowed to remain there because he kept the place clear of mice (and perhaps the odd small child?). Another snake used to live in the open drainage pipe of an old shower stall in the shed, regularly popping up his head to startle the bather.

So it's no surprise that today I am the designated "catcher and dispatcher" of any random wildlife in our household, from spiders to moths and anything else that creeps or crawls, while everybody stands by watching me with horrified looks on their faces.

Living on the fringes of a sugarcane farming district meant that once a year we experienced the huge burning off of the cane, prior to harvesting. As children, we found this time of year particularly exciting, as late in the afternoons we could see the fires burning far away on the horizon and suddenly the air would be thick with black flakes, sort of the tropical North Queensland equivalent of a snowstorm. We would run around in our pajamas, madly trying to catch the flakes, which were so dense in the air they would almost block out the sunset. I can't imagine what my mother thought about her home literally being covered in black soot, but we just loved it. It wasn't until many years later, at eighteen years of age, that I first saw real snow, but we had our local equivalent, I suppose.

Ever since I can remember, I have been drawn to music. When I was very small, I used to sit down in the back shed with a tiny old transistor radio to my ear and sing along to all the songs from the 1950s. I would spend hours lying on the floor, in front of our big gramophone, listening to LP recordings of Broadway musicals such as *South Pacific*, *Oklahoma!*, and *Showboat*. I knew all the words to the songs by heart, and as I listened, I would stare at the covers of the records, imagining myself in the middle of every scene.

the snake who swallowed a chicken (see the bump), my sisters Sally (holding snake), and Helen, circa 1968

I wish now that I could play a musical instrument, in particular the piano. However, in my early teens, I didn't take well to the discipline of piano lessons, probably because it wasn't my own idea at the time. In fact, one day, my exhausted and very frustrated piano teacher, Mrs. Croft, told my mother that I was the only pupil in all her years of teaching who had ever reduced her to tears. At that time, I was more interested in talking about boys and furtively smoking cigarettes in the laundry with her daughter, Helen, who was in my class at school.

I wish I could say that I was given a camera at a young age and never looked back, but that was hardly the case. I don't recall any avid photographers in our family. We owned one Kodak "box brownie," as most families did in those days, so I wonder now, had photography been offered to me as a subject at school, whether I would have found my calling and my passion much earlier in life. Certainly, at the time, photography as an inclusion in the school curriculum was not something that I was even aware of. But I'd always loved images of people and remember being fascinated by the concept of a single still image capturing an exact moment in time that could never be repeated. I suppose this sense of wonder has never left me.

Growing up in the 1950s and into the 1960s, we would receive subscriptions by post to each new issue of the *Encyclopedia Britannica* series and magazines such as *National Geographic* and *Life* magazine, my favorite, no doubt because it placed such a high value on the strength and quality of its photography. I would stare at the images for hours; I was completely drawn to them. But it simply never occurred to me, even remotely, that I could become a photographer myself. I had no idea then that one day I would have my own work published in *Life*. However, the seed for my future had been sown.

During my high school years, I excelled at any subjects connected with art or music—and sporting activities were second nature to me. But, both academically and personally, I generally felt quite lost, confused, and unmotivated. I recall painting backdrops for the annual school play and having a vague ambition to be a signwriter. Of course, this was back in the days when outdoor illustrations and signs were largely original and painted by hand. Regardless, I felt very out of step and uninspired with the education system as it was; nothing seemed to appeal to me, and consequently I had no interest whatsoever in going on to university or college. I couldn't see that there was anything I wanted to study.

When I was fourteen years old, my parents sent me to a Church of England girls' boarding school in Townsville, North Queensland for a year, an experience that I found to be very isolating and traumatic. For somebody who was a relative loner, that year spent crowded into a dormitory with so many other girls, and the strict environment of having to attend church, three times a week, was a catalyst for my wanting to escape schooling in general as soon as I possibly could. I had never felt so withdrawn and miserable. I was anxious to escape and get on with my life.

As a child, I'd always presumed that my entire life would be spent on the land, in some form or another, which is why I'm sometimes surprised, and more than a little puzzled, at where I find myself today. I remember those moments of solitude, riding out in the bush completely alone; it was the silence, I absolutely loved it. I felt out of place when I was first forced to live in a town. How on earth did I end up being married to a city boy who is afraid of being outside in the dark at night in case he's attacked by a moth?

Life invariably does not unfold the way we would expect. Certainly today, as I recall a lot of these memories, I am surprised and relieved that there are so many happy ones, as a balance to those moments of tension and distress. I have chosen not to dwell too much on the painful incidents, as many others have suffered far more than I and, in general, I consider my life to have been very fortunate.

above: (L–R) Kaye, me, Sally, circa 1966

starting a new life

At sixteen, I left school, and spent a year at a technical college in Townsville, learning office skills. I really just assumed that my working future would be in an office somewhere, though I'm not sure why I was thinking this way. Perhaps it was because this is what a lot of my friends were doing. There appeared to be no other choices for me and, at that stage in my life, not having any real parental direction, I took the path of least resistance. I had a vague and very brief notion that I would be a court reporter, back in the days when court reporters recorded everything in shorthand, a skill in which I became quite accomplished. For practice, I used to take down the evening news bulletin in shorthand and transcribe it.

I drifted for a while, occupying myself in local office jobs, until finally, when I was nearly eighteen years old, I answered an advertisement in my local paper. A chain of tourist hotels in New Zealand was looking for young Australian girls to work all over the country, on a twelve-month contract. I was not entirely honest about my age—the minimum age to apply was eighteen. But I was young and impatient, eager to savor life's experiences and discover what it was in life that I was continually searching for. A working holiday in New Zealand seemed the perfect solution—what I needed was an adventure.

my daughters, Stephanie (9 years) and Kelly (7 years), Auckland, 1993

I can vividly remember the morning I caught my flight out of Townsville to begin my new and exciting life in New Zealand. I was absolutely terrified at the prospect of leaving everything that was familiar to me and beginning a journey into the unknown. In fact, I cried for most of the ninety-minute flight south to Brisbane, in southern Queensland, which was the meeting point for everybody to embark on their flight to New Zealand. I was almost eighteen years old and this was to be my first trip overseas.

It was very exciting to be finally free and to feel as if, at last, I was in control of my own life. I made many new friends and reveled in my newfound sense of independence. We traveled the length and breadth of the country, hitchhiking a lot of the time (in those days hitchhiking was relatively safe) and life seemed to be one big party. I never really thought much about the future. I worked as a waitress, housemaid, dishwasher—you name it. And it was at this point, I also began taking literally hundreds of photographs. At first, I viewed my camera purely as a tool for recording my day-to-day adventures, but I very quickly became captivated with photography in general. The beautiful New Zealand landscapes were inspirational, and gave me my first experience of observing and appreciating the different qualities of natural light. In particular, I found that I enjoyed photographing the people around me, and my love for photography slowly began to develop. I suppose that had there already been a photographer or visual artist in the family, I may have realized photography could be an option as a career, but I don't think I had ever met another photographer at this stage.

In those days, the only way to have your exposed film developed was to post it off to Australia and then wait (for about two weeks) for it to be sent back to New Zealand. There was always great anticipation for my processed film to return and most of my limited financial resources went into buying and processing film.

I met my first husband, Lance, during that time in New Zealand. Like me, he was Australian, and also on a working holiday. We married in Brisbane, Australia, when I was twenty-one years of age. I was relatively happy, but always seemed to have a nagging feeling in the back of my mind that I was just drifting. I also remember thinking at the time that I was almost "over the hill," which is possibly why I married so young. Certainly, I was too young and emotionally immature to make such a huge commitment and, unfortunately, the marriage didn't last.

I worked for a time as a secretary in the office of a large shopping center in Brisbane, Queensland. The center was in the early stages of construction and retail stores were in the process of being leased. This exposed me to the "ins and outs" of the retail environment, and shortly afterward I ventured into a lease of my own: a small clothing store within the center. In hindsight, I was far too young to take on such a huge responsibility and, to be perfectly honest, I really saw owning a clothing store as a means to having more access to fabulous clothes. Of course nobody could have persuaded me otherwise and I would never have admitted it at the time. I called my store "Daddy Long Legs" for no logical reason that I can recall, and even today my daughters think it's hilarious. Of course a business such as this, based on the self-involved premise that it was, is bound to fail, and I (and my bank manager) soon realized that the retail life wasn't for me. Consequently, I sold the store and for the following six months spent every Sunday morning at the local markets, trying to offload my excess stock.

Shortly after the sale of the store, I noticed an advertisement for a secretarial position at a local television station and applied, thinking it would be an interesting and exciting industry in which to work, and that this would be my foot in the door, so to speak. I was twenty-two years old.

Looking back now on what ultimately proved to be a very tumultuous period, it is very clear that I had come to a "fork in the road" in my life. For this is where I met my soon-to-be second husband, Kel, who interviewed me for the position and hired me on the spot. Of course, at the time, we both had no idea as to how much our lives were about to change. We were eventually to fall in love—the quintessential office romance. Kel was then the programming director and had been working in the television industry for over fifteen years. He had begun his career in television at seventeen (his first job was painting the studio floor) and had worked his way up through the ranks. He

was, and still is, a larger-than-life character, and we got on well from the start. I know it's a cliché, but we really found in each other a soul mate. He's a true romantic and, at the time, presented me with a bound book of love poems that he had composed himself, culminating in the literary masterpiece "Love Is Like Elastic." Shakespeare was certainly under no threat. I have never let our girls near this book (indeed it has been safely hidden, though I know they occasionally search for it) for fear they will mercilessly mock their father for the rest of his days! Well, they do anyway, so I figure there is no sense in making things even more difficult for him . . .

Of course, while it's easy to be amused about the poetry book now, that period was a very fraught and difficult time. Unfortunately, at the time we met and gradually fell in love, we were both married to others, and Kel also had two young daughters, Trena and Renée. For us to be together, in this period of our lives, would prove to be very painful for all concerned. Only somebody who has been through these most difficult of circumstances can truly understand what I mean by this, as so many lives were affected on so many levels. Looking back, over twenty-five years later, I am so pleased that we were all able to reconcile, although it was a very gradual and poignant process.

There were many emotional struggles as we began our new lives together, not to mention the obvious financial difficulties, as Kel had a family to support as well. At one stage, we found ourselves living in a small unfurnished house without even a refrigerator. After work each day we would buy bags of ice to see us through the next twenty-four hours. An old wooden door we had found in the backyard was turned into our dining table, propped up on some bricks, with the doorknob facing downward—but what great dinner parties we had! Our daughters are very fond of this story and insisted that I mention it in this book. When we were finally able to afford a small pine dining table, I thought we were in heaven, and I still use that table in my studio to this day.

Even though my new job in television didn't directly involve me in photography, I was moving into an area where the visual medium was at the forefront, and I thrived in that concentrated, creative environment. There was a small photo lab on the premises, and I distinctly recall loving the smell of the chemicals from the darkroom as I walked by, and being intrigued by the whole process. Apart from those fleeting moments, I thought nothing much of it, except that I was gradually starting to accumulate a collection of photography books, and while most of my friends were reading fiction, I was immersed in beginner's guides to processing and printing, with the dream of someday having a small darkroom of my own, as a hobby at home.

In 1981, through my experience and contacts gained in television, I was offered a position in marketing and publicity for a large chain of department stores in Queensland. I thought this would be a great move, career-wise, as I was really interested in the area of public relations and promotions. I suppose I arrived at where I am today in a very indirect way, but, in one way or another, all of my experiences along the way have contributed to my success now.

When Kel was offered a position in Hong Kong in 1982, as president of programming for ATV, we both decided to make the move in order to make a fresh start. Since the two of us had been together, Kel had been particularly devastated at being estranged from his two daughters, a situation that he was constantly trying to remedy but to no avail at that time. On a positive side, but definitely secondary to our reasons for moving, the new position in Hong Kong would be a great career move for him. We were married in Hong Kong in 1983. The move to Hong Kong also meant that I would have to relinquish my marketing and publicity position, a job that I had grown to love.

I was uncertain about my career direction once we had settled, not just in a new city, but in an entirely different culture. Over the next few years, Kel's career in television would invariably lead to numerous moves for us, to different countries and different cities, and during this period, I always assumed I would be the one to play a supporting role to Kel in our partnership.

Finding myself in Hong Kong and having to re-evaluate my own career options, I decided to take the plunge and endeavor to establish a small portraiture business, photographing neighbors' and friends' children, on location, in either their homes, gardens, or local parks. Kel donated his old and very basic Pentax K1000 to the cause.

I suppose life is about taking chances but, in hindsight, this was a pretty courageous move, as I had absolutely no experience whatsoever. But there were young families living all around us, and portraiture seemed the obvious choice. Before I began to advertise, I enrolled in a short night course in photography, which at least gave me some confidence in knowing how to load my film and how to use the basic camera settings, but apart from that, I was learning on the job. My heartfelt thanks go out to those very first clients, who probably had no idea of my nervousness and inexperience, because they enabled me to slowly build my confidence and create a basic portfolio. For me it was a great way to begin a photography career, as generally parents are very forgiving. Let's face it, they already love their children and think them incredibly beautiful. Unless your images are completely out of focus, you can pretty much guarantee you're on a winner from the start.

I needed a work permit in order to continue building my business in Hong Kong, and at first it proved nearly impossible to obtain one. The authorities didn't seem to understand my concept of wanting to create a business by photographing babies. In fact, one perplexed government official informed me that everybody had a camera in Hong Kong, so he did not understand what was so special about what I wanted to do.

Undeterred, I forged on and prepared a handwritten notice, which I attached to the community noticeboard at my local supermarket. Slowly, calls came in. I was terribly inexperienced and literally terrified before each job, which is not necessarily an unhealthy thing! As encouragement, Kel bought me a professional-looking photographic case in which to carry my very limited equipment . . . the old Pentax and one lens. As long as nobody caught a glimpse of the emptiness inside my camera case (or heard my rapidly beating heart, for that matter) I could at least turn up on the job and inspire confidence in my clients. These days I wonder how I had the courage or the nerve, with such a limited knowledge of photography, to start my fledgling business, but then again I tried to trust my natural eye and not let issues of equipment (or lack of) and technique overwhelm me.

Photography was fresh and new to me, I was without preconceived ideas and rules, and I was simply ready to experiment and try anything and everything. And I tried to remain true to myself and not take it all too seriously. I found that once I began to discover how passionate I was about photography, I never wanted to be anywhere else. In a strange way, I felt as if I was returning to myself.

I remembered the various forms of child portraiture I had seen over the years and always knew that there must be another way, some-thing different from the formal images of children in their best clothes, often looking terribly embarrassed and uncomfortable, or just plain bored. Since the very beginning of my career, I have always felt rather "out of step" with traditional views on portraiture. To me, the reason for having a portrait created of your child is to capture not just their image at a young age, but also their wonderful individual character. For instance, when I look at myself in an early childhood portrait (see page 12) I really can't get a sense of what I was like at all.

Initially I found "photography speak" and all of the film and equipment details very intimidating. If you are just beginning a career in photography and you are feeling this way, don't be concerned, because it is absolutely normal. I thought that people who worked in photographic stores were speaking another language; in fact, sometimes, even today, I still do.

It took quite a few years for me to develop my own style and to gain the confidence that was crucial to carry me forward. Kel, seeing how nervous I was initially, was supportive and encouraging as I stumbled through my early learning curve, making all sorts of mistakes. I never could have done it without him gently pushing me forward, and constantly praising my (at that time probably quite average) images. The word "confidence" is very important to my story, because once I became comfortable with my equipment, and began

Kel, Auckland, 1989

below: Stephanie (2 years) posing for my first Christmas card, 1986

learning from my mistakes, my confidence steadily increased. Mistakes can be a very positive thing, as long as they teach you something. As my confidence began to build, my own personal style began to emerge. It was a natural progression.

After two years in Hong Kong, during which I had built up a fairly substantial portfolio, we made the decision to return to Sydney. Right at this time, I became pregnant. I'm sure every woman remembers the moment she first discovers this news. I remember late that day, walking down to the small beach in front of our house, and sitting there by myself trying to absorb it all—everything had taken on a new perspective. It seemed impossible to believe that there was a brand-new life growing inside of me and, until a little later when I was able to hear her heartbeat, it all seemed quite unreal. Kel and I were both thrilled from the very beginning. Stephanie was born in April 1984, shortly after our return to Australia.

My own experiences as a new mother gave me firsthand understanding of how isolating it can sometimes be when you are caring for a newborn, and living removed from relatives and other family support networks. This is the reality today for a lot of new parents, in particular mothers, who generally are responsible for the primary care of a newborn. I have always been a little envious of huge and close families who all live in the same area, with their lives intertwined. If this is your reality, you are indeed very fortunate.

However, Kel and I were new to Sydney and I had to cope virtually on my own in those early days. I remember the moment we first brought Stephanie home. She was three days old and lying fast asleep in her bassinet, in the middle of our lounge room. My sister Kaye was with me. Neither of us had any experience with newborn babies. We both just stood there, looking at her sleeping, and I turned to Kaye and said, "So, what happens now?" I was never really maternal in the traditional sense of the word, and was very nervous at the thought of being totally responsible for a brand-new baby. I have never been a cake-baking, craft-making mother. Many times over the following months, I craved adult company and conversation. I had dreams that I'd left her behind in a store, for instance, or in the back of the car, like a misplaced handbag or something; that I'd simply forgotten that I had a baby! I had a mental vision of a shop assistant saying to me, with an accusing look on her face, "Excuse me, but don't you think you've forgotten something?" and I would be exposed as a negligent mother!

I remember phoning Kel at work one day, sobbing that it was midafternoon and I hadn't even been able to take a shower, and another very early morning when (in tears again) I handed newborn Stephanie to Kel and said, "Take her, I'm afraid I'll poison her by feeding her something she could be allergic to!" I can still picture Kel that morning, lying in bed with this tiny baby on his chest, and a big grin from ear to ear. But I didn't think it was so funny at the time.

So, as you can see, I was not a "natural" mother from the start, but I struggled through and learned on the job, as most mothers do. I kept looking around at other babies and thinking to myself, "See, most of them survive!"

As my career developed, these personal experiences made me acutely aware of the needs and feelings of new mothers who came to my studio. I don't think it was being a mother that specifically made me a better baby photographer, as people often assume, but it certainly made me more sensitive and intuitive in my relationships with new mothers from all walks of life.

With the move back to Australia and a new baby, I needed to put my photography aside for a year or so. During this period, I naturally began to lose some of my initial confidence in myself as a photographer and I kept delaying picking up a camera once more, making any excuse not to have to begin virtually all over again.

Right around this time, on New Year's Eve 1984, Kel, Stephanie (who was by then eight months old), and I were with a group of friends, most with young babies, who had gathered at a vantage point overlooking Sydney Harbor for the annual spectacular fireworks display. Walking home after the show was over with our babies fast asleep, we all began making the bold New Year's resolutions that everyone is prone to at that time of the year. Suddenly I heard myself say, "I'm going to be the best-known baby photographer in the world." I recall that moment so well because, strangely, it didn't seem to be me speaking at all. I had managed to startle even myself. Of course, everyone was talking at once, and I thought probably nobody was listening, but when I mentioned this recently to one of the friends who was there at the time, she too remembered the moment. It turned out to be a real catalyst for me. I just don't know how I ever thought to say something like that, but I do know that everyone needs a passion to give their life meaning. After all, a passion is one of life's great natural guides.

Just before Stephanie turned two, I resumed my photography again, although in a very limited way. We were living in a tiny semi-detached house in Sydney, with three very small bedrooms. I set up a small amateur portable studio light in our spare bedroom, with a view to creating personalized Christmas cards for clients to send to friends and family. Our local suburban newspaper was generous enough to publish a brief story about my cards, including an image showing Stephanie posing beside a Christmas tree (top left). Stephanie and

I laugh together now whenever we look at that photograph, but I suppose back then the cards were quite innovative. Of course, these days it's very simple to create all manner of stationery and card designs on personal computers, but at that time they were rather unprecedented and unusual. Even today, Kel keeps the newspaper article about Stephanie and me in a small frame in his office, and I understand why, because it's always good to remember past struggles and continually remind ourselves to appreciate where we are today.

The cards were embossed in red with the words "Merry Christmas" (how very original!) and Kel (home from his own long days at work) and I spent many late nights together in the living room with a small, very smelly, and constantly overheating embossing machine, personally embossing each card, not necessarily with 100 percent success. Unfortunately, there was considerable waste! It seems astonishing now that within a few years, my greeting cards would be published worldwide. My small personalized greeting card business helped me to slowly regain my confidence as a fledgling photographer, and by the time Kel made another career move, this time to Melbourne in 1986, Stephanie was two and a half years old, and I was pregnant for the second time, with our younger daughter, Kelly.

I didn't find the constant moving at the time unsettling; in fact I embraced it. I'm a great believer in the fact that if your life doesn't change even slightly from time to time, you don't have a chance to brush out the cobwebs and go forward in your way of thinking. Especially as an artist, in order to stand out from the crowd, and have a point of difference, every photographer needs to have their own individual style, a sense that you can do it in your own unique way, and that can take years to develop. There is generally a moment, a pivotal point, when everything seems to fall into place and you realize that what you're doing is right for you. This happened for me soon after our arrival in Melbourne.

One morning, shortly before Kelly was born, while reading my local newspaper, I noticed a small article featuring a very simple portrait photograph taken by a Melbourne photographer who specialized in child and family portraiture. The image was a studio portrait of a young girl and I was quite taken with it. It took me a few days to pluck up the courage to call the photographer, and ask if she would like an unpaid assistant. Fortunately she said, "Yes." So, for the next year or so, I assisted her both in the studio and also at nights, in the darkroom.

Prior to this (apart from my tiny bedroom studio in Sydney when I was making my own greeting cards) I had only ever worked on location in houses or gardens, using natural light, so the studio environment was totally foreign to me. But when I walked into that photographic studio, in some sense, it was like coming home. I knew, instantly, that this was where I needed to be in order to achieve my own style, and I never looked back. The image of Stephanie (left) was taken there, and was my first ever studio portrait.

ANNE GEDDES
PHOTOGRAPHER

Naturally, from that moment on, I was keen to set up my own studio, not necessarily an inexpensive venture. We still had fairly limited financial resources at the time, so I had few options. At the back of our garden was an old, run-down, disused garage, which backed onto a small and overgrown laneway. The garage was full of the usual paraphernalia that old and deserted garages seem to contain—hundreds of spiders and their webs, and many other crawling creatures, including a family of mice.

Kel and I set to work emptying, cleaning, scrubbing, and light-proofing the windows to convert the small space into my "studio." One evening, shortly after we had finished, Kel proudly arrived home from work with a small brass plaque he'd had made for me (above). It read, "Anne Geddes—Photographer," and I placed it on the garage door. I have the plaque to this day. He'd obviously recognized that the key to my confidence was being able to refer to myself as a "professional" photographer, and for years afterward, whenever we traveled to various countries, he always insisted that I write "professional photographer" as my listed occupation, when filling out the immigration form. Kel's encouragement, enthusiasm, and total support from the very beginning has been the enduring reason for my success. I know for sure that I would never be where I am today without him being by my side. His unwavering reinforcement, especially in the beginning, was essential to my confidence as an

artist. He has always had more confidence in me than I have had in myself—in fact, he's my biggest fan by far.

In the image of the garage (above) you won't be able to see the plaque because this photograph was taken fairly recently, long after we had left Melbourne and I had become established in New Zealand. At the time, I was being honored by the New Zealand Professional Photographers Association, at a dinner in Auckland, and Kel secretly prepared a surprise slide and video presentation, covering my early years as a photographer. When he couldn't locate an actual photograph of my humble first "studio," he asked a photographer friend of ours in Melbourne if he would pay a visit to our old home and ask the new owners if he might photograph their garage. There was nobody home when he called, so he snuck through the garden gate and quickly shot this image. (So if you recognize this garage as your own, there is also a bit of history attached to it that you may not have known.) Recently I heard that a book had been published about successful businesses in the world that had their beginnings in the backyard garage—I'd like to be added to that list.

So, this is where my foray into studio work began. As I had two small children to care for, I only wanted to work part time. I bought myself a secondhand Hasselblad camera (that had certainly seen better days) from an elderly hobbyist, who had advertised in the local *Trade and Exchange* magazine, and set to work figuring out how on earth to load the film, not to mention how to master the intricacies of studio lighting. Thinking back, I'm shocked by how little I knew, but I'm also very proud that I managed to be so courageous (was it out of ignorance?). The saying "There can be no courage without fear" was certainly the case here but I kept moving forward, totally consumed by my new love for photography, and pouring all of my creative energy into learning as much as I could in as short a time as possible. My two girls became frequent models as I experimented with different lighting techniques and I found that I was able to quietly make mistakes and yet keep it in the family!

These days, remembering my early difficulties and insecurities, I am quick to counsel photographers who are starting out that there is no shame in a lack of knowledge. Never hesitate to admit how green you are, because green signifies new life and growth.

The language of photography and photographers can be quite daunting at times, especially when you are a beginner. I always tried to bear in mind that the energy in a great photograph is essentially about an emotional connection between photographer and subject— the camera merely a tool. Learn everything you need to know technically, so that operating your equipment is second nature, and then begin to photograph from your heart, because that is simply all that is required. There are many photographers who have a good eye, and many who are gifted technically, but rarely do they come together in one package. To quote artist Auguste Renoir, "The more you rely on good tools, the more boring your sculpture will be."

It wasn't long after Kelly's birth, in October 1986, that my local photographic lab announced they were conducting a portrait competition among their clients. I almost didn't enter because it simply never occurred to me that I would have a chance. To me, my work was so enjoyable and I didn't find it that difficult. So, I assumed that it also wasn't that great. I suppose this is a throwback to my childhood, when my sisters and I were never encouraged to believe in ourselves. It is very difficult, in fact almost impossible, to shake off some notions which are ingrained as children. However, I had nothing to lose. So I entered the simple photograph I had taken of Stephanie (on page 34) in her everyday dungarees and sneakers. The hardest part for me in the creation of the image was getting her to stand still on the one spot (she had a pocket full of jelly beans). I was totally surprised and thrilled when I won second prize.

It was shortly after this great confidence boost, that our family moved to Auckland, New Zealand, again to further Kel's career in television. Kel had been asked to launch TV3, a new television network. And, once more, I faced the prospect of starting my photography business all over again.

In Auckland, my plan was to work only one or two days a week, as the girls were still very young. I rented a tiny studio—450 square feet—not far from our home. The space was so small, the one canvas backdrop that I owned (it was brown!) reached almost from wall to wall. When, finally, I could afford to have a second backdrop painted (at last I could offer my clients a choice) the change-out meant that I would have to remove everything from the room, furniture included, into the corridor outside, and then move it all in again. Thankfully, I shared the building with understanding neighbors. At that stage I didn't even own a light meter, let alone know how to use one, and I was the proud owner of only one lens for my camera, which was now being put to very good use. For almost a year I never changed my lens or my lighting, and rarely changed my backdrop, for obvious reasons! I called my new studio, "Especially Kids."

At around this time, an important development occurred for us as a family, and this photograph of Trena and Stephanie always takes me back there. As I mentioned earlier, Kel's two older daughters, Trena and Renée, who were by then seventeen and fifteen years of age respectively, had been estranged from us, due to the painful circumstances of his divorce. It was not something that we had wished for, and over the ensuing years, this had been particularly distressing for Kel. When I first gave birth to Stephanie, one of my greatest wishes was that the two older girls would know her as their sister. It was a significant moment for us all when Trena came to visit us first in Melbourne, shortly before we left for New Zealand, and then again in Auckland, which is where this image of her with Stephanie was created. Stephanie was four years old, and in awe of Trena, while Trena, in return, was just getting to know her little sister. In fact we were all getting to know each other again, gingerly, as a different family unit.

Trena (18 years) with Stephanie (4 years), Auckland, 1988

top left: *Kel with Stephanie (18 months), Sydney, 1985*
right: *Kelly (2 years) and Stephanie (4 years), Auckland, 1988*
below: *Trena (17 years) with Kelly (12 months), Melbourne, 1987*
opposite page: *Kel with Renée (26 years), Brisbane, 1996*

12 MORE

I loved the image so much that I entered it in a portrait competition shortly afterward. The judges, automatically assuming that it was an image of a mother and child, were critical of the body language between the two, saying that they both looked slightly hesitant. Of course they weren't to know the circumstances, and when I look at this image today, I still see in the body language the beginnings of a new relationship between the two sisters. Sometimes the old cliché takes on real meaning—a single image is worth a thousand words.

And shortly afterward, Renée also came back into our lives. Kel, in particular, was absolutely thrilled to have his two older girls back with him. Now he spends his days happily surrounded (and unwittingly controlled) by all of his favorite girls! And he thinks he knows everything about them, but of course he's on a "need-to-know" basis, as are most fathers. All I seem to hear from the girls is "for heaven's sakes, don't tell Dad!"

But back to my photography. To me, simplicity was the key, especially in the beginning, as it allowed me to hone my skills, so the basics became second nature. I had no particular technique to speak of, just my own natural way of doing things. And it seemed to be working, because shortly after our move to Auckland, I got my big break.

The picture editor from a local magazine had heard about me from some TV3 colleagues of Kel's and asked to see my portfolio. I naturally agreed and hoped they might do a short story on my studio to help get me started in a new city. The editor fell in love with a hand-colored black-and-white portrait I'd taken in my Melbourne garage, of a little girl called Gemma, standing in a tutu, holding some flowers (OK, I know what you're thinking, but hand-coloring was almost de rigueur in the 1980s). The magazine printed Gemma, full page (above), with an accompanying promotional story.

The image of Gemma was my first ever published. When this issue of the magazine was first released, I remember going to my local corner store to buy a copy and couldn't believe that the image had been printed at that size. I was so excited I even rushed over to show the store owner—who didn't speak very good English and must have wondered what on earth I was talking about. That story launched my portrait business in Auckland, and my phone started ringing off the hook. It was very exciting, but for someone who had only wanted to work part time, it became a dilemma as well, as my business mushroomed, literally overnight.

Everyone needs a goal and a passion. This is one of Kel's favorite mantras, and the family all mock him for saying it so often, but of course, it's absolutely true. At the time, my aspiration was to be known as the most popular children's photographer in Auckland. Then, gradually, my ambition changed to embrace the whole of New Zealand, and then, of course, the rest is history. The New Year's resolution I had made four years earlier was slowly beginning to take shape.

I was already clear that I wanted to specialize only in child portraiture, and many people at the time were of the opinion that it simply wasn't possible—in a small country such as New Zealand—to specialize in one subject. Most portrait studios back then (and even today) found they had to cater to a broader audience in order to be profitable—most of them covered child portraiture, family groups, weddings, graduations, and so on. For about a minute, when I was thinking they could possibly be right about this, I tried my hand at photographing three different weddings. I personally know photographers who really enjoy covering weddings and are great at them, but the whole experience, for me, was mortifying. People probably mistakenly think that wedding photography is easy, but I can verify that this is simply not the case.

When looking through my proofs following the first wedding, I was horrified to discover that somehow I had misplaced the film of the bride and groom signing the register (perhaps because I was so incredibly nervous, I had no film in the camera at the time). At the second wedding, I managed to get my camera tangled in the bride's veil and tore a little hole in it—she never knew! The film wasn't even back from the lab following the third wedding, when the bride and

groom had separated! So you see my wedding experiences weren't at all positive, and I am more than happy to leave photographing weddings to the experts. I correctly took these experiences as a sign to avoid wedding photography altogether, as I didn't seem to bring a whole lot of luck to the proceedings, and in fact, I could have been jinxed. Give me a room full of two-year-olds, any day.

After my rather harrowing experience of photographing weddings, I was more convinced than ever that I couldn't be passionate about running a good general photography business. The saying, "Do what you love and the rest follows" is true for me and I kept thinking, "How many babies are born every day in New Zealand? Probably quite a few, so why couldn't I specialize?"

In order to achieve this goal, my philosophy was to utilize my previous background in marketing and publicity to create such a strong presence that anyone who was thinking of having their child professionally photographed would automatically think of me.

In the back of my car I carried mini exhibitions of my work to every large shopping center in Auckland, set up the displays myself, and spent many days sitting there promoting my portraiture and making bookings for sessions.

When I started to gain some confidence and could gradually increase my portrait sitting prices, I would stand in front of my mirror at home and practice telling people how much I charged. I know this may sound ridiculous, but it was my way of convincing myself of my own worth.

I joined my local professional photographic association in New Zealand and became involved in the photographic community. It was important for me, as a new photographer, to be around other professionals and to gain their respect. Their positive attitude toward my work was a huge confidence booster. I highly recommend this to new and aspiring photographers who are looking to gain valued experience, and develop their own personal style.

In 1990, I entered some of my images, for the first time, in the New Zealand Professional Photographers Annual Print Judging event, and in that year won the Portrait Section with this image (right) called "Crocodile Tears." I was surprised to find that, on the day of judging, the image became quite controversial due to the fact that it was not cropped in the traditional way; there was supposedly too much head room and the judges became deeply divided in their decision making. It was my first real experience of breaking the so-called rules. As I was largely self-taught, I hadn't had a chance to read the rule book. I still haven't, to this day.

I was thrilled to win the Portrait Section, and was told that my print would also be an automatic contender for "Champion Print," to be judged the next day. The so-called cropping scandal completely divided the panel who were judging the Champion Print and I narrowly missed winning. However, I was so excited about winning the Portrait Section that I hardly cared. As tradition dictated, each year the Champion Print was displayed on the boardroom wall of Kodak headquarters in Auckland (Kodak at the time was the main sponsor of the print judging event). When the Champion Print was announced, one of the gentlemen from Kodak came up to me and jokingly said, "Thank heavens you didn't win. How could we have a picture of a baby on the boardroom wall at Kodak?"

This is by no means an indictment of Kodak, which has been wonderful to me over the ensuing years; it was just a sign of the times. But from the very beginning, it was a struggle for me to have baby photography taken seriously as an art form. There is a misconception, also, that baby photography is easy, when in fact I believe that it's completely the opposite. People sometimes think that purely because of the subject matter, photographs of babies can't be viewed as art. Often photographers will say to me, "Oh yes, when I first started out I used to do what you're doing . . ." with the implication that they had moved on to more serious subject matters.

Of course, the age-old debate as to what constitutes art is always simmering beneath the surface among photographers. For me, a photograph is art if it does something more than record or decorate—if it causes the viewer to be awakened to an idea or visual experience they might not have otherwise had, or if it causes the viewer, in fact, to *see* his or her world afresh. In relation to my work, I can honestly say that I created some images simply out of a sense of fun, and others with a more serious purpose in mind. But more on that later.

For the rest of the 1980s and into the early 1990s, I worked hard to build my portraiture business. I quickly grew tired of the limitations of my tiny studio, and of the dramas involved in even changing a background. I found a much larger studio nearby and was finally doing well enough financially to warrant hiring my first full-time assistant. These days, of course, much has changed and I have a considerably larger team of very accomplished people. But back then, I was a "one-man band" doing everything, juggling a hundred things at once—answering the phone, making portrait bookings, running film to the lab, invoicing, organizing framing. I did it all. When I was finally able to employ a full-time assistant I thought I'd really made it as a professional photographer.

There was a tiny darkroom, about the size of a postage stamp, located at the rear of my new studio. The roof of the darkroom sloped steeply down to one side, making it impossible to stand up straight in some areas. In the summer, due to the uninsulated tin roof, my little darkroom became a sauna. I initially did some of my own black-and-white printing, as well as using a local black-and-white lab. As I became more well known and my workload increased, it became necessary for me to hire a full-time black-and-white printer. I was completely surprised when one of the best printers in New Zealand said he would be interested in working for me. This was a huge compliment, and Neil worked with me for many years. Sadly, he passed away in 1996.

Black-and-white photography has always been my first love, and the traditional black-and-white printing process is an art form in itself. The smell of those chemicals seems to get into your blood, a bit like sailors and the smell of the sea. It's a smell only a photographer could love! If I hadn't become successful as a photographer, I could quite happily have made a career out of printing in a darkroom.

It's such a pity that with digital photography becoming so popular, the black-and-white darkroom will eventually become a thing of the past. Fortunately, my two daughters, who are now keen photographers themselves, have been able to learn the art of darkroom processing and printing before it becomes rare, if not obsolete.

There is something magical about seeing an image slowly appear before your eyes in the developing tray, and I never tire of it. These days I have two full-time professional black-and-white printers who are producing my limited edition print collection. But even after all these years, I still marvel at the process.

"Crocodile Tears," Sarah 1990

my portraiture *years*

My many years of private portrait commissions were invaluable, as, by trial and error, I gradually learned how differently children react at various ages.

It is difficult, at the best of times, to connect with a child who considers you a stranger. To engage quickly and instinctively with them in order to create images that they and their families will treasure forever puts an enormous extra pressure on that connection. It requires incredible reserves of energy and focus, particularly with the very young ones. My reward was always when "portraiture parents" would say that I'd thoroughly captured their child's personality.

Yasmin *and* Dominic 1990

"babies are always more trouble than you thought— and more wonderful"

Roger Rabbit 2006

I quickly learned that photographing little children can, at times, be frustrating and exhausting—no big surprise, I'm sure. I also learned that, in return for the trouble, often the most difficult child delivers the most magic. That's handy to remember when you are trying to maneuver, bribe, cajole, or trick a small child into sitting on a chair even for just two seconds, when all they want to do is be off and running. The image of Rebecca, at fourteen months, is a good example.

I used to buy fresh flowers on the way to the studio every day, not necessarily just to enhance the portrait, but often simply because they served as another momentary distraction in my armory of tricks for holding the attention of a young child. But Rebecca didn't want to hold the tulips—when I handed them to her she promptly threw them on the floor. And she definitely didn't want to sit on the chair; there were too many other things to be done. Whoever came up with the saying "Make haste slowly" clearly wasn't a photographer of small children. Little girls her age always like to be busy. How do you get a fourteen-month-old to sit still? Show her the jelly bean, and then quickly put it down her trousers. In looking for the jelly bean, she discovered her navel and it kept her occupied for about ten seconds, plenty of time for me to achieve this image. It was then I remembered the saying "Babies are always more trouble than you thought—and more wonderful."

My theory is that, up until around five years of age, little children cannot conceptualize their image on film—nor do they care. They simply aren't interested in the result; they are totally in the moment. They also have extremely short attention spans. In order to achieve the best and most spontaneous results, I believe a portrait session involving children should never last more than twenty minutes, particularly with those under five years of age. Above all else, their time in the studio should always be lots of fun for them. Once they become bored and lose interest, well, I'm afraid, it's time to hang up the camera.

Tribute must be paid here to my old and trusted little friend Roger Rabbit (pictured above), who, for the past twenty-five years, has stoically entertained literally thousands of children, mostly successfully. His life has been checkered to say the least. He has been chewed on, dribbled upon, screamed at, hurled across the studio, and, on one unfortunate occasion, had his ear torn off and stolen (he was mugged by a two-year-old!). His once perky squeak has vanished and his eyes are very glazed, probably due to the fact that he has been washed and tumble-dried a thousand times! However, he was a real trouper through it all and adored by everyone. He now enjoys his well-earned retirement on a bookshelf in my office.

Apart from Roger, I used the small pink chair that Rebecca is momentarily perched on as an indispensable prop during all my portraiture years. I bought it for around five dollars at a second-hand store many years ago. It has been repainted numerous times—not to mention upended and thrown around during more than a few tantrums—but for me it was always a starting point when I photographed very small children. And I mean "starting point"—it is often nearly impossible to keep a young child stationary for even a brief period. We have taped and hidden treats on the underside of the seat on many occasions and I confess to much bribery over the years when I've endeavored to make it seem like a rewarding place to sit—as it eventually was for Rebecca.

Rebecca 1991

Aston, Mark, *and* Simon 1989

creating the *right* environment

In a portrait studio, it is essential to create the right environment for babies and young children, and it goes without saying that everything needs to be child-proof and child-friendly; a totally relaxed and non-intimidating space.

My studio has never been like a "normal" photographic studio; that simply wouldn't have worked for me. The environment was always very informal, with plenty of distractions for children of all ages. I had quite a comprehensive collection of "dress-up" clothing, which the little girls, particularly, adored. I didn't often use these pieces in my photography, but it helped to make the children feel happy and excited when they arrived in the studio. My daughters also loved the costume basket and, in fact, when Kelly was three years old, she took a particular shine to a long and slinky orange cocktail dress with purple lace and shoestring straps (I have no recollection of its origin—certainly it wasn't mine). She wore this dress constantly, for many weeks, occasionally accessorising with adult-sized high-heeled slingback shoes. To the horror of her then five-year-old sister, Stephanie, she even turned up in this most glamorous outfit one day at the school gate. I was instructed by Stephanie, in no uncertain terms, that this was never to happen again!

Ever since I began specializing in child portraiture, I made it a general rule to only ever photograph in the mornings. Everyone is different, but I discovered that my own energy, both physical and creative, is better in the mornings and, in general, so are small children. I used to limit myself to only two sittings per day: the first at 9:30 a.m. and the second at 11 a.m. I didn't feel that I could do more than that and give each session the full amount of energy that every client deserved.

Each morning, to get myself into the right mental zone, I would take half an hour alone in the studio while I dusted out the camera, fiddled around, and loaded my film. I suppose every photographer has their own way of finding creative focus, but that private time was essential for me—no interruptions, just thoughts and mental energy gathering for the two sittings ahead, and believe me, some of those sittings required the maximum amount of energy.

A week or so before the actual portrait sitting took place, I would schedule a consultation with the parents where we could sit and discuss plans for the shoot. At this meeting, I allowed plenty of time to talk and exchange ideas. This would also give me an opportunity to meet the children and get to know them a little before they returned for the sitting. I never wanted to fall into the easy trap of photographing to a formula and tried, even in some small way, to make each portrait sitting unique to that particular child. By meeting them beforehand, I was able to give some thought to the right approach, as after all, ideas can come from any direction and each client's taste is different.

Particularly with older children and especially teenagers, it was important for me to include them in plans for the shoot. A teenager who is "on-side" and positive about the sitting can make a huge difference to the result. Teenagers seemed to appreciate a more collaborative sitting, and I would get them involved in perhaps helping to set up, show them the camera gear, and generally get them to feel more relaxed before I started photographing. Good portrait photographers would probably make good psychologists. All children are naturally very intuitive, and they instantly know whether you are sincere or not.

Naturally, at the prior consultation, the subject of "what to wear" would also be discussed. It is very important to discuss clothing choices prior to a portrait sitting. A bad choice of clothing can completely ruin a photograph. Strong patterns and complicated and distracting clothing should be avoided at all costs—simplicity is the key. I would always stress the importance of not dressing formally in any way. I also have a particular idiosyncrasy in that I don't like watches in portraits. I think they are too distracting, and the viewer always feels compelled to see what the time was when the photograph was taken; at least that's what I always do.

The essence of a great child portrait is, for me, that the magic and the intangible individual energy of that child at that particular age is captured. And with a child, the magic or the energy is always in their eyes. By this I don't mean that they necessarily need to be smiling—in fact, some of my favorite images aren't of smiling children—but you can always tell by looking into their eyes whether the photographer has had some sort of empathy with the child, whether the child is engaged.

As parents, most of us want to look back on a portrait of our children—say, at two years of age—and get a sense of their wonderful, cheeky little characters at the time; to capture their individual nuances, such as their favorite sneakers, the jeans they wore day-after-day, the odd socks they insisted on wearing, or, in some cases, their bare feet. Apart from unreliable memory, this is all we have to remind us of what they were like. When my youngest daughter, Kelly (below), for instance, was around this age, she insisted on walking around with a piece of cotton cloth strategically placed on her head; often even one of her bibs would suffice. Heaven knows what a psychologist would make of that. Sometimes it doesn't bear thinking about too much!

Kelly (2 years), Auckland, 1988

keeping it simple

Some of the best portraits I've achieved were when the children actually dressed (or in many cases *undressed*) themselves—when they felt free and relaxed enough to *be* themselves. For instance, who would ever want to cover Lucie's adorable little tummy? My hard-and-fast rule was always to "keep it simple and real" and try to stay creatively flexible. It's unwise to be too rigid where the photography of children is concerned. Even now with my later work, where I am no longer doing portraiture, I try to keep a creatively open mind when I am in the studio. Without fail, I say to parents before we start, "Here's loosely what I am trying to achieve, now let's just see what transpires." Loose parameters are helpful in order to get the shoot under way and also to avoid total anarchy and chaos. But if you are too set with your ideas you will miss the magic. And often the magic happens suddenly, is very fleeting, and completely surprises you.

Of course, not all portrait sittings go according to any plan and the surprises are not always magical. I could probably write another book about my experiences of controlled chaos over the years. Although, as the saying goes, "What happens in the studio should stay there"—well, almost!

There were many times when I seriously wondered whether I'd be able to achieve even one photograph at a sitting. Luckily, I can't recall this ever happening, but I know that I came very close on a number of occasions. I often wished somebody would invent that elusive magic wand for controlling excitable or uncooperative children and, especially, one for getting babies to sleep.

Lucie 1990

never put all your eggs in *one* basket

One day, I did a portrait sitting for a family with three children under the age of five. They wanted a group shot of all three children together, plus individual shots of each child. I remember it as probably the most difficult shoot I've ever undertaken. The children were everywhere (except where I needed them to be). As the morning wore on, I could feel any sense of control that I might have had slowly slipping away. I couldn't even get them to sit together on a box.

It reminded me of a friend's story of their Border collie dog who was obsessed with rounding up every living creature he came across. They also had three cats, and he would spend all day trying to gather them together. He would finally get two together on the sofa, and almost seemed to be saying to them, "Just wait there and I'll be back in a second . . ."

After what seemed like a lifetime, but was actually just under two hours, I felt that I had finally achieved a few images that could have either been average or, if I was fortunate, perhaps really good. As I say quite frequently, often the most difficult children can deliver to you the most remarkable images—it's a combination of luck, the angle of the moon, good management, and quick reflexes on the part of the photographer.

After reassuring their exhausted mother that I thought I had some good images (after all, what else could I have said), I sent the film off to the lab. Around mid-afternoon I had a phone call from a most embarrassed lab technician to say they had made a mistake processing the film and it had all been ruined. Only twice in my entire career has this happened and one of them had to be with this shoot.

Needless to say, I in return had to make an embarrassed phone call to the mother to relay the news that we would unfortunately have to do the whole sitting over again. I went home that night and poured myself a big glass of wine. The second sitting went marginally better than the first, but of course I always wondered how good the lost images might have been.

As fate would have it, the second time my film was lost in the development process was also a shoot that involved a certain degree of difficulty. In 1994, over two days, I photographed forty-one six- to seven-month-old babies, each sitting in a large white paper bag. I know you're asking, Why? Well, I really love the fact that babies have very simple tastes and are happy to play with almost anything at all. When our daughters were small, they loved, as do most children, to crawl in and out of large cardboard boxes and the like; babies only ever seem to be interested in the gift wrap as opposed to the actual gift.

Every year my calendar included a four-month page, which is the first page with an image, and can be displayed anytime from September to December of the year prior, before launching into the new year. I figured that if somebody was going to look at an image for four months, I would need to try to make it as interesting as possible, and for a few years, to me that meant incorporating a large number of babies into one image. (*A Field in Provence,* on page 86, is another example of this theory.)

It was hilarious doing the paper bag shoot. I just love six-month-old babies and they all reacted so differently to sitting in the large bag. We went through quite a few bags over the two days, many of them ending up with tiny and very soggy teeth marks around the edges!

As you could imagine, it takes a lot of concentrated energy and organization to photograph forty or so babies over two days. In fact, it's hard enough simply finding that many babies of the same age at the same time, but I knew immediately I had some wonderful images, so it would all be worthwhile.

Unfortunately, on this occasion, I dispatched all of the film to the lab at once, a huge mistake on my part, because soon after came the dreaded telephone call to say that there was a fault with the temperature of their developer and my film had been ruined. It's a very sick feeling receiving one of those calls. There really wasn't a lot I could do under the circumstances except contact all of the mothers—who were very understanding—and organize the whole shoot over again. This episode lent new force to the saying "Never put all your eggs in one basket!"

sophie
and lucy

This image of six-month-old twins, Sophie and Lucy, was taken during my early years of private portraiture. Their father, Roger, was standing close by the chair just out of the image (to the right) and when he laughed suddenly at something we were saying, the twins both turned at exactly the same time to look up at him. They just looked so perfect, and what I particularly love about this image is the tiny gap between Sophie's cheek and the back of Lucy's head, pure luck in my case, but it seems to subtly emphasize the delicate beauty of their individual little round and bald heads.

a word of advice

As time went on, and I became extremely busy with my portraiture, I found that I was slowly becoming exhausted and more than a little creatively frustrated. Photographing small children can be very difficult at times, and creativity is often the last thing on your mind. Some days, it was a huge effort just persuading a child to sit on a chair in one place, and after years of interaction with many young children, particularly the notorious two-year-old age group, I felt that I needed a platform that would allow me more personal expression and creative control. (Well, not that anyone could have total creative control where babies are concerned!) I was very aware that I would need to continue with my portraiture for some time, as I simply couldn't afford not to and I was starting to feel a little trapped.

This frustration was the catalyst for my deciding that once a month I would take a day to create an image purely for myself, with no pressure from anybody else. It was to be a creative time, just for me. The image of Joshua (right) resulted from this first shoot. At the time, I remember looking at the first print I made of Joshua and feeling a huge sense of relief that I didn't have to worry what anybody else thought and that I was answerable only to myself. I really needed that outlet at the time.

Joshua's mother had initially brought him to the studio for a portrait sitting. He was such a beautiful baby and I asked if they would mind returning to the studio on another day for an idea that I wanted to try. The Plunket Society in New Zealand is a support organization set up in the early 1900s to help advise new parents on the general health and nutrition of their babies. They still, to this day, weigh newborn babies in cloth nappies (diapers) and this is where the idea for the image came from. Over the years, it's been amusing listening to people's theories as to why the hook is there. No reason at all, other than it was the most logical choice to me and it seemed the strongest and safest way to support Joshua's weight. (Incidentally, the father of one of my portraiture babies, Rebecca, pictured on page 47, was my local butcher and he loaned me the hook.)

It was a very hot day when I photographed this image. I was standing on a small, raised platform under a fan while cradling Joshua, already in position on the hook in the sling. The platform raised me slightly up off the floor to the height where he was suspended from a beam in the studio ceiling, and allowed me to gently rock him to sleep. Joshua was four months old at the time, and had I the knowledge and experience I have now, I would have chosen to achieve this shot with a much younger baby, because they are less aware of their surroundings and are easier to lull to sleep.

But I was a novice then and even though Joshua was lightly dozing, every time he felt his own body weight as I gently released him, he would wake and we'd have to start all over again. Of course, he was just fine but everyone else was becoming exhausted from trying to "will" him to sleep and my arms were also becoming very weary. Anybody who has held a sleeping baby for any length of time knows that even the tiny ones can become quite heavy. Also worrying for me was that I was directly in the "firing line" of a baby boy minus a nappy (diaper)! He finally went into a deep sleep and we all had a well earned coffee break, while he dozed away, slowly rotating . . .

A word of advice for what it's worth: I was less experienced then and now know, after twenty-five years and thousands of sleeping babies, that you cannot telepathically will babies to sleep. The secret is just to pretend that you don't care either way whether they sleep or not, then, the next minute you look down, their eyes are closed! (With due sympathy for new parents, this calm and nonchalant state of mind is difficult to achieve at 3 a.m.)

In hindsight, despite the difficulties, I'm so pleased that I used Joshua at this age. In the first few months of a baby's life, their bodies change so quickly. He has beautiful soft rolls—look at his plump little ankle—not so attractive on an adult, but just delicious on a baby.

Joshua 1990

joshua was one of my obvious choices . . .

. . . when I decided to photograph a few of the babies as they are today for inclusion in *A Labor of Love*. His baby image for me will always be symbolic of my first tentative steps toward total creative independence as a photographer.

Here's Joshua as he is today, at sixteen. When he came to the studio for this shoot, he was nursing a broken foot, which he had sustained in a game of rugby a couple of days earlier. This seemed ironic, because the last time I had seen him he was around eighteen months old and had come to the studio for a visit. He was running around in my reception area when he fell and cut his lip on the edge of our coffee table. It all happened so quickly, and of course I felt awful, but as every parent knows, little ones of this age are always very active and can move very quickly. They are brimming with the excitement and confidence of being independently mobile, yet without the common sense. We rushed him off to the doctor and he still has a small scar on his lip from that episode. So when his mother, Alex, told me that he would be coming to this latest shoot nursing a broken leg, we both nervously joked that perhaps we should wrap him up in cotton wool and keep our fingers crossed that nothing else would go wrong!

It was wonderful to meet him again after so long, and I'm sure I can still recognize some of the baby features from his earlier image, in the teenager he is today. Mind you, the sixteen-year-old Joshua may not relish my saying this! He seemed quietly proud of his earlier image, although he said that not many of his friends knew about it. Well, they will now . . .

Joshua 2006

"there are two things in life for which we are never truly prepared—twins"

Shortly after I created the image of Joshua, I photographed Rhys and Grant, seven-month-old twins who became known as my "Cabbage Kids."

There were two sets of twins in the studio on that day as, naturally, babies this age can't always be counted on as reliable performers. They have absolutely no respect for photographers and, for this reason, I always like to have more babies than I need on hand.

However, this age group is a lot of fun to work with. Some of them look as if they have rubber bands up their arms and legs and Rhys and Grant were no exception. They were sitting in two containers padded with foam. The containers were firmly fixed to a clear Perspex table, under which there was a light to illuminate the bottom of the cabbages. The cabbage leaves were built up around the outside of the containers. There were cabbages everywhere in the studio that day.

The hardest thing about this shoot, apart from the fact that the twins were constantly trying to eat the cabbages, was getting them to look at each other and not at everything that was going on around them. I had to be resourceful, so we tied a balloon to a piece of string, which my assistant lowered from the top of the shot, down between their heads. As soon as they looked at the balloon, she quickly pulled it up.

For me, part of the charm of this image is that they really have no idea they have cabbage leaves on their heads.

I mentioned earlier that there was another set of twins in the studio for this shoot. The difficulty with this is that even though I always try to photograph every baby, I am eventually forced to choose between them for a final publishable image; something I never like to do. The other two babies looked equally beautiful in the cabbages.

Rhys *and* Grant 1991

I am always concerned about disappointing parents, and I would like to say here that if you have been to my studio for a shoot over the years, and your baby did not appear in the final image, it's not that I consciously chose another baby over yours. To me all babies are equally beautiful and equally special in their own individual ways. At times, I choose the final images for reasons as minor as a hand placement, the angle of a head, or how a baby reacts to the camera at that time on the day.

In this image of the twins for instance, I chose Rhys and Grant for the simple reason that I was able to get them to look at each other! So you see, there is always an element of luck involved.

Encouraged by my success with Joshua and the cabbage twins, I continued to create other private images in this way, still at the time without any particular idea of how I would use the collection of personal images that were gradually accumulating.

Looking back, my portraiture years proved to be invaluable in that they had allowed me to perfect my craft and grow as an artist. And then both a new opportunity and a new purpose for my photography began to emerge. The new opportunity was the production of greeting cards and calendars, a conscious decision on my part, but the new purpose grew out of the fact that I was unconsciously concentrating more and more on younger babies as the subject of my work.

eight very good reasons

I distinctly remember the day I conducted my last official portraiture sitting. I closed the studio door and slowly sank to the floor with an incredible sense of relief from the pressure, as if I was taking a huge step forward into another exciting creative dimension. It had taken years to reach this point, where I felt that I could financially survive on the income from greeting cards and calendars and be able to totally switch my whole focus to creating my own images on a full-time basis.

And I know that if I ever became nostalgic for my portraiture days, I could always revisit this page. Photographing babies and small children requires endless amounts of patience, a sense of humor, and the understanding that sometimes it all comes together and sometimes it doesn't. Very often I have ended up with something totally different—even better—than what I originally planned.

I learned early on not to be too rigid; not to have a totally inflexible, preconceived idea as to how a shoot should unfold. If I had been too set in my ways, the lack of flexibility might not have allowed

things to develop into something absolutely unexpected or even more wonderful than I had hoped for. After all, some of my best portraits aren't necessarily of smiling children and, as is evidenced here, even the tantrum can become an art form! Today, when I photograph mainly newborn babies, I constantly remind myself to stay creatively flexible at all times.

Some wonderful little characters have passed through my studio over the years, and there has been great hilarity as we have reflected on some of their stories, in preparation for *A Labor of Love*. For instance, one day I came into our reception area to find a beautiful, seven-month-old baby boy sitting on the carpet looking up at me. All over his little, round, bald head—his face, his chest and arms—a budding artist had been very creative with a permanent pen! Of course he was totally unaware of this as he smiled up at me. His mother explained that she had left him and his three-year-old brother for just a second . . . needless to say, we postponed the portrait sitting until the ink had a chance to wear off!

to give up
portraiture . . .

At around the same time, another little six-month-old baby came to the studio with her mother for a portrait sitting. As is often the case with children this age, the little girl was completely bald. Her mother, who was quite flamboyant and outgoing, was wearing bright red lipstick. All over the baby's head were red lipstick kisses. Some moments are priceless. What a lucky baby!

One of the reasons I stopped doing portraiture after more than ten years is because I was finding that, as my reputation grew, and I became increasingly busy, the expectations placed on me to produce brilliant work each and every time became almost too much. In hindsight, I was putting an enormous amount of pressure on myself. I used to joke that even if I charged a million dollars for each sitting (wouldn't that be nice), if somebody brought a two-year-old to the studio who was having a bad day, they were still expecting value for money, therefore an image of a laughing and obviously happy child. Anyone with young children would know that sometimes it's just the angle of the moon that leads to their mood on the day.

greeting cards

While I was still trying to think of ways to reduce the amount of portraiture I was doing, help arrived in the form of an approach from John Sands, a greeting card company, to publish my first greeting card range. The greeting cards helped to give me independence from the constant demands of portraiture. The very first range consisted of some of my favorite images from portrait sittings over the years, with permission, of course, from the parents of the children concerned. These cards and subsequent calendars gave me a new and intense focus as I slowly worked toward the time when I could stop taking on portraiture commissions altogether and concentrate entirely on my own personal imagery.

This period quickly became creatively very challenging, because with the success of the cards and calendars, I was beginning to come under enormous pressure to create new images, especially those more specifically targeted towards the greeting card market, with seasonal subject matter such as Christmas, Thanksgiving, Easter, birthdays, and so on. I was aware that I needed to build a fairly substantial image bank of my own for future cards, and gradually this specific type of work began to take over from portraiture.

It was a lot of fun for me to begin to inject some gentle humor into some of the images and also to begin experimenting with props and costume making. However, when I look back today at some of these very early greeting card images, I can only think of how much I have learned over the ensuing years and of how much my work has changed and matured, which I guess is only natural. Most artists have the luxury of developing their style in the privacy of their studios—I have had to earn a living and mature as an artist in the public eye, which isn't always easy.

It was a real thrill for me to see the cards on sale in stores, and the reaction to them was incredibly positive. Soon after they were launched into the Australian market, for the first time, I started to experience the fact that my name was becoming well known outside of private portraiture. Initially, it felt strange to see my name printed on the cards, and to have my images in the public domain. And of course, once you are out there in the public domain, you can hear some pretty odd things said about yourself.

I don't know about you, but often when I am looking at greeting cards in a store and I come across something that I love, or is amusing, my natural inclination is to share it with the person next to me. Well, my sister-in-law, Jenny, was incognito by the greeting card stand, and she noticed a woman next to her smiling at one of my cards. The next minute she turned to Jenny and said, "Look at this baby—isn't he beautiful?" and of course Jenny agreed. Then the woman said, "You know, I heard Anne Geddes doesn't even *like* babies!" Sometimes you just can't win!

The instant success of the greeting cards in New Zealand and Australia took me by surprise—I had no idea that they would become so successful. By the following year, they were also introduced into the United States and Europe.

In hindsight, it's curious how opportunities indirectly present themselves, because right at this time the photographic company Agfa announced that they were conducting a photographic competition among professional photographers in New Zealand. There were to be four categories, landscape, portrait, commercial, and open. The prize for the winner of each category was a trip to Europe for one person, to attend Photokina, the world's largest photo and imaging trade fair, which is held every two years in Cologne, Germany. A photographer at Photokina is like the proverbial "kid in a lolly shop". I entered prints in both the portrait and open categories and, to my delight, won both, enabling Kel and me to go together. We took advantage of this prize to extend the trip to include London, which is where we made our first presentation to poster and greeting card publishers in the United Kingdom. Had it not been for this win, Kel and I would never have been able to afford the trip.

Shaun, Tait, Elizabeth, Kendall, Jonathan, *and* Christopher 1993

I don't for a minute think that this image is a work of art, but it's hard to not include it in this book. Apart from the obvious charms of the babies, it was a challenge to keep them all standing at the bathtub and not looking in my direction at the camera, or simply just wandering off! One of the mothers came up with a bright idea, and jumped into the bathtub to distract them all. Very resourceful woman!

the old saying "it takes many years to become an overnight success" for me is true . . .

It was ten years between the time I began photographing friends' babies in Hong Kong, and the publication of my first calendar.

These days, my work is published in seventy-nine countries and twenty-three different languages, and my calendars are available all over the world. In the beginning, however, it was very difficult to find a publisher.

It was the success of the greeting cards that led to thoughts of producing a yearly calendar. I felt that a calendar would provide a further vehicle for the publication of my private images and give me the necessary focus and encouragement to create more on a regular basis. It also meant I could vary the kinds of images I was making.

In my mind there was, and is, a definite difference between a greeting card image and a calendar image, in that the calendar images needed to be more timeless, have aesthetically pleasing formal qualities and a certain strength to them—in other words, qualities of art. Greeting card images, on the other hand, needed to clearly convey some sense of the message intended when the card was sent. The message could be anything from a light-hearted playfulness to heartfelt congratulations—qualities of ordinary human exchange. This means that some of my images have been created as "art" and others purely fun or expressing sentimental feelings. Some of them have, for me, far more artistic value than others, and that is exactly how I intended them to be.

The first calendar publisher we approached said, "Why would you want to produce a calendar of baby photographs? There are already too many of them out there," which was puzzling to me because I had researched this for myself and could hardly find any at all. Around that time, a London publisher we had approached also told me, "If I can give you some advice, just photographing babies is never going to work for you. You need to broaden your portfolio to include adults and animals."

In order for my first calendar to become a reality, we had to produce and publish it ourselves. Released in 1992, the first calendar was available only in New Zealand. Partly financed with the help of generous local businesses who individually sponsored a particular page, a portion of the proceeds from the sale of each calendar was donated toward raising awareness of the prevention of child abuse. Since then, we have done the same each year.

In the early 1990s, issues concerning child abuse and neglect were not discussed as openly as they are today, and initially it proved to be very difficult to find twelve companies who were willing to be directly associated with raising funds for this cause by publicly becoming sponsors of a calendar page. There seemed all sorts of negative connotations as well as many other worthwhile charities with which it was far more socially acceptable to be identified. Despite the many published memoirs uncovering abuse and the resulting media coverage, to some extent, this reticence is still the case today. The most vulnerable in our society still do not attract the financial support needed to help protect them.

As we were also unable to attract a publisher, the first calendar couldn't be distributed and made available to the wider public through regular calendar retail outlets—something that is vitally important for this type of product, particularly with its limited selling season.

A relatively small chain of camera stores in New Zealand, with around thirty outlets, came to the rescue and offered to sell the calendar in their stores. It was a great start. Unfortunately though, this is not where the average person goes to buy calendars, and although the sell-through was good for a camera store, at one stage we had so much excess stock (thousands of calendars were stacked on my studio floor) it presented quite a dilemma. I would lie awake at night panicking about what on earth we would do with them all.

At around this time, Kel was becoming increasingly jaded and frustrated with his thirty-year television career. He was then working for a television network in Sydney and commuting to New Zealand on weekends, or in turn, the girls and I would travel to Sydney to be with him. We seemed to be living our lives on airplanes, which in fact was true. It was not an ideal arrangement by any means, and we soon came to the inevitable conclusion that it was more important for us all to be together as a family, and that we would sell our home in Auckland and return to Sydney.

One weekend during this time, Kel and I were sitting up late one night in Sydney, sharing a glass of wine. He had spent a lot of that day voicing his frustrations about his job in one way or another, and finally I turned to him and said, "So, why don't you just resign and come back to manage my business?"

It was another one of those pivotal moments, because that is exactly what he did the following Monday morning, and by the next Friday he was back in New Zealand. Kel and I both have quite strong personalities, and I must admit to having a few panicky moments during that week, wondering what on earth we were getting ourselves into. No doubt Kel was feeling exactly the same way. There are so many negative stories of couples not being able to work together successfully. However, we both knew that in order for the business to continue to grow, I not only needed Kel's expertise, but that his presence would also free me substantially from the day-to-day details, and allow me to concentrate on my photography. Most importantly, I was with a partner I could absolutely trust.

Through his many years of working in television, Kel was able to bring a global perspective to the future direction of the business. Without him being alongside me in those early days, and certainly even today, there is simply no way I could have managed it all, nor could I have envisaged that he would provide me with such an incredible platform for my work. He also has been the one who has always encouraged me to reach for new heights, when as an artist I have often been riddled with self-doubt—something I suppose is the experience of anybody who is creative. We have a unique partnership in this regard.

We are often asked how we manage to work together harmoniously, and I have to say that at times it hasn't been easy; we definitely have our moments! Probably the reason for our success in this regard is that we try to have clearly delineated areas of responsibility and not infringe upon the other's area of expertise. And we endeavor, not always successfully, to not constantly talk about work in the evenings or on weekends.

Of course, when Kel first joined me in the business, we were still very small. The first and most pressing problem we had to tackle was how to clear the excess calendar stock. So we became door-to-door calendar salespeople! It must have been a big mental leap for Kel to go from programming a television network to selling calendars from the back of a car, in only a matter of a few days. Every weekend we would pile calendars into my small car. I would drive, with Kel doing the door-knocking. Often the girls would be sitting in the back seat with plenty of books and toys to entertain them. It was a good day if we sold two dozen calendars. We also came up with a plan of enlisting the help of local art college students to sell the calendars on street corners on a commission basis.

In that first year, we didn't manage to sell all the calendars, but we sold enough to enable us to give a generous donation toward the prevention of child abuse and neglect. Our continuing association with this cause had begun, if only in a small way.

My second calendar, in 1993, was available in both New Zealand and Australia and followed the same basic formula of page sponsorship by companies and organizations. In Australia, Kel's previous employer, the Ten Network, generously offered to sponsor the entire calendar. However, the problem again was that, with no publisher, we were unable to secure wide distribution. Our only form of distribution that year was through a newspaper distribution company, on a commission basis.

By this stage, we had sold our home in New Zealand as we had been planning to return to live in Australia. Without a publisher to absorb printing costs, we elected to invest all of our savings from the sale of our home into the printing of the calendar. Initially, the print run was 20,000 calendars.

We have both always believed that life is about taking chances, but here we were, after finally owning our own home (or at least a mortgage), risking everything, our life savings, on an unproven baby calendar. Baby photography is definitely not for the faint-hearted! Had the calendar not sold well, we would literally have lost everything. However, I don't recall either one of us losing a night's sleep over it, as we so totally believed in the product.

We held our breath when it first went on sale, but we needn't have worried, because the calendars sold out within three weeks, presenting us with another unique, albeit positive problem. It was only October and there was no more stock.

Based on the income from the sale of the first 20,000 calendars, we were able to finance the printing of another 20,000, which also sold out prior to the holiday season. It was this success that attracted the attention of one of the major calendar distributors in Australia at the time, who was then distributing the phenomenally successful Elle Macpherson calendar.

By this stage, my calendar was beginning to attract some media attention and I had been invited to do a few interviews—no mean feat as Elle's calendar was literally everywhere and attracting a lot of publicity. In one of these interviews I jokingly quipped, "My nudes were better than Elle's," and soon after we received a telephone call from Elle's publisher, offering to publish my calendar the following year. We were on our way. In 1994, over 200,000 calendars were sold in Australia.

At the same time, Kel was looking toward breaking into the American market. My greeting cards and posters were doing very well there, but our greeting card publisher, who also published calendars, felt unconvinced there would be a similar success with our calendars in the United States as there had been in Australia and New Zealand. In particular, the larger size of our earlier calendars

was not in line with regular twelve-by-twelve calendars that are standard in the American market. Accordingly, we elected not to release the calendar in the United States until the following year, when we were able to find a publisher who also believed in the product as it was.

This proved to be a good decision, as the 1995 calendar was eventually a huge success. For the past seventeen years, the calendar has been a bestseller all over the world—proof that baby photography, and babies themselves, should be taken seriously. I don't mind saying that I feel incredibly proud of what we have been able to achieve, both in terms of building a business and raising awareness and funds for the protection of children.

Hannah 1992

"All that is necessary
for evil to triumph is for
good men to do nothing"

Edmund Burke, eighteenth-century English political philosopher

my personal motivation

Over the exciting days of this "early calendar" period, I was gradually beginning to realize that my work had gained a momentum that wasn't just about me as a photographer; the babies were taking on an energy of their own. From the shadow of my early childhood experiences, I slowly emerged to hope that, through my images, I could make a positive difference in the world in terms of the nurture and protection of babies. I felt that if I could truly convey the exquisite, yet vulnerable, beauty of each baby, perhaps I could also help strengthen awareness of the need to protect them. My association with the prevention of child abuse and neglect, beginning with that very first calendar in 1992, continues to this day.

Apart from my own personal childhood experiences, when I first became associated with this issue, I had absolutely no idea of its terrible extent and would like to take a moment here to say that child abuse has been, and still is, a shocking crime in all societies worldwide.

Unfortunately, it's a fact. Everybody knows somebody who has been abused in some way as a child, whether they realize it or not. Little children don't have a voice, or any control over their own lives, which makes them vulnerable.

*We are **all** responsible for **all** of the children **all** of the time. Please don't think child abuse can't happen to a child you know.*

When I first became a strong public advocate for the prevention of child abuse and neglect, I felt as if, finally, some of my negative experiences as a child could be turned into a force for good. The publication of my first calendar also opened doors for discussion within my family about our early days, and gradually another very distressing story emerged which caught me completely unaware. Abuse can take many forms, and this very personal story is of sexual abuse, though it does not belong to me. But I tell it with the permission of the person concerned and her identity will remain private. However, she hopes that others may benefit from her experience. She had been sexually abused as a child, over a long period of time, by a teacher at her school, and had lived with this painful secret into adulthood. One of the saddest elements to her story was that the abuse was "allowed" to continue for so long, because she had felt, at the time, that there was nowhere to turn for help. Even her mother had been unwilling to listen to her, feeling it would somehow bring shame upon the family.

I was shocked and distressed to discover this news, and completely unprepared for the tidal wave of emotions that engulfed me. However,

out of this grew an even more fierce determination to help prevent this from happening to other children.

This is why I am dedicated to raising the level of awareness of child abuse. Every child deserves to be protected, nurtured, and loved and, unfortunately, for some children, this is simply not the case. Child abuse and neglect is very hard for most people to believe, or indeed understand, which is often the very reason why the abuse is able to continue undetected. Because the victims are *always* children, and the abuser usually someone that they know and trust, it becomes too easy for the abuse to happen and the chances of the abuser getting away with it, very high. The child victim suffers for a lifetime, and the abuser often escapes justice and continues to abuse and damage more lives—it is a terrible imbalance. We need to shift that balance to one that favors the child.

If any good came out of her story, it is that, in adulthood, she courageously chose to confront what happened to her and reported the abuse to the relevant authorities. Consequently, I was given the opportunity to gain an even better understanding of the effects of child abuse, and how we as a society are dealing with it.

In the course of her pursuit for justice and in order to provide her with much-needed loving support and assistance, I found myself thrust into the world of those dedicated professionals who deal with the devastating effects of child abuse on a daily basis—police officers, lawyers, doctors, and social workers, who impressed me with their determination and commitment. They also helped me to more deeply understand my motivation, not just for wanting to raise the level of awareness of the issues of child abuse and neglect, but to provide much-needed funding to those organizations who are desperately in need of reliable, ongoing financial assistance simply to function.

Discovering this story of such terrible suffering by somebody close to me was pivotal. I clearly understood what my life's passion and commitment would be—that moment I spoke of earlier in the book where as a child I had a clear premonition that I had some sort of calling in life. From then on, I realized that my photography would take on even more meaning, and that there was an important reason for me to not just continue with my photography of babies, but also to convey the message that they are incredibly precious and vulnerable human beings who deserve our full protection as they grow and develop. Babies are a unique gift, and should be treated as such. From my own experience I have seen the devastating effects of child abuse and know all too well that they can often last a lifetime.

sugar plum *fairies*

As I have mentioned before, I'm not ashamed to admit that bribery is always at the top of my list for entertaining babies, especially ones at this young age. They are easily distracted by food, but then aren't we all? Quilaine (top right) was featured in my 1999 calendar as the Christmas Fairy, and up until now, the others have not all made an appearance together. I was therefore delighted to revisit the film from the shoot and find the other four babies, all looking fabulous as sugar plum fairies.

When I first looked at these images again after so many years, I wondered how we ever got them to keep their headgear on. Then, on closer inspection, it was obvious that the usual form of bribery was the order of the day. All over their faces, hands, and little round tummies were bits of soggy biscuit, which we had to remove on the computer. There were even bits of biscuit between some of their toes.

The set for this image was especially constructed, and in fact the babies were photographed one at a time. The specially made seat (pictured empty, below right) was atop a steel pole, which had been bolted onto a heavy metal base.

You can see that there is a soft wide seatbelt that goes around the baby's tummy, and fastens at the back of the seat, out of sight. At the end of the shoot, I noticed some pieces of costume lying on the seat, and thought the image was quite lovely in itself, a bit like the leftovers after a party; basically, that's what it was.

potted babies . . .

If there is one enduring concept in people's minds regarding my work, it seems to be the babies sitting in flowerpots. When I was creating the first of the flowerpot images, the thought crossed my mind that not too much should be made of all this, after all it was just an idea that I had for one or two images. What an understatement. They became instantly popular and remain so to this day, even though it has been at least ten years since I have used a flowerpot in my work. At one stage, I even noticed that Britain's Prince Charles had planted his two sons in pots for a photograph that was designed to appear on one of his personal Christmas cards. The flowerpots had certainly taken on a life of their own.

In 1991, when I placed my first baby in a flowerpot as a fun idea for a portrait sitting, little did I know that the seeds for my first coffee table book, *Down in the Garden,* had been sown. These two images (right and overleaf) were taken within days of each other. The whole flowerpot idea stemmed from the fact that, at the time, I was photographing many six- to seven-month-old babies. I really love to photograph babies this age because they are beginning to sit confidently and a lot of them still have lovely little bald heads. They love to interact with people, their personalities are wonderful, and they like to be entertained with an abundance of noise and color. The thought of a little head popping out of a flowerpot sounded intriguing to me, but first I needed to determine the perfect pot size.

I asked a few mothers with babies of this age if they would like to come to the studio for a test shoot. They all thought it was a lovely idea. We bought a few different-sized pots for the experiment and Stuart, Tessa, Thomas, and Johnathon (pictured overleaf), all six months old—made flowerpot history! What I love about the image is the different reactions of the babies; and for the record, the pot second from left became my standard size.

The babies are all sitting on small soft foam pillows placed in the bottom of each pot. Eventually I built up a huge collection of these pillows, to accommodate babies of different heights (smaller babies could sit on two of the stacked pillows in order for them to be able to see over the top of the flowerpot). One day, a little boy who was accompanying his baby sister to the studio commented that they looked like "dinosaur biscuits," an interesting observation! For years afterward, that is exactly what we called them.

Chelsea (right) came in for a portrait sitting a few days later. As it was winter at the time, she was wearing a gorgeous tiny woollen cap, and when I sat her in the pot, she reminded me of one of the miniature cactus plants I had on my window ledge at home.

Later, as I became more experienced at flowerpot photography (I suppose that's what you'd call it), through all of the various flowerpot images in *Down in the Garden*, I used to tape little bells or colorful toys to the inside front of the pot to keep the babies suitably occupied.

For a while, I became completely carried away with the whole flowerpot theme, which in 1992 culminated in the pièce de résistance of flowerpot photography, "123 Pots" (page 82). Now that I am fifty years old, I know for sure that some undertakings were definitely suited to the far younger and more energetic photographer I must have been at the time!

Chelsea 1991

Thomas, Johnathon, Stuart, *and* Tessa 1991

123

pots

The organization behind the scenes to achieve this image (overleaf) was quite daunting, to say the least. The whole shoot, in fact, had been scheduled to happen six months earlier. I had calculated that ideally I would need 160 six- to seven-month-old babies in order to achieve impact in the image, and of course had to allow for the fact that perhaps up to thirty or forty babies might not want to sit in the pots on the day. I had researched many locations and finally settled on a large greenhouse at a local garden center, which not only was perfect as a setting for the image, but could also accommodate all the necessary facilities required for so many babies to be in attendance, all at the same time. An undertaking on that scale requires quite a lot of care and attention to detail.

There were rows of change tables with individual change mats for each baby, supplies of nappies (diapers) had been donated by a local company, refreshments were on hand, bathroom facilities, parking arrangements, you name it. Everybody had a name tag, and model releases of course needed to be signed; it was a bit like a polling station on voting day! I have included some behind-the-scenes images, which I hope give you more of an impression of what it was really like on the day. My recollections are that it was all a blur!

In order to find 160 babies exactly this age, I needed outside help, and a local radio station volunteered to interview me and assist with announcements. In no time at all, our phone was ringing off the hook.

The criteria for our six-month-old models included that they be confident sitters, but still unable to pull themselves up to a standing position, as I didn't want them to stand up in the pots. Of course, on the day, lots of assistants were on hand in case of this eventuality and, in fact, a few babies were quickly plucked from the pots when this happened at the start of the shoot, hence some empty pots in the final image. I used to smile when I heard my Studio Manager on the phone as she was booking babies for shoots.

"Does your baby sit confidently?" she would ask.

"How confidently do you mean?" the mother would reply.

"Well, if you sit him on the floor in the living room surrounded by pillows and leave the room for five minutes, is he looking at the ceiling when you come back?"

Eventually, we had booked all of the babies and were a few days away from the shoot when a measles epidemic struck in Auckland. Six-month-old babies are not inoculated against measles, and of course to have 160 children together at one time in a warm garden greenhouse just wasn't an option. I immediately canceled the entire shoot, which was a feat in itself, as everybody who was booked needed to be informed that it was postponed. There were a lot of disappointed mothers, as of course by the time the shoot could be rescheduled in the summer, their babies would be too old to be able to attend. I faced the prospect of having to locate and rebook another 160 babies.

In fact, I almost didn't reschedule the shoot at all mainly through lack of intestinal fortitude. For the amount of planning and work we'd already done, I was starting to have serious doubts, not just whether the concept had merit, but simply whether it was achievable. However, the thought of all those little bald heads peering out of the flowerpots finally drove me to it, and it was certainly worthwhile in the end.

From the camera angle in the image, it appears as if the pots are all really close together, but in fact there is plenty of walking space between them, to allow easy access to each flowerpot in order to safely place the babies in and out. All of the pots contained a little foam pillow (or dinosaur biscuit). A parent stood by each pot with their baby and watched while I quickly demonstrated the best way to place the baby in the pot, which was with their legs crossed as if they were already in a sitting position. All of the babies were then placed in the pots at precisely the same time, then the parents quickly and quietly walked away to one side. I specifically asked the parents to not try to attract the attention of their baby once they were in the pot, as ultimately I wanted the babies to be looking toward the camera, or at least in that general direction. It's always good to have a basic plan!

I had two cameras operating simultaneously, and I knew that I would have to shoot quickly, as I would only get one chance to achieve the image. So as you can imagine, I was a little anxious at the time. I remembered the fantastic desert scene in the movie *Lawrence of Arabia,* directed by David Lean, and wondered if he would have liked to have changed places with me in terms of crowd control . . . certainly, at the time, I wouldn't have minded swapping.

You can see that some of the babies are looking to the left of the image—this is where the parents were standing. To the right on the opposite side, one of my assistants was waving an enormous bunch of balloons to try to distract everybody, not necessarily with much success! Of course, once one baby started to cry, a few others joined in; however, the babies were probably in the flowerpots for about two minutes at the most. The general consensus is that we can count 123 babies in the final image, and that name kind of stuck. I admit, though, that it was a while before I could look at this image without having flashbacks to the sheer amount of effort it took to achieve.

When I first went to the plant nursery to check if the space was going to be suitable, I noticed a sign about some seedling plants for sale. Our version (below) was copied from the real thing.

a field in *provence*

Charlotte   Riven

Bailey   Connor

or two. Sometimes I photographed them in groups of two or three, and sometimes individually, but what people say they love about *A Field in Provence* is the reactions of the babies. Everybody seems to have their favorite baby in the crowd. I do too, but of course I would never tell.

I explained to each mother when they arrived that it wasn't at all necessary for their baby to be smiling in the image, and, in fact, lots of different reactions would make the image more charming. Babies this age can be very funny—one of the reasons I love working with them. Some are happy to sit in a group, and others don't want anybody else sitting next to them. A lot of the babies were looking at each other as if to say, "Do you know you're wearing a funny hat on your head?" and a few thought the hats were very tasty indeed. None of the babies have been repeated in the image and I'm pretty sure that every baby who came to the studio is included in the "field," even though a select few weren't too thrilled about it at the time!

When I look at this extravaganza (what else could I describe it as?) now, I marvel at the energy it took to photograph 309 six- to seven-month-old babies, all wearing various flower hats. As anybody with a baby knows, sometimes they just don't want to wear anything on their heads and there's nothing you can do about it.

A Field in Provence (overleaf, and keep turning) was photographed over several days in March 1994 and was featured in my 1995 calendar. The size of the page in the calendar probably didn't do it justice, but it was reproduced more effectively as a poster as well.

I love images of the beautiful flower fields in Europe in spring and summer and of course they were the source of inspiration for my own *Field in Provence*, although with a decided twist. Aside from the logistics of finding and booking this number of babies, and the organization beforehand, the whole experience was lots of fun for everybody involved.

The hats which represent sunflowers, poppies, lavender, and daffodils received quite a workout from the babies, who all came to the studio at their rostered times, and sat in their green pants with their hats on in front of a white background for no more than a minute

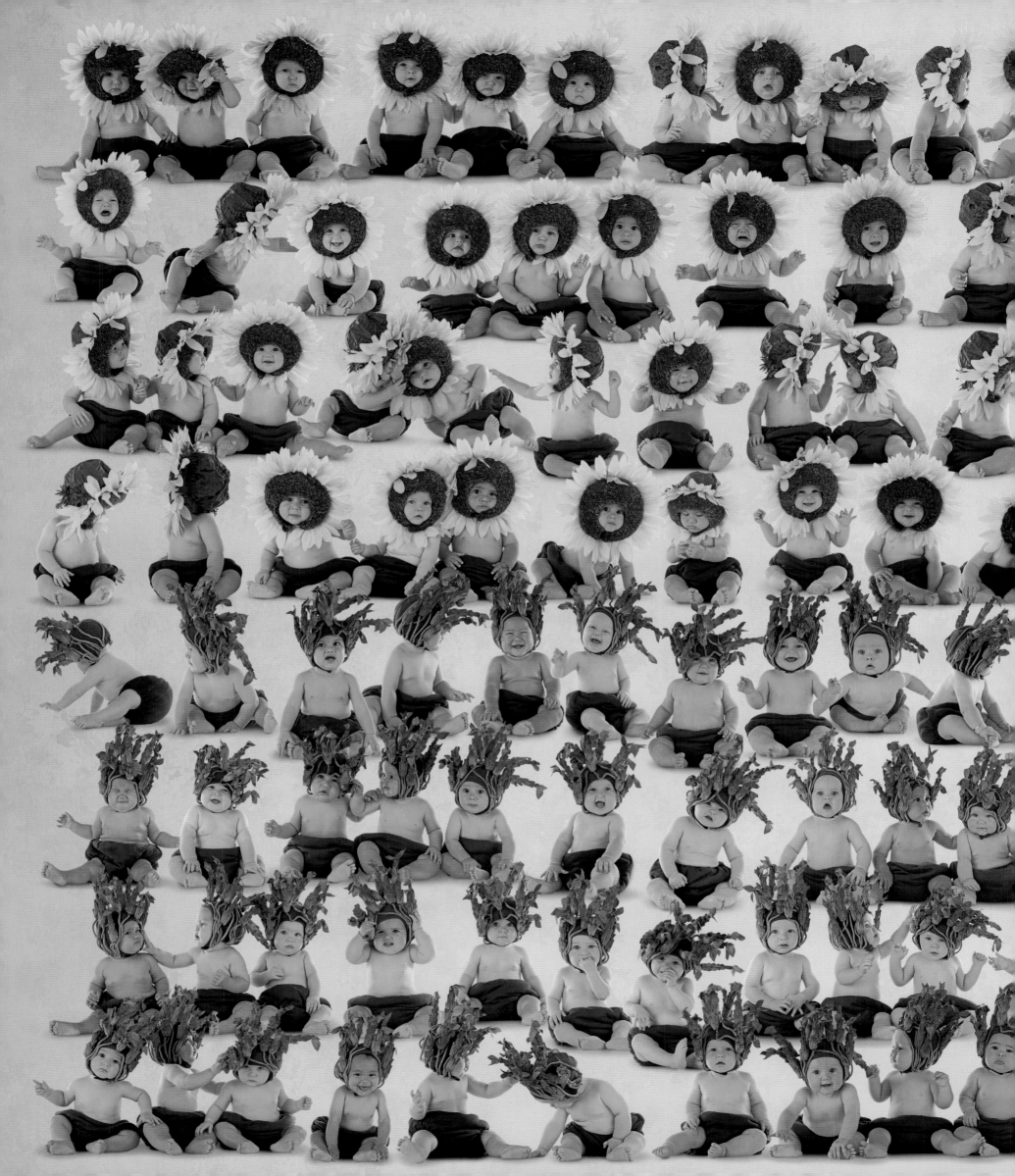

The Twelve Days of Christmas

Following the success of my early greeting cards, somebody suggested that I should think about creating my own version of the popular traditional song "The Twelve Days of Christmas."

As is often the case with me, once I start with a simple idea it can invariably become something else completely, and this series of images is a great example. For a six-month period in 1994, when I was shooting these images, we couldn't get the song out of our heads. My daughters eventually banned the song from our home because they were so tired of hearing it. Everyone was literally in a Christmas zone for that whole time; we didn't have much choice.

The Twelve Days of Christmas required much creative planning and very comprehensive prop making, which meant that Dawn, who makes my costumes and props, was in her element. When I was in the planning stages for writing *A Labor of Love,* I knew that I would like to capture in the book the essence of not just what is involved in the physical creation of my images, but the spirit and gentle humor required when working with babies in these sorts of situations. The images themselves come from my sense of fun and my feeling that not all images of babies need to be serious. *The Twelve Days of Christmas* is for those who feel the same way.

Before I started shooting, in fact right in the middle of prop preparations, I was overseas for a short time, overseeing some printing. This was in the days long before e-mail, and even private facsimile machines in hotel rooms. One morning this report, which has now become known as "The Blue Fax," and talks about prop preparations back at the studio, was delivered to my hotel room, and I remember thinking that I hoped nobody in the hotel reception had read it, otherwise they would have thought me quite strange.

(In order to save confusion, "Rack" was our nickname for my assistant at the time.)

In preparation for this book, we spent two weeks searching through literally dozens of boxes of old files trying to find "The Blue Fax," and eventually were able to locate it!

The phone is featured in "Four Calling Birds," the duck feathers were used to make the beautiful swan who featured in "Seven Swans a-Swimming," and the muslin, gold paint and hair spray were used to make the "Five Gold Rings." We did not eventually use the turbans, and in fact I can't even recall what they were for. The spotty bandanas were for the "Three French Hens." The "Eight Maids a-Milking" are sitting in the buckets.

The "Partridge in a Pear Tree," "Two Turtledoves," "Three French Hens," and "Four Calling Birds" are not computer-generated images, meaning that the babies are all in the images at the same time. From there onward, the babies were photographed individually and each image compiled on computer.

As you could imagine, it isn't easy holding the attention of four six-month-old babies (who are wearing bird outfits), and when we were shooting the "Four Calling Birds," my studio manager, Natalie, whose job it was to try to keep their attention, was extended to her full capacity. She told me later that she had a small surreal moment in the middle of that shoot, when she was running back and forth between the babies and the camera and thinking, "What on earth am I doing?" At that stage, I would have totally agreed with her. Of course, the babies were more interested in playing with the phone and looking at each other than paying attention to Natalie.

FACSIMILE

TO: Anne and Kel Geddes

FAX: 00613 650 2119

FROM: The Studio

DATE: 14th June 1994

PAGES: 2

RE: Today's happenings

Dear Anne and Kel

Great to talk to you this morning and to hear that everything went so well.

On with the more serious things, well serious to us any way.

Rachael does very good phone in cream or ivory and it works too. She also has the problem of duck saturated nostrils even when walking through Newmarket it still follows her.

Turbans are done and the gold hair spray looks great on the fabric. Don't think we will need to put the pale gold paint on now but would like to put some sort of fixer on top of the glitter so that it stays.

The muslin dyed in the duck bucket, the smell was so bad it turned yellow, but not the right yellow so we will add some orange to it tomorrow.

Milk Buckets!!! RacK has found some maids are milk'n buckets. They are tin with a brass edged to the bottom and brass handle loops to hold the handle. Understand?. Are they to be bashed and aged like the billy lids and is RacK doing them?

RacK has also done good bandanna, spotty in fact. Blue and maroon fabric. Very French Very Chic.

Ron is now called "Dusty" and will be mixing up the gold paint to match the tubes directly.

Sent Dawn the wings and she is now plucking, also spoke to David the hairdresser about dying the feathers and he is trying another method this evening and will report results tomorrow morn.

Branch didn't arrive but will be here tomorrow morning.

Well that's about as serious as we can get here.

Speak to you both tomorrow.

Happy printing.

As mentioned earlier, the images from "Five Gold Rings" onward were compiled on computer, and you can see how some of them were shot, using the individual babies . . .

The funniest and most endearing shoot of the twelve images to me would have to be the "Three French Hens" (below). The eggs in this image are very large props. The French hen costumes were made with real exotic chicken feathers. These feathers were expertly adhered to three, especially constructed, soft round foam shells, which quickly slipped around the babies and fastened with Velcro at the back. You can see the little feet of the baby on the right.

When shooting with babies of this age, it is necessary to be very quick, and have a minimum of handling and fuss. I knew I would only get one brief chance at sitting them all together and I was right, because they eventually became very busy looking at each other and trying to pluck and taste the feathers.

Knowing that I would need lots of feathers over the coming months of shooting an angel calendar, and also parts of *The Twelve Days of Christmas,* somebody had the bright idea that we could contact some chicken farmers on the North Island of New Zealand and have them send us whatever feathers we needed. They were more than happy to do so, and said that a huge bag of feathers would be dispatched the following day.

It happened to be mid-summer at the time and very hot. Unfortunately, the bag was dispatched on a Friday and, due to one mishap after another, it ended up spending the whole weekend sitting outside in the sun at a railway station mid-route to us in Auckland. By the time the bag of feathers arrived and we opened it to check the contents, the smell was unbelievable. Into the bargain, there was still flesh attached to a lot of the feathers, and a few chicken's feet had been thrown in for good measure.

I remember that I had a new assistant who was starting work that week, and her first job was to sit, for hours on end, separating the flesh from the feathers and soaking them all in a bleach solution. I'm sure the smell must have permeated the whole street, and out of desperation we found a commercial laundry who agreed to wash the feathers in one of their huge machines. As a result, the smell became permanently embedded in their machine as well, which ultimately needed to be replaced. For the record, the new assistant did not resign after or during her first assignment.

As for me, even now, I have trouble sleeping on feather pillows; I can still faintly smell those chicken feathers, more than ten years later.

Christopher, Olivia, *and* Sarah 1994

Down in the Garden

In 1996, when my first book, *Down in the Garden* was released and became a phenomenal success, nobody was more surprised than I was. While I was shooting for the book over approximately a two-year period, I had absolutely no idea that it would be so popular. In fact, the idea of me producing a "gardening" book at all was a constant source of amusement to my family and friends, who know how I truly feel about toiling in the garden.

However, I do love admiring other people's gardens, and during shooting for *Down in the Garden* I spent a lot of time imagining what else could be happening in those gardens—hence the idea for the book. It was a perfect combination, I thought—beautiful flowers, beautiful babies, and all manner of interesting goings-on down in the garden.

Fiona (pictured left) reigned supreme over all of the other characters in *Down in the Garden*, by becoming the cover girl. At the time I shot this image, her family was our next-door neighbor. Fiona's mother is Japanese and her father Malaysian, hence her delicate features. She was three weeks old at the time, and looked exquisite in her little outfit, lying on top of huge hand-painted butterfly wings. I really like the simple and yet delicate impact of this image, which is why it was chosen for the cover.

Many of my images are taken from above as Fiona's has been. In my studio, I have a large overhead balcony (pictured on page 279) with a specially constructed hole through which I can take the photograph looking downward.

Now as I look back through *Down in the Garden* it seems incredible to me that we were able to achieve so much with minimal use of computer-generated imagery, which was then in its infancy. Nearly all of the props in *Down in the Garden* are real, which, to me, gives the images legitimacy in that reality has helped to create the illusion. For instance, Sophie, my first Woodland Fairy (page 117), is actually sleeping on top of an enormous piece of real driftwood. Erin, the Toadstool Fairy (page 103), is sleeping on a huge toadstool made of foam (and various other components). Fiona Butterfly (the cover girl for *Down in the Garden*) has her own full-sized hand-painted wings and costume, as does Thomas the Monarch Butterfly (page 99). Nowadays, of course, with all of the clever technology readily available, nobody would bother to go to so much trouble, which I think is a shame.

During the production of the book, I was fortunate to meet many dedicated garden lovers, who were very generous with their time, advice, and anecdotes, not to mention the fact that they kept me constantly supplied with beautiful flowers for my imagery. They made me look like an expert on everything horticultural, even though the book does tend to sometimes make a mockery of serious gardening advice.

In journeying back through *Down in the Garden* I am reminded that I was trying to tell a kind of fairy tale through my photography. At the time, our girls were small and every night at bedtime we would read wonderful children's stories, full of fantasy characters. This is where my headspace was, creatively, as well. I hope the following images, taken out of context of that story, still give a sense of the fantastical world I wanted to create.

cactus pots

At the time I created this image, I had a collection of miniature cactus pots along the kitchen window at home. These cactus plants are always so pretty, and some of them so colorful, they were the inspiration for this image, which has proved to be very popular over the years.

Dawn, my prop maker, painted the pots and of course made the hats, which are constructed from very light foam and fastened under the babies' chins. With images such as these, I had to be very quick. The hats were on and off before the babies even realized.

all
good things
take time . . .

Monarch butterflies were everywhere in Auckland when I shot this image. Our own daughters were still quite small, and it was a wonderful nature lesson for them to see the magical transformation of a caterpillar into a butterfly. In New Zealand, where my studio is still located, everyone knows the most effective way to see this metamorphosis is to buy a couple of relatively inexpensive swan plants and place them in your garden or on your deck. Soon you'll have literally hundreds of caterpillars, who will proceed to demolish the plant, in short order, then promptly turn themselves into chrysalises and, in a matter of days, beautiful butterflies. We had little green chrysalises hanging from every outdoor piece of furniture on our verandah, and wet butterflies drying in the sun every day; hence, the inspiration for this image in *Down in the Garden.* A "real" chrysalis from my own garden is hanging underneath Thomas, the baby butterfly. Of course it's empty, as I had filmed the butterfly emerging in the studio just prior.

The chrysalis prop, into which the babies are nestled, was hand-crafted. At the back of the chrysalis is a door that opens and closes; this is how we placed the babies in and took them out. Inside is lined with soft wool wadding and foam padding. The babies were wrapped in soft blankets before being fed by their mothers and dropping off to sleep. They were then gently placed inside.

In real life, a chrysalis slowly turns darker as the butterfly develops until, eventually, it becomes almost transparent and the "unborn" butterfly is quite visible. I wanted to portray this sequence in the book. I first photographed some of the babies in the lighter green prop and then over a period of days the chrysalis was gradually repainted until it was finally very dark, as if in its last stages. It took about two weeks to shoot this whole sequence. The caption with the image in my book *Down in the Garden* says, "All good things take time . . ."

Many beautiful costumes for babies were featured in *Down in the Garden,* but the monarch butterfly suit that Thomas is wearing is one of my all-time favorites. As I recently looked through the old film from this shoot, I remembered that Thomas was actually photographed on our studio ironing board (pictured below). Not very glamorous, but it did the job well!

Thomas on his ironing board

Danielle, Elijah, Nicholas, Tara, *and* Thomas 1995

moth orchid *triplets*

Triplets Alesha, Chantelle, and Kailee were my first moth orchid babies. When this image was created in 1994, I was just beginning to experiment with combinations of babies and flowers, my two favorite subjects, and a continuing theme throughout my work ever since. I never tire of the endless combinations.

I photographed the girls when they were eight months old. They were wearing beautiful hand-painted moth orchid hats, and kept glancing upward every now and again, as they could glimpse the curly tops of the hats out of the corner of their eyes. In order to easily integrate them with the flower, which I had photographed previously, I simply photographed them one at a time sitting on a box and had them hold on to a white cardboard cut-out which exactly copied the shape of the flower petals.

Alesha, Chantelle, *and* Kailee 1994

pool party △

toadstool fairy ▷

A few weeks after I photographed the girls for the moth orchid image, I also popped them into three small green buckets. They were so funny, sitting there looking around at everyone and at each other, probably wondering what on earth was going on, not to mention what we were all smiling at. Now I wish I had not put the yellow roses on their heads—as they weren't necessary and they look too fussy—their little round heads over the top of the buckets would have made for more impact in composition, but of course we'd all love the benefit of hindsight.

I like to mention the fact that the girls are identical triplets because a number of people have commented to me that they thought I'd photographed the same baby three times over. Even their mother said sometimes she had trouble telling them apart. They were like little China dolls, all with similar expressions. Identical triplets are relatively rare, and the girls are one of two sets of identical triplets in *A Labor of Love*—the other triplets are featured on page 220.

This toadstool was constructed to be very large in order to make Erin, the fairy, look tiny. I know I could have done this image on computer, using a real toadstool and then enlarging it, but I wanted everything to be absolutely real. The top of the toadstool was made especially soft and wide so it would be comfortable for Erin to sleep on and had been gently warmed with a hot-water bottle beforehand. Her fairy wings were attached by florist's wire to the back of the toadstool, and lowered gently onto her back once she was in position and fast asleep. Erin, who was two weeks old at the time, lived next door to my prop maker.

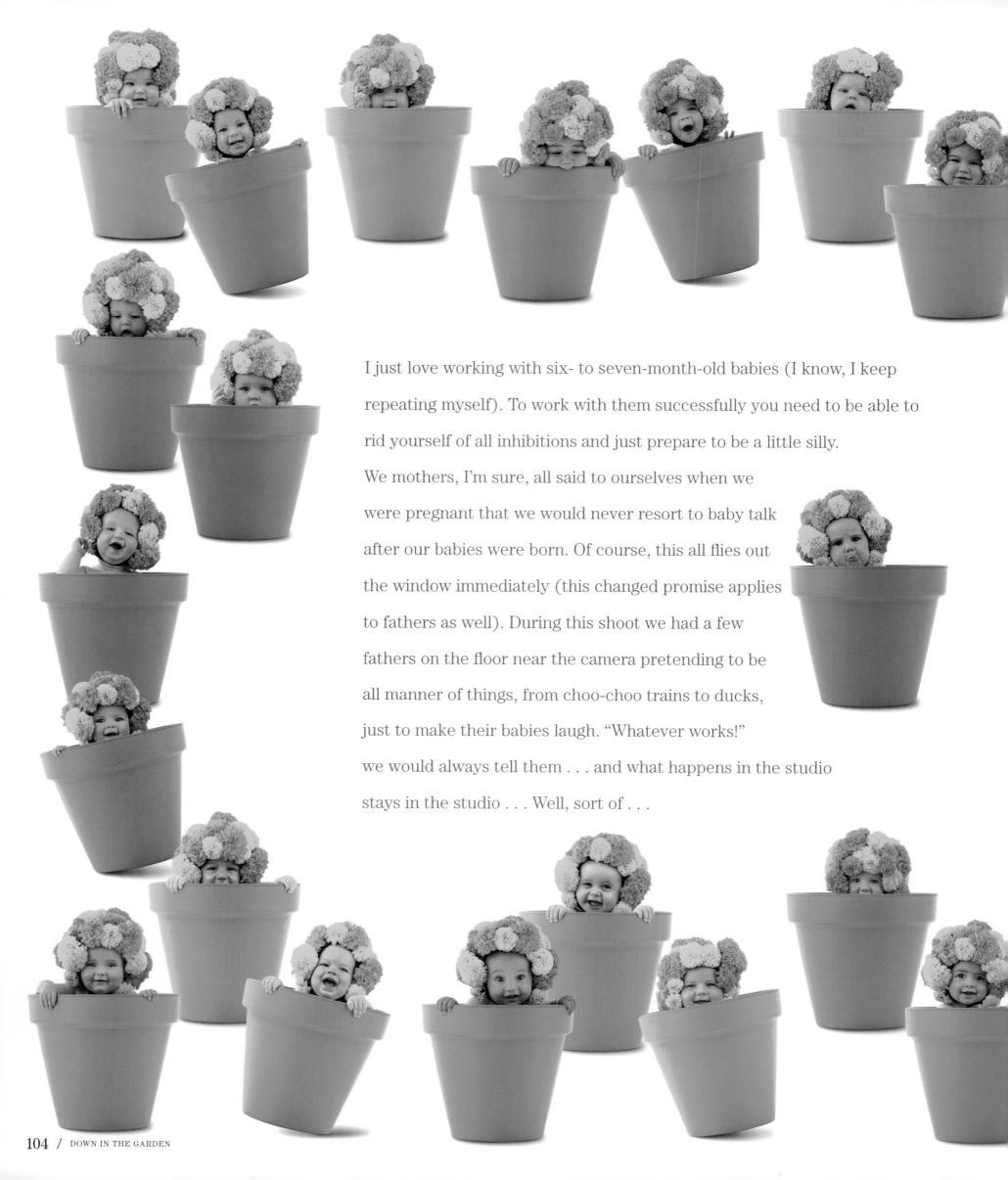

I just love working with six- to seven-month-old babies (I know, I keep repeating myself). To work with them successfully you need to be able to rid yourself of all inhibitions and just prepare to be a little silly. We mothers, I'm sure, all said to ourselves when we were pregnant that we would never resort to baby talk after our babies were born. Of course, this all flies out the window immediately (this changed promise applies to fathers as well). During this shoot we had a few fathers on the floor near the camera pretending to be all manner of things, from choo-choo trains to ducks, just to make their babies laugh. "Whatever works!" we would always tell them . . . and what happens in the studio stays in the studio . . . Well, sort of . . .

There are many six- to seven-month-old babies featured in *Down in the Garden*, mainly sitting in flowerpots. The slightly older children of some of my staff were happy to feature as gnomes and various other characters. Mind you, when I say "happy," some of them, as mentioned earlier, were initially reluctant to wear the large foam tummies required to be worn under the gnome outfits.

The bride and groom featured in the "Gnome Wedding" (page 138) scene were not very thrilled, at first, about holding hands, and the bride, who wasn't at all keen on her fake bosoms, adamantly preferred to hold her bouquet upside down. I generally know how to get around most situations with children of all ages, but I also know when it's wise to just go with the flow. If there's a choice between a tantrum and upside-down flowers, I know which one I'd choose any day. Every day presented me with new and unique challenges!

"through the eyes of a child, all wonderful things seem possible"

Some of these fairies didn't want to put their costumes on,
and some didn't want to take them off afterward. Generally, the ones who didn't
want to take them off afterward were the same ones who didn't want to put them on in the first place.
A couple also tried to fly!

Elizabeth, the newborn in the center of the branch, is one of the sweetest little fairies I think I've photographed over the years. She has become
the iconic fairy in my range of fairy clothing—released earlier this year. She has such an old-fashioned little face. Of course, all of these fairies
were photographed separately and placed on the branch later.

Pictured right is my author photograph from *Down in the Garden*. Whenever I look at this image, I remember the letter from little Stephanie, who asked,
"How did you get a fairy on your hand?"

Room 10
Waimairi School
Tillman Ave
Christchurch 5

15 May 1998

Dear Anne Geddes

Hello my name is Stephanie. I really want to know how you make costumes for your baby photos because there so fantastic. Also how did you get the fairy on your hand? One more question. How do you do the backgrounds and did you go to a kind of school or something because you are so good at taking baby photos.

Yours Sincerely
Stephanie

sweet peas

When I was small I used to help my mother shell peas from our vegetable garden. It might seem strange to see babies in pea pods, but I used to imagine back then that the peas nestled inside the pods were little pea babies, and even now a pea pod reminds me of a pregnant form. Fortunately I love peas, because when I was shooting this image the whole studio smelled very strongly of them. Again, this is not a computer-generated image. The babies are actually encased in soft cloth pods and lying on top of 130 pounds of fresh green peas. On top of the babies in the pods are very light oversized peas, crafted from foam. Each page is a separate image, so I suppose you are looking at 260 pounds of peas altogether, with a different baby inside each of the pods. Getting the babies asleep at the same time wasn't really too difficult. On a "difficulty scale" of one to ten, this was probably about a four; newborn babies love to be wrapped snugly—even though not, normally, in a pea pod.

My only problem on the day was that I wanted a very dark-skinned baby included in the image, as I always like to have babies of different races represented in my images. There are many Maori and Pacific Island babies in New Zealand, and they are often included in my work. However, sometimes at birth their skin can be relatively light, becoming darker as they grow older. So I was waiting to do the image until I found a baby with very dark skin, to add contrast to the scene. Finally we heard about Nana-Yaw (lower right-hand corner).

I had extra lighter-skinned babies on hand in the studio, in case some of them didn't fall asleep at the time, but only one dark-skinned baby, which meant that the success of the image really hinged on whether he would go to sleep or not. True to form, he was the brightest and most wide-awake baby on the day. The others were all dozing away in their pods, but he was quite ambivalent about starring. I was very relieved when he finally dropped off to sleep, but it was only briefly.

I know you must be wondering what we did with all those peas after the shoot. They went to the Auckland Zoo to feed the elephants. Whenever I look at this image, I have visions of elephants with very bad wind. I'm sorry, but I just can't help it.

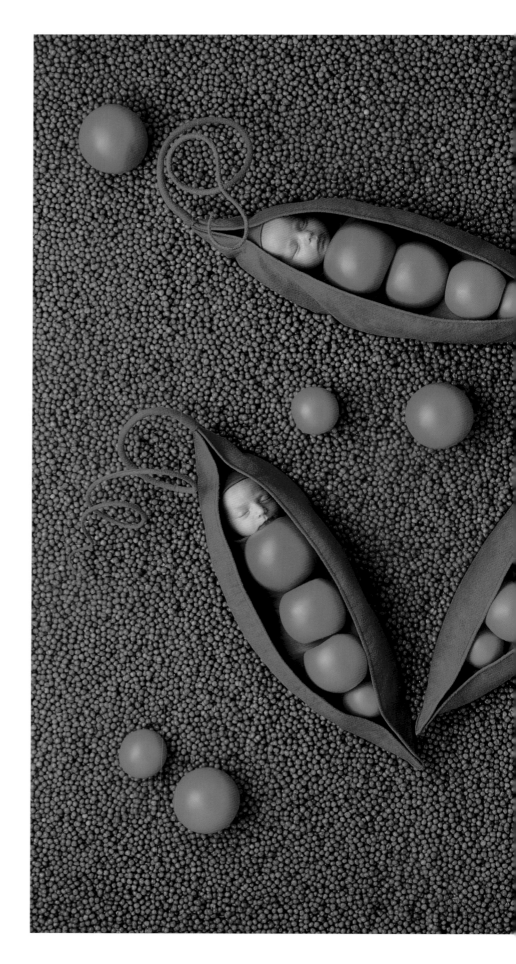

Thomas, Holly, Elise, Rebekah, Sophie, *and* Nana-Yaw 1995

Cara *and* Danielle 1995

◁ watermelons

Shooting for *Down in the Garden* allowed me to become acquainted with all kinds of trivia regarding fruits, vegetables, and flowers. For example, families are generally much smaller nowadays than some decades ago, so there is very little demand for larger watermelons. Finding the right-sized watermelons for this image was the most difficult part. Even though Cara and Danielle were very tiny, for this image I needed some very large watermelons to lay them in. We eventually found a couple at the bottom of a huge container of watermelons at the early-morning fruit markets (the ones that open at 5 a.m.!).

The watermelon costumes, made of foam and hand-painted, were really beautiful; they even had real watermelon seeds incorporated in them. The babies were lying in the carved-out watermelons on top of plastic and soft foam, so they were very warm and dry, and to get them to sleep we walked around with them actually in the watermelons.

Many people think this image is computer-generated; however, as with all of the images from *Down in the Garden,* if it's not completely obvious that an image is computer-generated, then it probably isn't.

teddy bears
picnic ▽

The teddy bears picnic sequence in *Down in the Garden* is one of the most popular with children. Babies love looking at pictures of other babies. I once had a seven-month-old baby sitting on the floor in my studio, kissing each page of one of my books.

The bear costumes were so beautiful on their own, but when we dressed the babies in them they seemed to come alive. I have a baby bear suit and a small baby bear plush toy included in my clothing range. They have been extremely popular ever since their release five years ago.

waterlilies

The year or so I spent researching this book meant looking through all my old film. One of the great things to come out of this exercise was that I frequently came across beautiful images of babies who had been in to the studio for specific shoots, but had not been featured in any of my books or calendars. As an example, for years one of my most popular images has been little Tayla as a waterlily (right), so I was absolutely delighted when I revisited the files and found that, in fact, there were other babies there that particular day who had done just as good a job of posing in the lily pond. Immediately Monet's paintings of waterlilies sprang to mind, so I set to work creating my own version. The other babies, who are now teenagers, are finally able to achieve the "stardom" they deserve.

For some strange reason, time and again over the years, I have found that while babies love to splash around in the bath among a myriad of floating toys and other paraphernalia, they quite often draw the line at floating flowers or leaves. I have no idea why. I'd forgotten how lucky we were on the day of the waterlily shoot that everyone was so cooperative. In fact, most of the little stars were content just to try to devour the waterlily leaves. I must have had some good karma that day.

In the basement of my studio, we constructed a small rectangular pool from large wooden planks lined with a very big sheet of strong black plastic. This was filled with water and connected to a warming system—which theoretically would overnight transform the cooler water into a perfect temperature for the babies. The next morning we arrived to find that the pool had sprung a leak, so unfortunately I had to cancel the shoot and start the whole process over again. Eventually the perfect pool was prepared, the water beautifully warm and our lily leaves—brought in from a waterlily farm just outside the city—were ready and floating in the pond. At the bottom of the pool under where the babies would sit was a piece of dark toweling cloth so the plastic that lined the pool wasn't slippery.

The babies arrived for the shoot and as soon as we put the hat on the first baby, I knew it wasn't right. It was too bulky, and what's more, very absorbent. As soon as the first baby began splashing in the water, the hat was soaking wet—not quite the look I had envisaged. Dawn, my prop maker, agreed and tried to make a few quick adjustments, but unfortunately this delay caused the lily leaves in the warm water to go floppy and soft and they started to sink! Having not anticipated this development, I had no extra leaves on hand and had to call off the shoot for the day and have the babies come back a second time. I've discovered over the years that creating props that actually work well is essentially a form of problem solving. Thankfully, the next time we attempted this shoot the hat was much improved and everything went according to plan. A perfect case in point of never giving up against all odds when you think you have a good idea.

I would like to mention here that babies at this age generally have quite short attention spans, so as soon as we sat them in the pool, my assistant was busy distracting them with a colorful toy and the shot was completed even before they realized what was going on.

This is a good example of how much work sometimes goes into one image, when very often the planning goes on for months before the babies are even on the scene. Babies who have been in to the studio as newborns are often invited back if I am shooting six or seven months later.

As I mentioned earlier, for many years little Tayla was the only waterlily baby I had published. When she was about six years old and had just begun school, the image was included in an episode of the television series *Friends*. It could be seen hanging on the wall in one of the scenes.

When the producers asked for permission to use the image (they in fact used two or three other images as well), I called Tayla's mother to let her know that the episode was to be telecast that week. Tayla was very excited and the next day when she went to school and informed her bemused teacher that she had been on *Friends* the previous night, nobody initially would believe her!

woodland fairy

Every time I look at this image of Sophie, I think of her lovely head of black curly hair, which unfortunately nobody ever gets to see. Sophie was five weeks old when she became the first of my woodland fairies. At the time, I was shooting not just for *Down in the Garden*, but also for a possible calendar with a fairy theme.

I had spotted the very large and extremely heavy piece of driftwood Sophie is sleeping on from the top of a steep cliff face on one of the coastal beaches in Auckland and became quite fixated on using it for this image, despite the fact that there would be obvious difficulties in retrieving it. Being a great believer that "what doesn't kill you makes you stronger," I managed to persuade a group of strong men, led by Neil, my black-and-white printer, to haul it 300 feet up the side of the cliff. I, of course, went with them to supervise and lend moral support, which I thought was most generous. But as you could imagine, by the time they heaved it to the top, they were clearly having serious doubts as to its artistic merits. Of course, I could have used a driftwood prop, which would have been much easier for all concerned, but I wanted to be as authentic as possible.

I love some of the quotes we used in *Down in the Garden*, and on Sophie's page it says,

"In quiet corners of the garden,
Mother Nature takes care of her own."

Sophie 1995

peggy's *worm farm*

If I were to single out any one favorite image in *Down in the Garden* it would have to be Peggy's Worm Farm. Peggy Fleming was a wonderful elderly lady who was our next-door neighbor in Sydney, Australia, when our daughters were very small. She had lived by herself for many years, and was remarkably artistic in many ways. Sadly, she passed away in 2002. Here is my favorite photograph of Peggy (opposite) as I always remember her, sitting in her big, comfortable chair in the front room of her house, surrounded by all her arts and crafts. I don't think I ever saw her without her pearls. Her home was a veritable treasure trove for small children, with handmade teddy bears, dolls, butterflies, all manner of little things peeking out from every corner. She taught our daughters how to make all sorts of objects, including their own handmade butterflies. She would send them beautiful hand-embroidered handkerchiefs and other personally crafted gifts for years after we had moved overseas to New Zealand.

Gardening was one of Peggy's great loves, and she used to tell our daughters that when it rained the fairies would come out on the leaves with their tiny bath towels to shower, because that was the only opportunity they had to bathe. If you look out your window next time it rains, you will surely see them if you look closely enough and with the eyes of a child.

Outside and underneath her kitchen window, Peggy had cultivated an amazing worm colony. Most gardeners would know that worms are great friends to have in your garden. The girls loved to watch her feed the worms with whatever food scraps she had on hand—worms aren't very fussy eaters, I'm told. Charles Darwin once wrote, "Of all animals, few have contributed so much to the development of the world, as we know it, as earthworms." In *Down in the Garden,* I dedicated this image to Peggy, and kept it a secret from her until she received one of the first copies of the book. She was really thrilled.

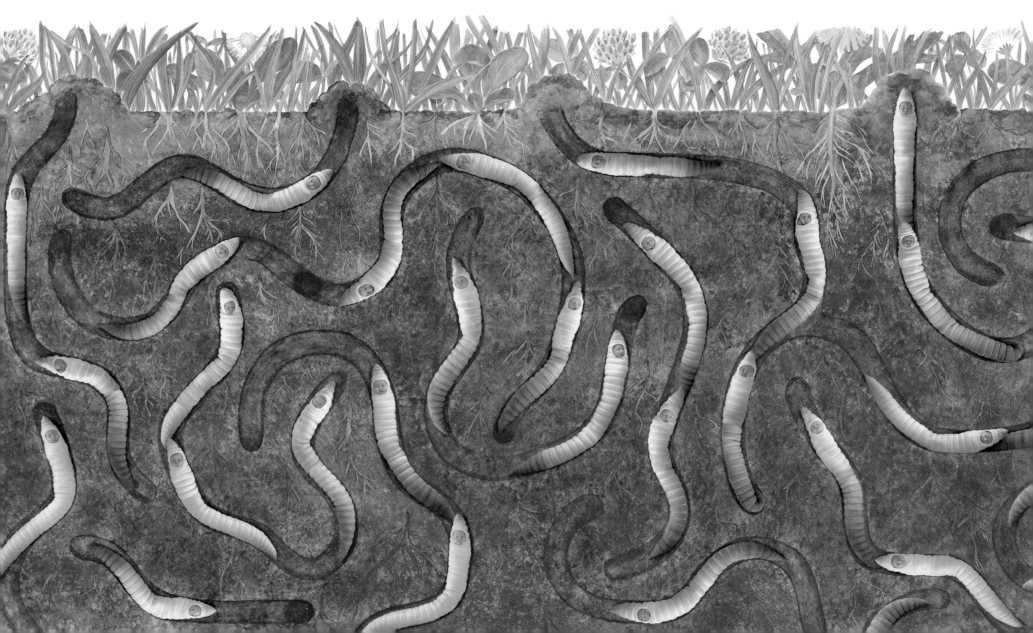

Fifty-five newborn babies have brought their own unique charm to "Peggy's Worm Farm" (no one worm repeated). They were photographed over a period of six months.

There are many images over the years where I wish I had videotaped background footage while I was shooting and this is surely one of them. Once word got out that we were shooting with new babies, people were calling from everywhere, and there wasn't one baby who came in that we didn't include in the final image. My worm farm just kept getting bigger and bigger.

The costumes were made out of soft foam, with an opening down the back. The babies inside were wrapped in one of my soft studio blankets. Once the babies were in the costumes, we laid them in various shapes that were carved out of foam to resemble tunnels. Many of the babies slept right through their entire visit to the studio. The mothers thought it was hilarious to see the babies in their costumes, this shoot really was so much fun. The whole image was later combined on the computer, and we were very excited to see the final result.

Peggy, in her favorite chair, Sydney 2000

julia snail

This image has become a classic from *Down in the Garden*. Julia, who was three weeks old at the time, is comfortably lying on various pieces of soft foam, thin enough to be artfully hidden in the final image. Under the foam, plaster-coated snail shell, she is encased in a very wide version of a seatbelt, which held her snugly to the beautiful old fence post we found at a farm outside Auckland. In the outtake you can see the remnants of the scene after I had finished photographing the image.

Sometimes titles for images become more obvious once they have been created, and this image is an excellent example. "Julia Snail"

sounded perfect. A few years after Julia had been photographed, I was talking to her father, John, and asked him if Julia was still their baby, or had they had any more children. He said, "Definitely not, we stopped at the snail."

Julia also makes a cameo appearance in the vast woodland fairy scene on page 186—I couldn't help myself.

Here is Julia as she is today. It was hard for her to imagine that she had ever been tiny enough to be almost completely covered by that shell.

above: Julia 1994

right: Julia 2006

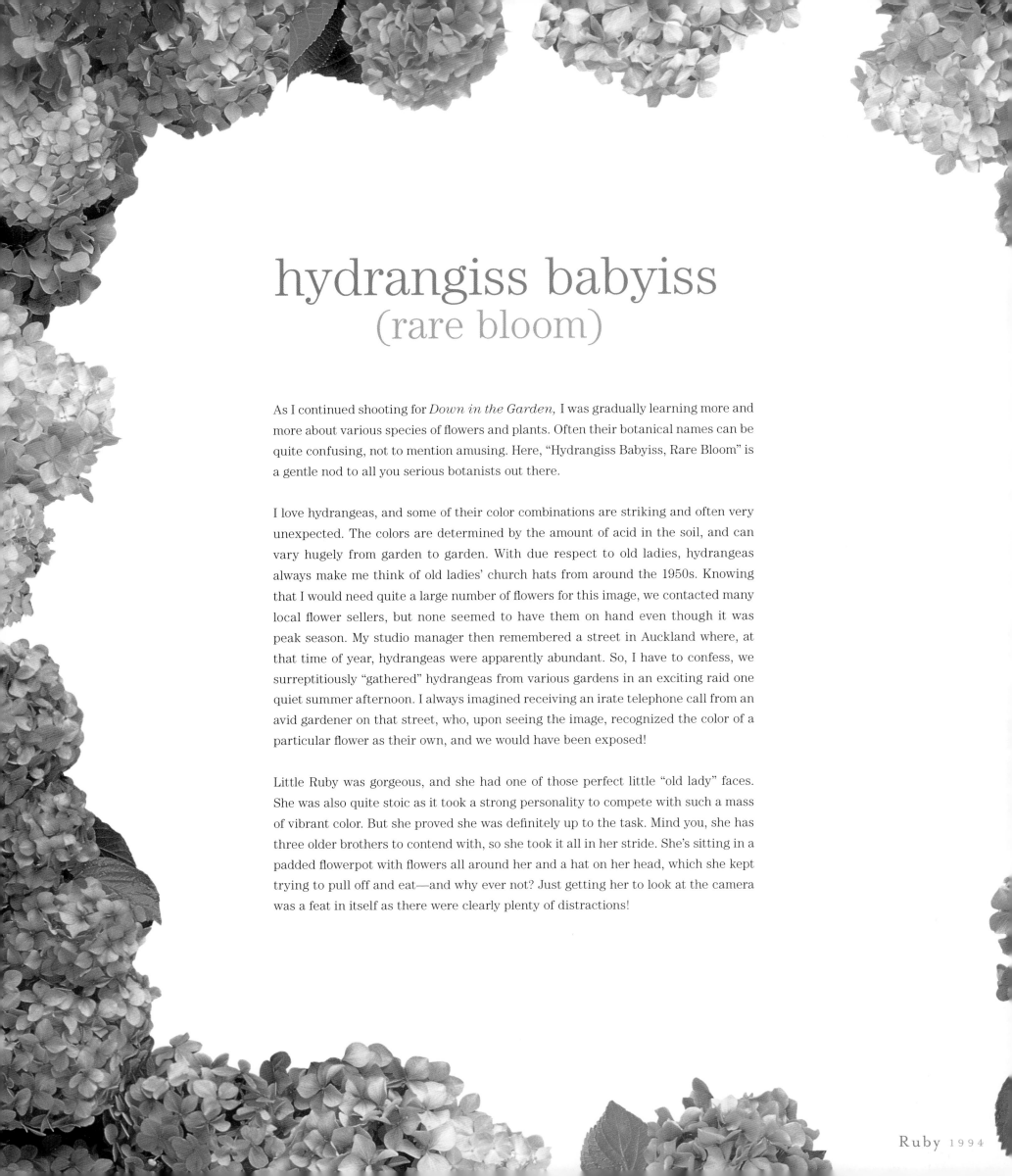

hydrangiss babyiss
(rare bloom)

As I continued shooting for *Down in the Garden,* I was gradually learning more and more about various species of flowers and plants. Often their botanical names can be quite confusing, not to mention amusing. Here, "Hydrangiss Babyiss, Rare Bloom" is a gentle nod to all you serious botanists out there.

I love hydrangeas, and some of their color combinations are striking and often very unexpected. The colors are determined by the amount of acid in the soil, and can vary hugely from garden to garden. With due respect to old ladies, hydrangeas always make me think of old ladies' church hats from around the 1950s. Knowing that I would need quite a large number of flowers for this image, we contacted many local flower sellers, but none seemed to have them on hand even though it was peak season. My studio manager then remembered a street in Auckland where, at that time of year, hydrangeas were apparently abundant. So, I have to confess, we surreptitiously "gathered" hydrangeas from various gardens in an exciting raid one quiet summer afternoon. I always imagined receiving an irate telephone call from an avid gardener on that street, who, upon seeing the image, recognized the color of a particular flower as their own, and we would have been exposed!

Little Ruby was gorgeous, and she had one of those perfect little "old lady" faces. She was also quite stoic as it took a strong personality to compete with such a mass of vibrant color. But she proved she was definitely up to the task. Mind you, she has three older brothers to contend with, so she took it all in her stride. She's sitting in a padded flowerpot with flowers all around her and a hat on her head, which she kept trying to pull off and eat—and why ever not? Just getting her to look at the camera was a feat in itself as there were clearly plenty of distractions!

field mice

Of course, mice are a constant problem in and around the home and particularly in the garden shed, but who could resist these two? I have tried to give the impression that they were snoozing in a dark corner of the barn and the door had just been opened, letting in some light.

Mitchell and Taylor are twins, and even though they were tiny, I couldn't find an existing pair of shoes that were large enough to accommodate them. Eventually we had to have an extra-large pair made, which would be the equivalent of U.S. size 22—16 inches long. As the shoes were brand-new, they had to be specially aged to make them look as if they were very worn and had been discarded. The insides were lined with soft padding and the mouse tails were slipped inside each boot after the boys fell asleep. They looked absolutely adorable in those little hats, and I actually wish I'd filmed some video on the day, because Mitchell was so comfortable in his boot, he was snoring.

Mitchell *and* Taylor 1995

pansies

Many of us, including myself, are old enough to remember when jam came in tins, and the rusty old discarded ones were often used for planting seedlings (with a few nail holes punched in the bottom for drainage!).

The idea for these pansy tins featured in *Down in the Garden* originated from a story that Natalie, my studio manager, once told me. At around three years of age she recalled being out in her grandmother's garden when she bent down to pick a pansy. Her grandmother, who was gardening at the time, hid behind a bush and just as Natalie was about to pick the flower, she heard what she thought was the pansy say in a tiny, squeaky voice, "Oh, please don't pick me." So you see, pansies perhaps really do have faces.

The tins, which were in fact new, had been made to look old and rusty especially for the shoot. The labels were enlarged from an illustration of old jam labels in a library book we found. The babies were fascinated with each other's hats, probably not realizing they were wearing the same themselves.

Aisha, Taylor, and Grace 1995

lawn daisies

In the corner of my studio I constructed a set, which consisted of a ten-by-twelve-foot plot of real turf, built up around a small hole, which contained a flowerpot in which the babies sat. Over two or three days, I photographed each of the babies sitting in the pot wearing a daisy hat. As the shoot progressed, the babies were gradually pulling the grass out from around the edge of the pot. Lawn daisies are abundant in the garden, and are largely ignored or considered a pest, but whenever I see them, I can't help but think of this image.

sometimes the
best flowers arrive
unexpectedly . . .

It was impossible to find a ready-made glass vase for this shoot, as naturally it needed to be quite large to accommodate a seven-month-old baby. I also had to be able to get the babies in and out easily. Eventually, I decided to have one specially hand-blown. Christopher (above right) happened to be the only boy out of the four babies we had at the studio on the day. They were all more or less happy to sit in the vase; however, I thought he looked the best in that hat, and until now, the other babies have not been published.

I suppose the most difficult part of this shoot was keeping the fresh flowers attached to the hat, because the babies kept pulling them off and trying to eat them. At this age, everything goes in the mouth!

It's also not an easy task to stick real flowers to fabric; they tend to keep dropping off onto the floor. I have absorbed a lot of trivia over the years—what sticks and what doesn't. What you also cannot see is that each baby is sitting on a pile of soft plastic kitchen wrap (for practical purposes!) and not actually on the glass balls, which were placed at the front of the vase. A lot happens in the background during the making of my images, to ensure the comfort of the babies.

The caption that goes with this image in *Down in the Garden* is "Sometimes the best flowers arrive unexpectedly." I suppose that also applies to some babies . . .

right: Charlotte *and* Brittany 1995

above: Ashleigh, Brittany, Charlotte, Christopher 1995

▽ small *is* beautiful

The newborn ladybugs and bumblebees were among the most popular characters from *Down in the Garden* and continue to be popular even to this day. Many of them were photographed in the United States, as it is very difficult in New Zealand, where my studio is located, to find newborn babies with very dark skin. In fact, over the years I have traveled quite often to the United States to photograph African American babies and darker-skinned babies of other nationalities because it is important to me to have babies from various ethnic backgrounds represented in my work. I have photographed at various times in Los Angeles, New York, San Francisco, and Las Vegas.

In 1993, before the release of *Down in the Garden,* when I first went to the United States specifically for this purpose, it wasn't as easy for me to find babies as it is nowadays, because I was still relatively unknown. As I describe on page 285, on one of my more recent visits to Los Angeles for a shoot, I needed twenty-five babies, and we received over 2,500 phone calls from people who were interested in taking part.

A good percentage of the bumblebees and ladybugs are African American, so as often as possible, when a dark-skinned baby was at the studio for another shoot, we would pop them in the little costumes and photograph them for the book. They were photographed on any available surface that was convenient at the time, even the studio ironing board. Babies don't mind at all; in fact, they are quite forgiving—handy for new mothers to keep in mind.

The saying "Small is beautiful" is certainly appropriate here; I can't tell you how beautiful these newborns looked as I photographed them. I wanted the ladybugs, whose shells were crafted from very light foam, to lie on a straight line in the design for the book, hence the foam pads under the feet (above right).

jim, flora, *and* pearl ▷

Jim, Flora, and Pearl are triplets. Jim is actually in the middle, with Pearl on the left and Flora on the right. Whenever I look at the three of them in that pot, I just want to pick them up and cuddle them. Their mother, for obvious reasons, laughingly called them the "spew crew." At the time, Jim still wasn't very accomplished at sitting on his own, so the girls are lending him support.

This image features in *Down in the Garden* and the caption reads, "Don't forget to separate your bulbs before they become too crowded." Jim, understandably, perhaps wouldn't have wanted to be "separated" at the time!

Jim, Flora, and Pearl 1994

props *and* pots

Recently, while researching and writing for *A Labor of Love*, we were rummaging through the vast storage area where many of the old props are stored. I have never been good at throwing things away, and the storage area has grown quite large. I often joke that I should set up a prop museum. Noticing some of the odd signage on a collection of boxes that were stacked on top of each other, we all laughed as we started to remember their contents and someone suggested we photograph the wall of boxes and include it in the book. I thought you might enjoy seeing them as well. For us, they certainly brought back many fond memories.

In the back of the storage area I also came across the beautiful painted flowerpots used in *Down in the Garden*, which had been carefully wrapped and hidden away in a corner. It felt quite nostalgic to see them again as it had been many years since I shot the images and I had forgotten how beautiful the flowerpots actually were. They really are all original works of art in themselves.

When I first began to shoot for *Down in the Garden,* I invited a group of students from an art school in Auckland to each paint a few pots using their own interpretation of a garden theme. They were all very enthusiastic about the brief and each left with a couple of plain terra-cotta pots as their blank canvas. Here is the result. Some of the budding artists were so proud of their pots they signed them as well.

Looking at this compilation now, I don't think we did too badly with our limited computer work in those early days. Even though it is tempting to revisit the original concept with today's generation of computer magic, I resisted, and for *A Labor of Love* have left all of the *Down in the Garden* images in their original form in the book.

Some of the garden gnomes who are featured are the children and friends of my studio team. The little guy standing on the pot in the image (top right) initially wasn't too keen on wearing his foam tummy under the costume. He took one look at it and shook his head adamantly. It took some gentle persuasion (not to mention bribery) to bring him around.

leaving the
garden

A garden wedding in the

There was an innocence in my approach to this book and the possibilities seemed endless. As I mentioned earlier, *Down in the Garden* was created as a storybook, with all of the images linked by the narrative of an imaginary and magical garden. *Down in the Garden* was simply meant to be fun—and that is the spirit in which the images were created.

As shooting for *Down in the Garden* continued, more and more ideas sprang to mind and we found ourselves frantically making props as we tried to include extra images. It was hard to finally stop as the deadline for the book loomed. We were all so exhausted in the end that I have to admit to not being able to look at the book for a couple of years after it was published without feeling somewhat stressed!

Summertime is always delightful.

Sometimes it seems that people still think of me as the "flowerpot baby" photographer. When my three subsequent books were released, for instance, I was hoping during interviews to be able to talk about my new imagery, but most interviewers wanted to revert to "cute and funny" conversations about babies. I'd almost always be asked how I got the babies to sit in the flowerpots. I suppose it was inevitable, but for a while I found it very frustrating. Of course, however, if it hadn't been for the success of *Down in the Garden* I would not have had such a solid base on which to build my future career.

Down in the Garden was pure fantasy springing from my own imagination. It must have connected to the imagination of many others because it has been in constant reprint since it was first released. The tenth-anniversary edition was published in 2006.

works *in* progress

There are a number of images I have made which are either "works in progress" or perhaps part of an idea which I have not pursued. Sometimes I take some images that I am pleased with but they do not end up being part of any book because they just don't fit with the theme or they are part of a series that I haven't finished.

For example, the following images were created as part of a nursery rhyme series that I am still working on, and have been for the past ten years. It seems like a never-ending project, probably because there are far too many nursery rhymes to choose from and also because other projects seem to continually get in the way. I don't suppose there is any rush, though, as the rhymes themselves have been around for hundreds of years. It was actually interesting doing some initial research as to the origins of some of the rhymes, which are surprisingly dark and quite disturbing, to say the least!

Susan the stork (left) was quite a magnificent-looking creature, a work of art, in fact. She was taller than me, and I'm five-ten. She looked so fabulous that after the shoot I kept her in the back corner of the studio for many months, where she would watch over everybody with a discerning eye. She impressed many small children, not to mention adults. Most importantly, she reminded everybody of where babies really come from (I wish). We even dressed her up for our staff Christmas party with presents under her wings. Then she started to go a funny shade of yellow from the glue in her feathers, and had to be dispatched to stork heaven.

antique dolls

I was always planning to use this image in the nursery rhyme collection and, of course, I may do so in the future. There was a doll fair being held in Auckland, and we went along to see what was on offer. As it turned out, the choice was incredible, with many antique dolls of all shapes and sizes. The most unusual of them all was the dubious-looking fellow (middle of top shelf) who, at the time I purchased him, had a cigarette in his mouth, which I of course removed immediately. He looks like one of those characters who hang out in dark corners of bars late into the evening. Not that I would know of course.

The four babies featured are actually two sets of twins. They were around four months of age, not yet sitting on their own, but small enough to be of similar size to the real dolls. Their beautiful outfits were especially made at the studio to blend with the antique clothing the dolls were wearing. The faces of the babies seem to mirror the expressions of some of the dolls (but not "cigarette man"!).

The shelves in the image were purpose built, and around each baby (underneath the outfit) is a soft wide fabric seatbelt which threads through the back wall and fastens behind to keep them secure and upright. The babies were photographed one at a time and the image completed on computer. We moved the dolls around as each baby was photographed, to provide variation in the end result.

When the image was published the following year, I received a lovely letter from a very excited woman in Australia who said that she recognized one of the dolls as her childhood favorite which had long since been lost. She was absolutely certain the doll was hers and was so relieved to see it again that I sent it to her as a gift.

Rachel, Brittany, Tara, *and* Georgia 1998

lines of sunflowers
and pretty maids

Fortunately, the creation of these next two images, which were shot in Los Angeles, was captured on video. Recently I watched the footage, and remembered how concerned I was beforehand that both shoots go seamlessly, especially as we had quite a large number of babies in the studio at the time. The images were created on two consecutive days in April 1998.

When twenty-five six-month-old babies and their parents are gathered together in the studio for a shoot, it pays to be extremely organized. In a case like this, my motto is always "A fast shoot is a good shoot," and I kept repeating this to my studio team beforehand. As anybody who works with young children can tell you, things can very quickly become chaotic, and where babies are involved, well, they come with excited parents and lots of baggage (literally).

As is always the case, everything was prepared the day before the babies were to arrive. The lighting was exactly right and everything in place for the next day. The seats were all tested and retested. The safety aspects of the lighting set-ups were constantly double-checked. All cables were taped to the floor, ensuring nobody tripped over them, especially because babies are likely to be carried around the studio. All sharp and pointed objects, such as the ends of lighting stands and poles, were covered. The video stills (right) give you an idea of how much happens in the background that people would never imagine.

These two particular images involved quite extensive prop building and preparation. The background canvases were especially painted for the occasion and the line of seats on which the babies sat was constructed beforehand in my studio in New Zealand. I had used them a few months prior to this when I directed two television commercials for Target USA. Even though in the images featured here there is a long line of babies, in fact there were only six seats in the row and the image has been extended as different babies were placed in position.

A structural engineer supervised and tested the construction of the set before it left New Zealand. Each of the seats is atop a strong steel pole which has been bolted into a heavy metal base. The seats themselves had been especially molded for the comfort of the babies, and were padded with soft foam. At the back of each seat there were two openings to accommodate a six-inch wide softly padded green "seatbelt." Once each baby had been placed in their seat, an assistant would hold and distract them while two others worked quickly behind the babies to bring the seatbelt around their little tummies and fastened securely out of sight at the back.

In order to achieve an image with this many babies, everybody needed to work quickly and efficiently. As I was hoping to achieve a perfect (and real) image with six babies all in the seats at the same time, I knew that I would need to have babies waiting in the side-lines, already dressed and wearing hats, so we could quickly replace any baby who decided they didn't want to be in their seat any longer. And when they didn't, they let us know loud and clear! Just getting the hats on their heads without them realizing was a feat in itself, so we had to be very quick, unobtrusive, and extremely organized.

There was an assistant assigned to each baby sitting in the seats at the time, so whenever we had to replace a baby in any particular seat, someone would step forward in front of each of the other babies, to keep them entertained while the replacement was made. A couple of the babies in this image were perfectly happy to sit in their places for the whole time, and in fact thought the whole situation was hilarious.

above: video stills from the sunflowers shoot, Los Angeles, 1998

My studio manager, Natalie (in action, bottom right), is marvelous at entertaining babies. Her task was to try to have all of the babies looking at my camera more or less at the same time—no mean feat, but she always delivered. She was running back and forth from the camera to the babies with all manner of distracting toys, bells, whatever worked on the day; but, a lot of the time, all the babies wanted to do was pull each other's hats off. Poor Natalie was thoroughly exhausted afterward.

Of course, the babies weren't all I had to worry about. Before we started shooting, I explained to the parents what we were trying to achieve and asked them to please stay out of eyesight of their babies when they were being photographed, as we wanted the babies all to be looking at the camera. It must have been very hard for them, but they were all good sports on the day.

I wish I could show you video footage of all the babies up there in their seats, their little legs kicking away and the hats looking so charming as they were all looking at Natalie being silly, and then at each other; it was a delightful sight. At times like this, I know why I continue to photograph babies.

Naturally, with so many babies in the studio, it wasn't possible for me to include all of them in the image that was published soon afterward, so when the time came to research *A Labor of Love* I looked back through all of the footage, and have tried to include here all of the babies who played a part on the day. The lines have been extended through the genius of computer generation!

Until Now

By the time *Until Now* came along, I was well and truly ready for a creative change. Shooting for *Down in the Garden* had been fun, and even though it had been a huge success, creatively I felt the need to finally escape from beneath all of the flowerpots, ladybugs and bumblebees.

In tandem with all of the colorful and highly propped imagery in *Down in the Garden*, I had also been creating more classic imagery, and in particular a lot of work in black and white, which is my first love. In these images I was striving for simplicity and expressive power, trying to let my subjects, the babies, speak for themselves with their own natural beauty. However, few of these images had been published. They were of a very different style to *Down in the Garden* images and they needed a separate book in which to feature. *Until Now* was the result, and while some saw the new images as a radical departure, most of my *Garden* fans came with me on my journey.

We included thumbnails of the images, in the back pages of *Until Now,* along with a short explanation of how some of them were photographed. This section of the book proved to be really popular. At the time, I didn't realize how interested people were in behind-the-scenes stories.

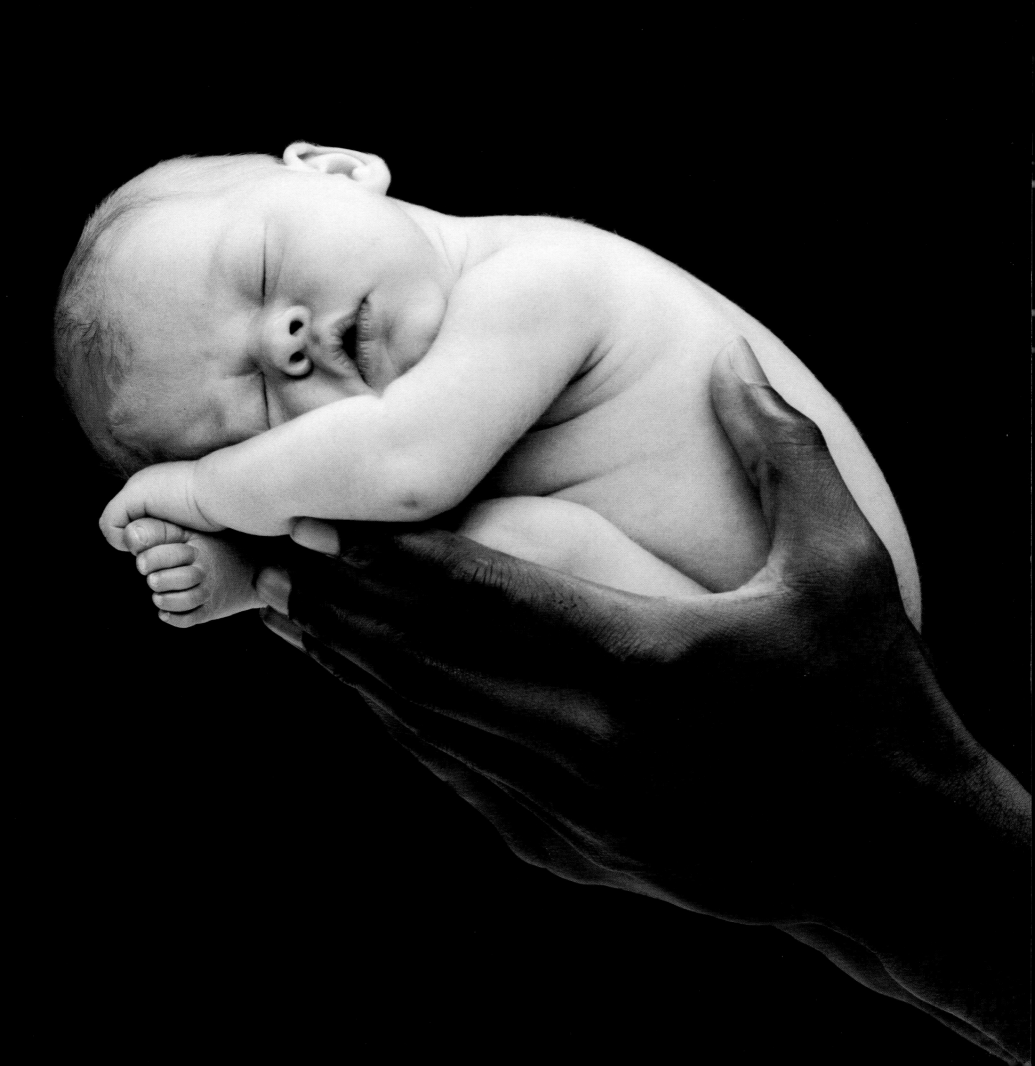

jack *holding* maneesha

Maneesha is the smallest baby I have ever photographed. She was born prematurely at twenty-eight weeks' gestation, weighing a little under 1.5 pounds, and was just about to leave the hospital after her long stay. I am fascinated by the continual medical advances to save babies who are born too early and would not otherwise survive.

At around this time, I was beginning to photograph more and more newborns, as opposed to older babies. I thought it would be wonderful to show how tiny these premature babies are—but also how perfect. I felt the best way to do this would be to contrast the baby in some very large hands—but where to find them?

I telephoned the local police station and fire brigade—after all, aren't policemen traditionally supposed to have big feet and hands? Of course they all thought it was hilarious, but were most helpful because the fax machine ran hot with outlines of hands coming through. I also placed an advertisement in the local paper for "A man with very large hands for a photo shoot." As you can imagine, we had some interesting replies. Eventually, I auditioned about ten (mostly embarrassed) men, some of whom were brought in by their wives, not necessarily willingly! Jack's hands happened to be the second largest, but he had a warm, gentle personality, which was essential for the shoot. I just felt he was perfect for the job.

In the meantime, I started making inquiries to the neonatal ward at our local hospital. I had a meeting with one of their specialist pediatricians and outlined my idea for the image. Naturally I was concerned that there be absolutely no risk involved; in fact, I was so concerned that, without realizing it, I must have kept repeating this point to the doctor. He finally said that I should stop worrying so much; he understood what I was trying to achieve, and he would help to put me in touch with the parents of a baby at the hospital whom he thought would be perfect.

I was introduced to baby Maneesha's young parents, who agreed to be a part of the shoot. Maneesha would soon be ready to go home for the first time, and they were understandably very excited. When I first saw Maneesha, in her incubator, she looked so incredibly small and fragile. She was attached to all manner of wires and tubes, which, to a layperson like myself, can be quite intimidating. On the side of her incubator was a label saying, *"I'm in the Kilo Club,"* and I learned that 1 kilogram (2.2 pounds) is a significant weight milestone for premature babies. Maneesha weighed just 1 kilo at the time of the shoot. Even her dummy (pacifier) was minute; they make a special size for premature babies.

Maneesha's shoot took place at the hospital in an anteroom directly outside the neonatal ward. I set up a small background in this very limited space, with some simple lighting and a chair for Jack. One of the reasons for using this small room was because it could be effectively heated—most important, as Maneesha would be naked and the temperature needed to be similar to that in her incubator.

I can't imagine how emotional it must have been for Jack to hold such a tiny and precious human being; watching them both was certainly one of my most moving experiences. That day was the first time Maneesha had been completely disconnected from all of her machinery, and I remember, when I settled her into Jack's huge hands and was photographing her, the look of amazement and wonder on her mother's face.

I next photographed Maneesha when she was a very healthy four-year-old. I wanted an updated photo of her for my book *Until Now,* to show what wonderful progress she had made since she left the hospital. By then she had a baby brother and they both came to the studio. They were sitting side by side on a chair in readiness for a portrait of them together and, in true "sibling rivalry" form, Maneesha obviously decided that she was not prepared to share the limelight. Without taking her eyes off the camera and with a huge smile on her face, she promptly pushed her brother, Aakash, sideways off the chair! No harm was done, apart from some slightly wounded pride, but I suppose that's what all the little brothers of the world have to suffer from time to time.

Jack *holding* Maneesha 1993

As I was preparing for this book, I thought it would be wonderful to show Maneesha as she is today, a beautiful

twelve-year-old. I recently asked her how she felt now, looking at the photograph of herself when she was so tiny,

and whether she would like to write something personal for *A Labor of Love* . . .

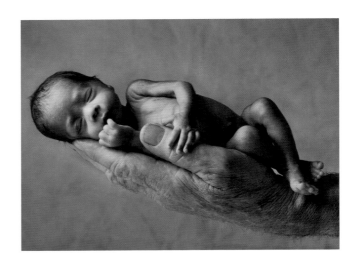

my picture
by maneesha, age 12

" *Anne says that to her a great image is one that you can look at for a long, long time. I often gaze at the image of myself in Jack's big hands, and wonder how I could ever have been so small. To be honest, it's really hard to believe that it's actually me.*

Of course, I don't remember anything from that time, but in my mind I have a picture of a 'gentle giant' holding me so very tenderly. My mother has told me how nervous Jack felt when he had to hold my tiny and fragile body, but I think he did a wonderful job.

Over the years my parents have told me many stories about the time when I was born and everything that happened. But I still used to wonder what all the fuss was about. Now I am older and can understand a bit more—the word "miracle" really has special meaning to me.

I'm just an ordinary twelve-year-old, no different to my friends, except I guess I am very aware of how lucky I have been since the day I was born so prematurely, lucky that I had such wonderful medical care and also to have such a beautiful image to look back on.

My school friends think it's really cool that I was such a small baby. They say they can't believe it's really me in that photograph. My little nine-year-old brother, Aakash, sometimes gets a bit jealous, but on the other hand I know he tells everyone at school he has a famous sister!

I'm so proud that my photograph has been in lots of books and nearly around the world, so I guess I can say that I am a little bit famous, even if people don't know me, but especially for those people who do know me. These are strange feelings, but it is nice to have the attention sometimes. Thankfully though, everyone still treats me the same and that's the best thing!

Perhaps everything I have been through has been worthwhile. If I had not come into the world so early, I wouldn't have been fortunate enough to have met Anne, who from day one has been such a big part of my life and really has made me feel so special. Thank you, Anne, for continuing to be a part of my life as I grow. "

Maneesha

above: Jack *holding* Maneesha 1993
right: Maneesha 2006

phillipa ▷

Sometimes life can hand you wonderful moments, and this image, originally done as a portrait sitting, is surely one of those. It's a great example of everything coming together totally unexpectedly, with a bit of magic thrown in.

A few days before the sitting, Phillipa's mother called me to discuss the details of the upcoming shoot. She mentioned that she had a beautiful rose garden, so I suggested that she bring either one perfect rose or lots of them, whichever she preferred. She arrived with buckets full of de-thorned roses, and one lovely little red-headed baby. When I walked into my reception area to say hello to them, Phillipa was sitting on the floor looking up at me with this beautiful smile, and her mother said that if you smiled at her the same way, she would invariably copy you. I wish we had some video footage of my assistant and me during the shoot, up on a ledge near the ceiling, looking down at Phillipa lying in her bed of roses and trying to get her to smile like that again—and then she did.

Phillipa was eight months old at the time, and I knew we would have to be very quick if we wanted her to be lying on her back in the roses. Babies of that age are generally confidently sitting and a lot of them are also crawling. Understandably, they like to be mobile as opposed to lying on their backs, because for the first six months of their lives they spend a lot of time looking at the ceiling! As we were laying her in the roses we distracted her with the rose she has in her hands, and also a lot of noise and color from above. The shot probably took, in total, about a minute to complete.

Rebecca *and* Courtney 1997

◁ rebecca *and* courtney

Rebecca and Courtney were premature twins, who weighed 2 kilos (almost 4.5 pounds) each. They were petite and perfect, just out of the hospital on an "early release" program. Although very tiny, they were healthy enough to go home.

Whenever I look at this image I remember that on the day of the shoot it was proving difficult to get them both to sleep at the same time. Whenever one of them was asleep in position, the other would wake, and so on. I can imagine what it must be like to have twins or triplets at home; it must at times be extremely hard work. However, to me, it was really just a matter of being very patient and waiting for the planets to line up! Finally they were both asleep, looking perfect. Just as I went to take the first shot, the fire alarm at the studio went off—a false alarm—but of course we all had to gather outside the building, naturally, babies included, and wait for the fire brigade to give us the all-clear to go back in . . . and start all over again.

Finally, for the second time we got them both asleep and in almost identical poses, apart from the fact that Rebecca was determined she wanted her arms exactly where they were, and not the same as her sister's. Who was I to argue?

Phillipa 1992

country pumpkin ▷

There was a giant pumpkin competition at a local fair, which is where I first met Reece Jones, pictured here with his grandson, Wade. Reece grew not only giant pumpkins, but giant sunflowers, giant beans, all manner of oversized vegetables. This is not his winning pumpkin, however; that particular one wouldn't even fit through the studio doors! As it was, the pumpkin pictured here took three people to carry up the stairs into the studio.

When I look at this image today, I think to myself that if I knew then what I know now about babies and their behavior at different ages, I could have made my job a lot easier. Of course, it's not easy at the best of times to get a nine-week-old baby (as Amelia Rose was then)

to sleep on top of a huge pumpkin, and I don't recommend trying this at home. Nowadays nearly all of the babies who are sleeping in my images are newborn, which to me means under the age of four weeks. Newborn babies, if they are warm, comfortable, and well fed, will sleep almost anywhere, which can come in very handy at times.

I also broke one of my golden rules here, and that is never to photograph babies in the afternoons, but of course it was 1993 and I hadn't yet written my rule book.

Amelia wasn't the only baby who was in the studio on that day and I'm afraid I wasn't having much luck with any of the babies sleeping well. Every time one of the babies was sleeping and I tried to gently place them on the pumpkin they would wake. Finally I decided to call the whole thing off and planned to try again the next day, but Amelia's mother said, "Look, she's asleep, why don't you try one more time?"

The top of the pumpkin had been gently warmed with a hot-water bottle and it was a lot wider than it appears in the image, so it was more comfortable than it might look. When we finally got Amelia Rose up on the pumpkin she looked so gorgeous I found myself mentally willing her to stay asleep so I could achieve my shot, and I'm positive everyone else in the studio was doing the same. I managed to get a shot of her first without the pumpkin flower on her back, but knowing how beautiful the pumpkin flower was, I knew it would complete the image perfectly.

It's moments like these when our nagging little inner voice pops up and says, "Come on, forget the flower, it looks just fine as it is, take the easy way out."

The texture of a pumpkin flower is quite furry, and I didn't want to tickle Amelia's back and, therefore, possibly wake her. As I gently lowered the flower onto her back, she twitched her shoulders slightly and gave a little sigh. There was a collective holding of breath in the whole studio. I was able to get only one image before the flash woke her. It was an anxious couple of hours waiting for the film to come back from the lab before I could be certain that my one image was perfectly focused, as my hands were shaking so badly when I was operating the camera.

Reece Jones, giant pumpkin grower, holding grandson Wade, 1993

Amelia Rose 1993

Tyrone 1995

I learned from Reece that pumpkin flowers do not last very long at all after being picked. We had planned for Reece to bring a couple of freshly picked flowers to the studio just before the shoot was to begin. The flowers were still closed when he brought them in, and as one slowly opened under the studio lights, a small bumblebee crawled out, looking slightly confused. Reece explained that as bumble bees don't have homes of their own, they often spend the night inside the pumpkin flowers, hence the idea for this image (above). They crawl in before the flower closes at sunset, and fly out when the flower opens in the morning light. This particular image shows what happens when you break the curfew.

Following the pumpkin shoot with Amelia, I got to know Reece and his wife, Mrs. Jones, quite well, and loved to visit them at their small farm outside Auckland to see what Reece was up to as far as his giant vegetable cultivation was concerned. He loved to show us around the farm, and was always growing something oversized and interesting. Mrs. Jones would invariably prepare a delicious

morning or afternoon tea and I remember fondly our times on their porch, where we'd sit and survey the next batch of giant pumpkins ballooning in the front paddock. As the pumpkins became larger and larger, Reece would cushion their weight using bales of hay and straw.

One day, just as we were leaving, Mrs. Jones said to me, "Oh I think I have something you might like," and brought out a tiny flower. It was a parachute flower from a small vine growing on their front porch, and was only about an inch long. Obviously, Reece had little to do with this tiny flower's cultivation! I photographed the flower as soon as I returned to the studio and then we made the costume for Elise, the baby in the image (right). Elise happens to be the twin sister of Thomas, the monarch butterfly on page 99.

Sadly, both Reece and Mrs. Jones have since passed away. I have been very lucky to have met so many wonderful people over the years, and Reece was one of those gentle, kind, and unforgettable characters.

Elise 1995

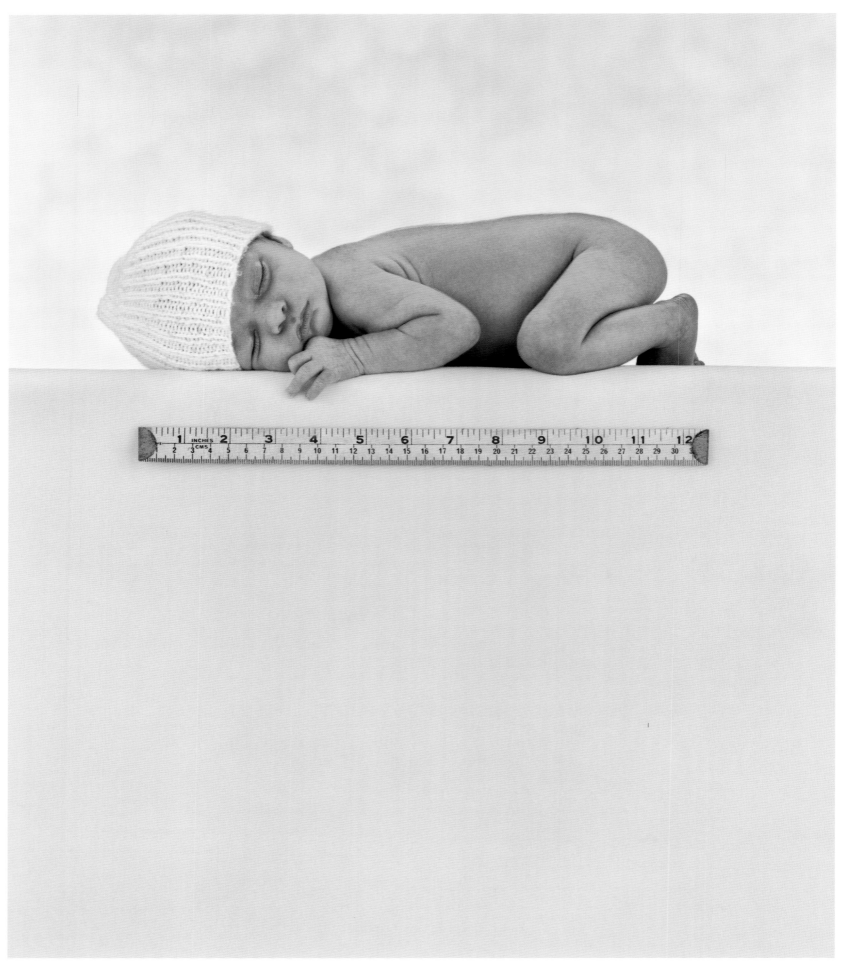

Ariana 1997

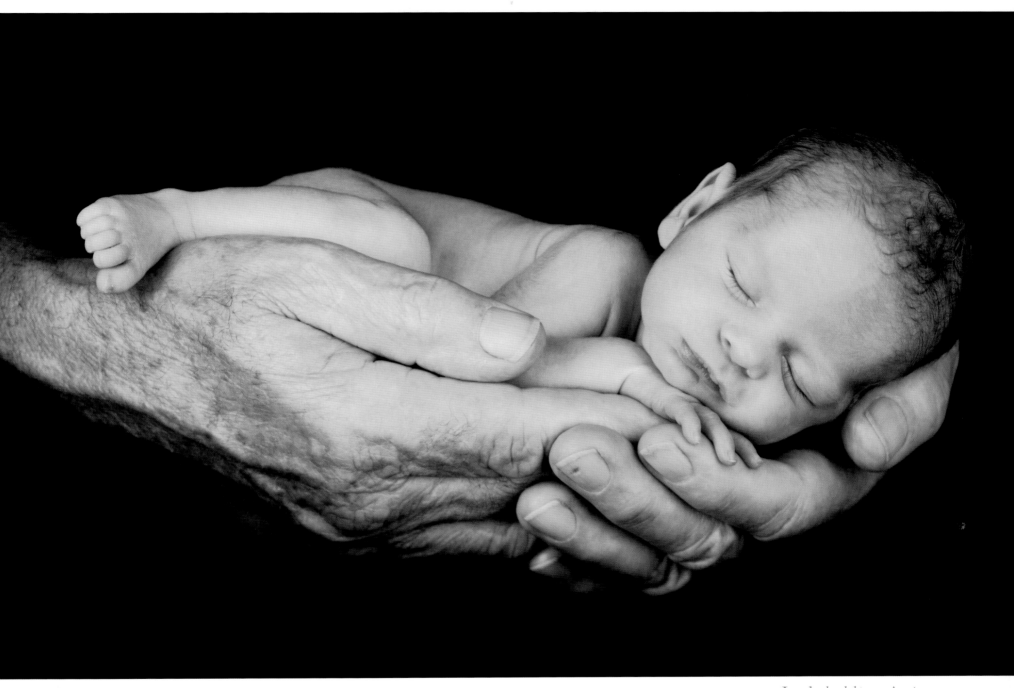

◁ ariana △

This was the second time I had used Jack's hands in one of my images, the first being when he held the little premature baby Maneesha (page 157). Ariana, who as you can see is very tiny, was on an "early release" program from the hospital—she had been born twenty-five days early, and weighed just under 2.3 kilograms (about 5 pounds).

Ariana is also featured in another image (left). Those of us who are parents often forget how tiny our newborn babies were. I have no photographs of myself as a newborn baby, and when I was in the darkroom watching this image slowly appear in the developer I thought again how wonderful it would be for Ariana to look back on when she is an adult.

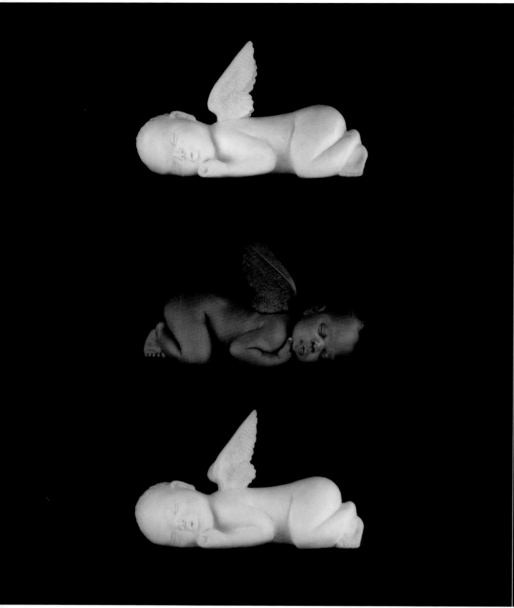

John 1996

Kofi 1997

john *as an* angel

kofi *in a* nautilus shell

This is another example of arm placement that didn't quite happen perfectly on the day. John, the only real baby in this image, modeled for the two pale angels a few days before the shoot, so they would appear to be identical to him. Then Dawn created the two plaster likenesses of John as quickly as she could. The trick at the shoot was to have John sleeping in exactly the same position. He was quite happy to sleep, but he didn't want me to move his hand. In fact, every time I tried to move it he would start yelling at me. That's fine!

I thought I'd have to carry this prop shell all the way to a shoot in the United States; then I was lucky enough to find Kofi, who was born in Auckland.

The idea for the shoot came while I was holidaying in North Queensland, Australia, the home of the magnificent Great Barrier Reef. I love the amazing shells to be found up there. Mother Nature never seems to get confused about color or design, but she certainly never made a shell this large.

varjanare
as an angel

This image was shot during one of my trips to photograph in San Francisco.

Varjanare was four weeks old. At the time I photographed her, I was planning a calendar with an angel theme and she was perfect for it. Her very light wings, made of foam and plaster, are attached to a small and flexible piece of wire at the back of the pillar. Once she was asleep, the wings had to be carefully lowered onto her back without waking her.

◁ ebenezer *and* adnan

To find two newborn African babies in Auckland at the same time was a miracle. In desperation, I had even done an interview on local radio, asking for people with babies of different nationalities (in particular those from Africa) to contact the studio. There was no response at all, and then we received a telephone call from a man on his mobile phone who was riding on a bus. He said that he had heard the interview, and that he had just spotted a very pregnant African woman standing at the last bus stop he had passed. So my studio manager, Natalie, jumped in her car and rushed down to the bus stop, but of course the woman had obviously boarded a bus and left.

Over the next few days Natalie went to every corner store in the area to ask if anybody knew the pregnant woman, but nobody could recall her. Then one day as she was driving to work, Natalie passed an African man who was riding a bicycle. So she flagged the astonished man down and, to her surprise, he turned out to be

the baby's father. Just when we were thinking our luck could not get any better, he told Natalie that he and his wife had a friend whose baby was due at the same time. They were all from Ghana.

In this case, the shoot was the easy part. On the day, both babies slept through the whole proceedings. I just try never to give up on an idea, despite the inherent difficulties involved. In hindsight, whenever I look at this image I wish that I hadn't used the cherries. At the time, I thought the richness of their color would add an extra element, which wasn't really necessary. However, they did come in handy in the same way fig leaves did for medieval painters. (I'm not prudish, but I think it's important that babies are not unnecessarily exposed in this way.)

peony angel(s) ▷

Whenever I look at this image, I remember the amazing sight in the studio of literally hundreds of peonies. They were absolutely magnificent, and their sweet scent pervaded the whole studio. I had to wait for precisely the right time of year to shoot this image, when peonies were right at the peak of their season and a local grower was able to supply so many flowers at the one time. When this image was originally published, I only featured one baby, and I don't really know why because, upon revisiting the film, I discovered that there were five other babies in the studio that day, and they all performed wonderfully. Most of us would feel slightly daunted by competing with a whole bed of peony roses, but it didn't seem to faze them at all, in fact, they thought the flowers quite tasty!

For a week or so after the shoot, we had peonies everywhere in vases around the studio and at home—they were glorious. Ever since then they have been one of my favorite flowers. I later featured the peony as one of my six flowers in the *Miracle* project—on which I collaborated with Celine Dion. In fact, Celine stars on the cover of the book, resplendent in a peony gown.

Danielle 1995

bumblebees

This image was created in San Francisco, in 1993, for the first shoot I ever conducted in the United States. The very large honeycomb prop was made in New Zealand, and transported to San Francisco, probably the starting point of my interesting relationship with the customs departments at airports in both countries, who are now used to weird and wonderful things being transported back and forth!

When I was planning the image, I knew that I would need at least fifteen six- to seven-month-old babies. Photographing this many babies in one image has its unique difficulties, and as my career progressed, I avoided crowd scenes like this more and more. There is a huge element of luck involved in pulling something like this off and, after a while, I found it too stressful to plan an image and know that there was a good chance I wouldn't be able to achieve it.

These days, I always travel with my own very experienced team of people, but back in 1993, I was a novice in terms of knowing the particular difficulties that can arise, organizing a shoot in a foreign country, with people whom I'd only just met.

I had hired a talent scout in San Francisco to find the babies for this shoot, and stipulated that they be six- to seven-month-olds. I explained once again that when babies are older and more mobile, they aren't content to sit for too long.

On the morning of the shoot, however, as everybody was arriving, I discovered that almost half of the babies were much older than I had stipulated, in fact, one was over twelve months old. I was horrified, but of course had to proceed with the shoot as everybody was there, ready in the studio, and excited about taking part. Some of the costumes were far too small for the older babies so some quick adjustments were made. I needed to have all of the babies dressed in the bumblebee outfits before the shoot commenced; needless to say, there were three or four bees who were actually walking around the studio—hilarious in hindsight—but I didn't think so at the time.

I knew that inevitably, as we started to place the babies in their positions (and tried to keep each one occupied and amused for the time it took to place everybody else), one or two babies would decide that they didn't want to be in the honeycomb. When this happened, we would need to quickly replace them with another baby, and still keep everybody else happy. Sometimes this isn't easy, or necessarily successful, and the mood can change at any time! I try to work very quickly and calmly in these situations but on the odd occasion it can soon become noisy and chaotic.

Directly behind each baby, out of sight, there was a small pole built into the structure. At the back of each bumblebee suit there was a very large Velcro seatbelt. This seatbelt went snugly around the babies' tummies (inside the costume) and then around the pole, to keep them safely in place and make them feel very secure.

As I was shooting, we were changing the babies in and out of their places and they started to become very interested in each other, as you can see. At the very end, when I was pretty sure I had my shot and we were just about to take all of the babies out, I turned around to find that one of the oldest babies who came to the shoot was fast asleep in his mother's arms, so I gently placed him in position at the bottom of the honeycomb. This just goes to prove that sometimes my theory on the ideal age of the babies I needed was proved totally wrong. I'm very happy in this case to admit that!

phillip *and* arin

I love the composition of this image, the strength of the white pillar in contrast to Phillip's strong

(yet softly rounded) body and dark skin, and the pale plumpness of Arin, the newborn baby.

This image of Phillip and Arin was also taken during my first shoot in the United States. I had traveled to San Francisco mainly to photograph African American babies, and in particular create the (previous) image of the bumblebees in honeycomb.

So there I was, surrounded by beautiful little African American babies, and into the studio came Arin with her mother. One of the lovely things that happens to me frequently is that people bring their babies just to say hello, and as far as I can recall, Arin's mother was friends with, or related to, somebody from the studio I was working in at the time. Arin was so beautiful and her skin was like porcelain. I knew that I had a spare afternoon the following day, so I asked her mother if she would like to return with Arin for a photo shoot as I had something in mind. After all, if I had come to the United States specifically to photograph African American babies, who was to say there was an age limit on this. Phillip, although not quite as young as the rest of my models, provided the perfect skin contrast to Arin.

There was a white pillar prop already in the studio at the time. I sent my young female assistants out to find a very dark-skinned and well-toned bodybuilder. As you can imagine, they were most enthusiastic about their mission and resourcefully positioned themselves in the car park outside of a local gym. Eventually Phillip emerged and they pounced! He must have initially thought they were crazy but he was a good sport and immediately agreed to come to the shoot.

When I first met Phillip I asked if he had any experience with young babies. He said no, but that he and his wife were very keen to start a family of their own. In hindsight, this shoot was probably good training for him, as I asked him what he would do if he felt the inevitable trickle down his back and he said he'd be absolutely fine. People who have not had much to do with young babies need to be forewarned! Arin was true to form; halfway through the shoot, poor Phillip said, "Oh my goodness . . ."

jonti *as an* angel

I had to shoot this image twice. The first time we didn't leave enough room in the prop to accommodate the baby, and I didn't realize this until right in the middle of the first shoot, when I had a newborn fast asleep and perfect. When I tried to place her into position, she simply wouldn't fit! I had even organized to shoot video footage on the day, which I sometimes do with my shoots as it's useful to show in the background when I am doing television interviews. So, as it turns out, the footage that is often shown of this particular shoot is not actually of Jonti, who ended up in the final image a few days later when we had made the opening in the hands much larger.

Jonti was fourteen days old, and had already been in for a shoot prior to this. She was just so delicate and tiny and she was the obvious choice for this image. Once I had corrected the size of the opening she was to lie in, and I placed her into the hands, she just seemed to melt into the spot and then lie there so comfortably with her little mouth open.

The stone angel prop itself was impressive. It was very light and had been especially carved out of one huge block of foam with a reinforced steel dish incorporated into the hands to make the structure strong. I had photographed my assistant's hands beforehand in exactly this position, as a model for the sculpture, and Dawn, who has made all of my props for many years, did a wonderful job of bringing the sculpture to life. It is always difficult to find ready-made props for the special needs of babies, and therefore we take a great deal of time and effort to make suitable, safe, and comfortable props for individual shoots. My dilemma is what to do with them all afterward.

Jonti is such a lovely name that one of my staff members who became pregnant in 2002 also named her baby Jonti.

boys *and* doves

James, Diontah, Niam, Greg, *and* Mutunga 1993

This is another of the images I created on my first overseas shoot in San Francisco in 1993. I had been thinking about the concept for this image for a number of years, specifically using very dark-skinned children and contrasting their smooth, rich, and silky skin texture with the whiteness of the doves.

I thought it would initially be difficult to find trained doves, but of course, in America, where there is a huge movie industry, people are used to sourcing all things weird and wonderful, so my birds were not a problem at all. The dove trainer arrived with them at the studio and they behaved perfectly!

The beautiful boys in the image—James, Diontah, Niam, Greg, and Mutunga—ranged in age from seven to ten years. Not only were they *very excited* about taking part, they were also very keen to see the doves. I remember thinking, "If there's a recipe for potential chaos, this must be it." Apart from having to persuade them to put their arms around each other, my main objective was to keep the boys relatively calm and focused while they had the doves on their heads; but I needn't have worried; they were wonderful. Halfway through

the shoot, one of them said to me, "Will the doves do anything on our heads?"

"Of course not, they're trained," I said (with my fingers crossed).

In 2003, an e-mail arrived addressed to my Web site, and it was a wonderful surprise for me. I'd like to share it here:

Hi Ms. Geddes,

It has been about 9 years since you have seen me. My name is James. I was in the picture "dreamers" which you took in San Francisco in 1993. I never knew you had a website and today marks the first time that I have been to your website. I am 17 and at Diablo Valley Junior College. It was funny for me to see myself on the internet. I had to go to the calendar gallery to see myself. I would like to thank you so very much for letting me partake in what I believe is photographic history. Oh, I am on the far left, looking as if I am sad. Continue your wonderful work.

Thanks, James

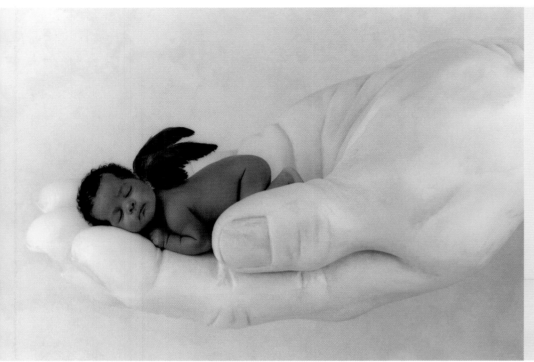

C.J. 1996   Claire, Alexander, Hazel, Jamie, *and* Madeline 1992

C.J. *in the* marble hand   bathtub babies

This image was taken in San Francisco. Many people assume it has been computer-generated, but that's not the case. The enormous hand was crafted in Auckland from foam and plaster and transported to the United States for the shoot, in a huge crate. When we were packing the hand at the studio, Dawn came up with the clever idea of using a special form of expanding foam which is often used in the building and marine trade for insulation and gap filling, to encase the hand in the crate, and protect it on the journey to the States. The foam comes in a two-part mix and when both parts are combined it expands very quickly. Unfortunately, we added too much foam all at once and as it rapidly expanded around the hand and filled the crate, we all had to sit on the lid trying to stop it from rising to the ceiling.

Can you imagine the U.S. customs officers asking, "What's in the box?" I don't think I'd know quite what to say.

Claire, Alexander, Hazel, Jamie, and Madeline were all six- to seven-month-old babies. I've found that babies this age generally don't like sitting too close to one another and I'm not quite sure why. All of the babies at the shoot were beautiful, but it was hard not to take a special shine to Hazel, who is sitting in the middle. She was the epitome of a Renaissance-style baby—lovely, round, and plump—gorgeous. Recently, Hazel wrote to me and sent a photograph of herself as a teenager—a beautiful tall, slim, and gangly fifteen-year-old, who now has a baby brother who looks exactly like Hazel did when she was sitting in the bathtub!

For a shoot like this, there are always twice (or even three times) as many babies on hand as are needed, so if anybody didn't want to sit in the tub it wasn't a problem. I need that many babies in order to be reasonably sure I will be able to achieve a shot with five who are happy to participate, and all at the same time. Babies, in general, have no respect for photographers' plans. When they decide the show is over, it's definitely over.

Trent *and* Joel 1992   Jordan, Trent, Amber-Marie, *and* Joel 1992

trent *and* joel

mud people

Trent and Joel are twins, and were six years old when this image was taken. What I love about twins, as is evidenced in this image, is their closeness. The boys were naturals, and with their beautiful faces, it was hard to take a bad photograph of them. They modeled for me a number of times when they were around this age, and along with their sister and cousin became my "Mud People."

These children are all related. Trent is second from the left and Joel on the far right. Between them is their sister Amber-Marie, and on the left is their cousin, Jordan. They were all really enthusiastic about the shoot, and very good about being covered in a mixture of moisturizing cream and potters' clay. Into the bargain, the clay kept drying very quickly, so we had to spray them with water during the shoot. Unfortunately, the day of this shoot dawned as the first cold day of the year.

When it was all over, there was a mad scramble for the showers!

woodland fairies

The original version of this image, created in 1997 and first published in *Until Now,* included twenty-six little woodland fairies. All of the original babies were photographed separately over a two-day period, which was quite an undertaking in itself. I don't often have that many babies in the studio at any one time but, when I do, it induces such a wonderful atmosphere. Everyone thought their babies looked so gorgeous in their tiny outfits.

It has often been said that every mother thinks her baby is the most beautiful in the world and, of course, each and every one of them is absolutely correct. As I write this, the thought crosses my mind that these twenty-six babies would now be ten years of age.

Long before the babies were even photographed we were collecting props. The driftwood and various other bits and pieces that make up the woodland were collected over two months, during numerous trips to the wild and beautiful west coast beaches near Auckland. I fondly remember those walks along the beaches with our daughters and my small dog, Poppy, bounding on ahead, the black sand constantly underfoot in the car for months afterward.

Included in the woodland scene is the huge piece of driftwood I had kept since the 1995 shoot of Sophie, my first woodland fairy. On page 117 you can get an idea of how large it is compared to little Sophie.

It took almost a week to meticulously place all the components included in the woodland setting, and photograph the scene, minus the babies. Once I determined where each baby would be placed within the image, soft foam shapes were crafted for them to be photographed on, enabling them to fit precisely into position. Then, the babies came to the studio for their part in the project.

For the two days it took to photograph the babies, I placed a large print of the woodland scene on the studio wall, with the position of each baby marked and numbered. This was done for two reasons: first, I thought it would be helpful to explain to the mothers exactly what I was trying to achieve; second, I could work methodically to save any confusion later when I was combining everything on the computer.

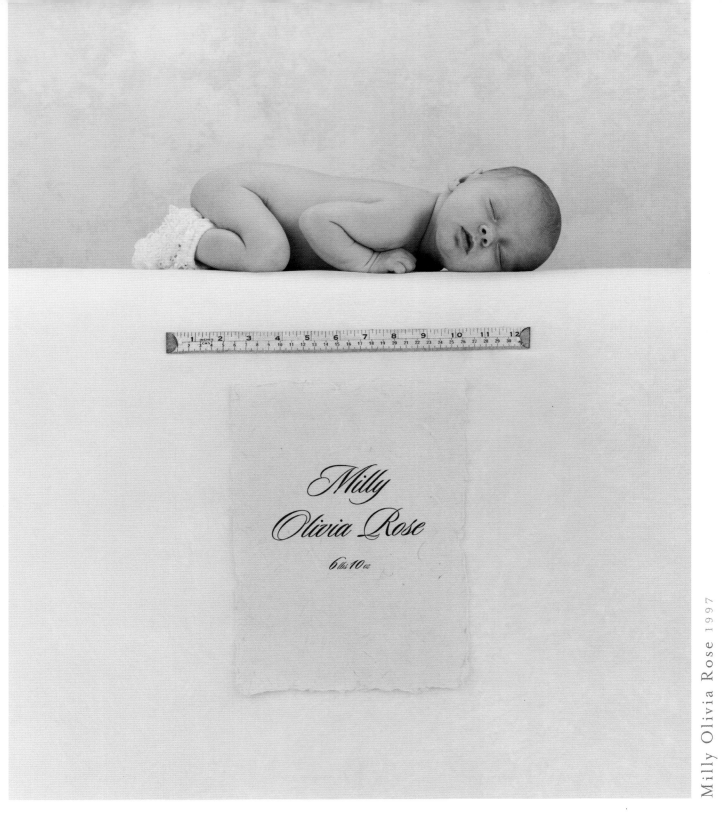

◁ olivia *and* milly olivia rose △

These images are so very special to many people. They are symbolic of grief, but also of the renewal of hope. Little Olivia, our "Baby Bald Eagle" (left), tragically drowned about a year after she was photographed. All of us who had worked with her were devastated. At the time of this terrible tragedy, she was also featured in the left-hand pot on the cover of my 1995 calendar (pictured). Understandably, I thought her parents would not want the images published afterward, but her mother, Clare, said that she wanted to see Olivia's beautiful face everywhere, as a celebration of her life. In 1997, Clare brought her new baby, Milly Olivia Rose, to the studio for this image (above). Milly was undeniably a very precious baby. She restored our faith in life and, whenever I look at these images, I am reminded that we should never take any of our loved ones for granted. Indeed, we should celebrate and cherish our children every single day.

barbara *holding* maynard

Often newborn babies are born with a soft layer of downy hair on their bodies, which gradually disappears soon afterward. This is entirely normal.

Barbara is not the mother of Maynard. Her own baby had been into the studio for another shoot a few weeks earlier. But she had such fabulous hair that I asked her if she'd model for me. Maynard still had that suppleness unique to a newborn.

Barbara *holding* Maynard 1994

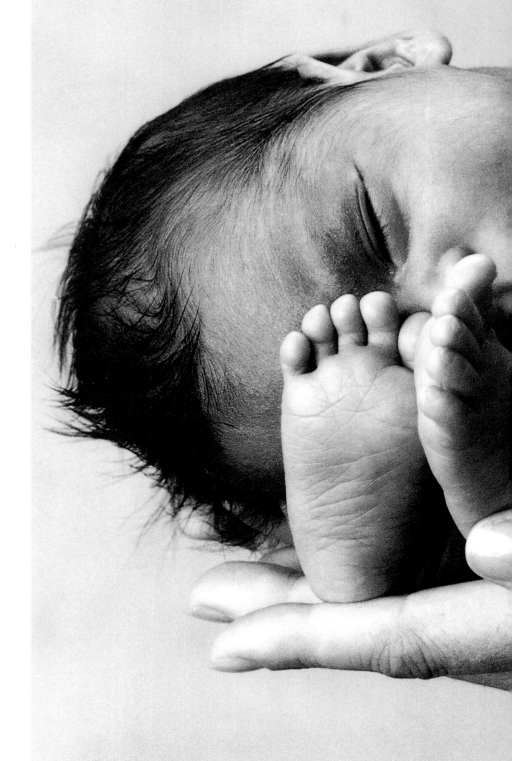

The beautiful fairy costumes were all individually designed in remarkable detail, specifically to match the scene. I am still amazed at the amount of work that went into making them. But, I had never been totally happy with the image in its original published form. I felt that the whole concept had far more potential and that the twenty-six original fairies were being overpowered by the woodland scene; hence, almost ten years later, I've decided to rework and enhance the image for *A Labor of Love.*

Adam *and* Benjamin 1997

The original image was shot in black and white, so as an experiment we spent time on the computer selectively and subtly introducing color into elements of each fairy and enlarging them slightly to make them more noticeable. I then remembered that some of the babies I had photographed for the *Miracle* project had not been featured in the book. So, I set about incorporating them into the scene as well; something I thought would take only a day or two. It turned into a month-long marathon of computer work, as we kept adding different versions of the outfits to all of the new babies, some of whom happened to be naked in their original images.

Then, to complicate matters further, someone suggested that "Julia Snail" (featured on page 120) would be delightful in a cameo appearance. That was also when I remembered that I had photographed some birds belonging to the owl family during a holiday a few years back. I love owls and so I incorporated them into the image as well. These two are of the tawny frogmouth variety. By this stage, I was becoming obsessed with the whole scene, and then a friend found another owl in their back garden and sent a photograph with a message to say that the little bird had heard there was a vacancy going in one of my images and could he apply. It was all getting way out of hand!

In this new version of "Woodland Fairies" there are forty-seven fairies, one snail, and three tawny frogmouths (who are doing their best to be invisible).

woodland fairies

Julia 1991

Alexandra *and* Myles 1993

◁ mary *and* charlotte

alexandra *and* myles △

This was my very first image of a pregnant woman, and I have continued to explore pregnancy themes throughout my work ever since. I photographed Mary and Charlotte in 1991, when I was shooting for my very first calendar. I loved the image so much I even wanted to use it as the cover.

However, I was dissuaded from using it because at the time it may have been too explicit for a baby calendar. So when *Until Now* was first published, in 1999, I was relieved that I could finally include "Mary and Charlotte," as this image is one of my all-time favorites.

The little girl, Charlotte, is the sister of the unborn baby, Julia, who featured less than a week after her birth in the image above left.

Alexandra and Myles are seven-month-old twins. They were just classic, lovely, round, soft, and spongy, with faces straight out of an old advertisement for something like Pears Baby Soap. Notice the rolls down their arms and legs, and their fabulous tummies. They are the very essence of what I love about babies.

Mary *and* Charlotte 1991

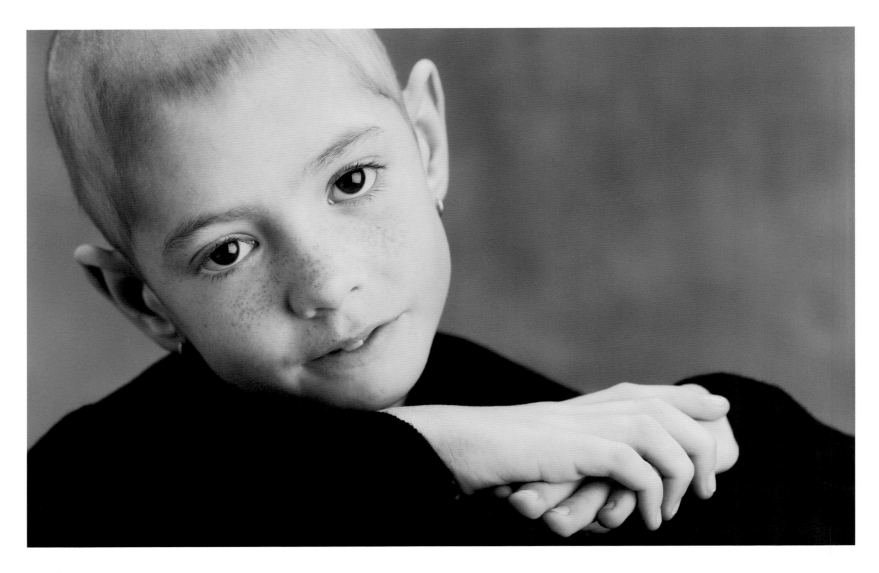

stacey

Stacey was a very special little friend who came into our lives when she was six years old, and for three wonderful years gave us far more joy than we ever could have given back, although we tried. Her many long hospital stays were spent in the Starship Hospital in Auckland, which we can see from the balcony of our apartment. We would flash our apartment lights on and off in the evenings to let her know we were thinking of her while she was in isolation in her room, and she would blow up surgical gloves and float them out the window as a return signal.

She had a wickedly wonderful sense of humor, and one of our favorite things to do together was drive down a busy street in my car and turn on the spray for the windscreen wipers and see if we could sprinkle passers-by. She would be doubled up in hysterics if we were successful. Somehow, when we were together, we both turned into a pair of naughty kids.

Every year, in Stacey's memory, I like to deliver some of my special plush toys to all of the children in her old hospital ward who are unable to be at home for Christmas.

These two images were taken the day after the doctors told her that there was nothing more they could do for her, and that she possibly had only weeks to live. We had already planned the photo session prior to this news, and I naturally thought that she wouldn't want to go ahead with it, but she was adamant she wanted to. She was so tiny and fragile by that time.

The two of us worked quietly alone together in the studio and the atmosphere was incredibly peaceful. Her parents, Gill and Tony, were taking her on a special trip to the Gold Coast in Australia the next day, and she was chatting excitedly about everything she was planning to do there. She told me afterward that she had a wonderful time. I knew while we were doing the shoot that for her own reasons she wanted to make the images special. She died, of cancer, just after she had turned nine.

I wish Stacey was able to know that she lives on through the *Miracle* project I created with Celine Dion in 2003—she was the catalyst for bringing the two of us together. I explain how this happened in the *Miracle* chapter, beginning on page 262.

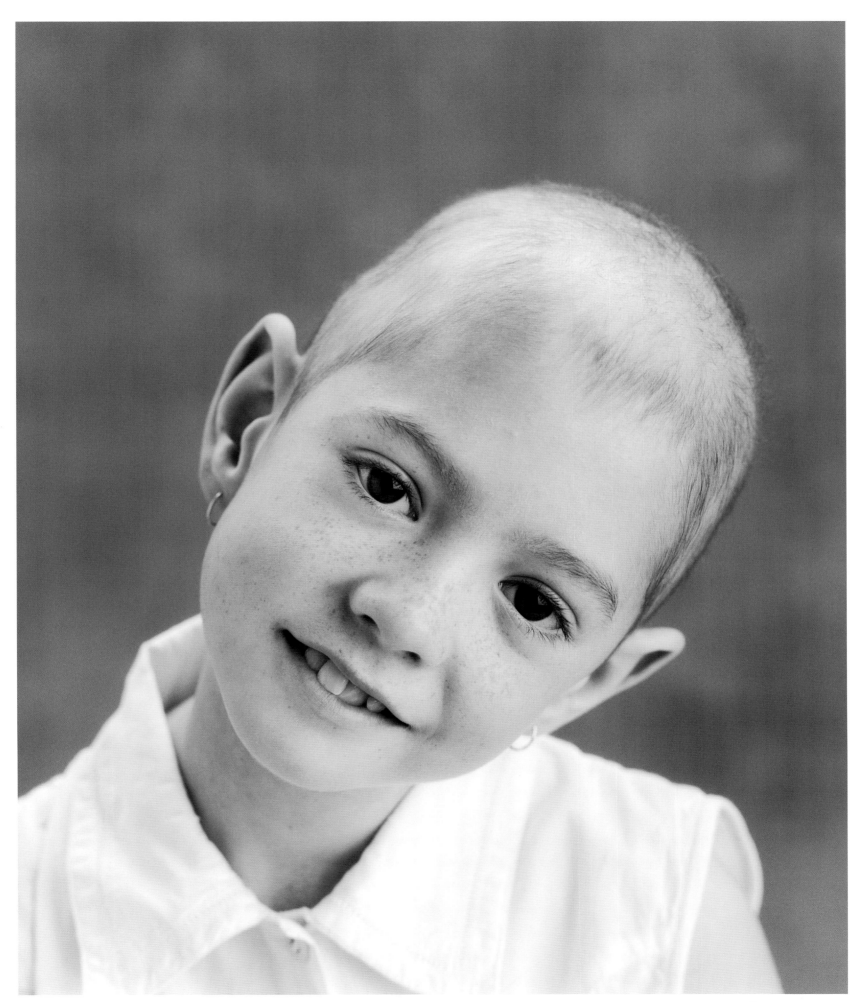

Stacey 1997

rock oyster

Being Australian, when I was shooting for *Until Now,* I wanted to include some Australian Aboriginal babies in the book. However, finding the babies proved more difficult than I had anticipated.

The logical first step was to begin my search in the capital cities of Australia, where I knew that I would readily be able to hire a studio and equipment for the shoot. However, as I soon found out, most pure-blood Aboriginal people do not live in the cities and densely populated areas.

Further research led me to the Tiwi people of Bathurst and Melville Islands, in the far north of Australia, and from there began our extraordinary adventures among these remarkable people. I needed a special permit to gain access to Bathurst Island, and an Aboriginal guide for our time there. The Tiwi have a unique way of looking at the world, and it was a privilege to work with them over the three days it took to prepare for and achieve this image.

It was terribly hot, in fact mid-summer, when we were there, and my studio was an extension off the back room of the art gallery, a large galvanized iron shed next to the school. Everybody was very interested in what we were up to, so we had lots of visitors and an audience of children at all times. On the day we left, all of the local children gathered to farewell us, with an offering of a celebratory bucket of witchetty grubs, as a delicacy.

Gathering the rocks for the shoot took a full day, and quite a precarious trip up the hillside in an old four-wheel-drive vehicle, which (I discovered too late) had no handbrake. The rocks were covered in very dense red clay soil, not to mention thousands of angry red ants, who didn't take kindly to being disturbed and transported in the back of the truck. Once back at the schoolyard, we hosed off all the rocks and laid them out to dry on the ground at the back of the art gallery before placing them in position inside.

As there was no accommodation for us on the island, each morning we would fly over in a small light aircraft from Darwin and then back again in the evenings. I remember taking off early from Darwin on those mornings, just as the sun was rising, and the landscape and light were magnificent.

The oyster shell prop had been made at my studio in New Zealand and flown to Darwin and on to Bathurst Island. Needless to say, the customs officers were a little confused when I told them there was an oyster shell in the enormous box we were transporting with us.

Alexis *and* Rochelle 1993

black pearl

After I had finished on Bathurst Island and we were back in Darwin preparing to leave for home, I was introduced to the Paspaley family, who own Paspaley Pearls, one of the largest pearling companies in the world and based in Darwin.

As we were chatting about the image I had just created, which I intended to call "Black Pearl," a thought came to me for another image. I asked if it would be possible to do a shoot with quite a lot of pearls, and they said, "How many do you mean?" Not knowing how pearls are measured or accounted for, I merely said, "Well, perhaps three or four buckets full." In true Australian style, they didn't flinch, and the following year what was to be known as the real "Black Pearl" image was created when I returned again to Darwin with a huge pearl prop (right).

For purposes of security, the shoot was done in a small anteroom directly outside an enormous safe, where the pearls were stored. It was at precisely the right time of year when the pearl harvest was in and the pearls were all still gathered together in one place. We erected scaffolding over the top of the scene, and the space was so small there was barely any room to move once the scaffolding was in place. Certainly, from my vantage point at the top of the scaffolding, there was only room for me to lie flat on my stomach, as the ceiling was only a few inches above my head.

In a contained area on the floor, which was padded with soft cotton wool, we tipped literally hundreds of the most magnificent pearls from plastic bags, as if they were marbles. The colors were incredible, from warm gold, through pinks, grays, and silvers, to the classic creamy white. I guess you can tell that I am a fan of pearls!

Little Adam, who was two weeks old, was the only one of three babies who came to the shoot who even remotely wanted to sleep, and I knew that we wouldn't be able to reschedule the shoot if I wasn't able to achieve it on that day. So, it was a little tense in the room when we finally got him sleeping very lightly in the large pearl. I wanted to also place some pearls on Adam's tummy and to discreetly cover his private parts, so we were warming the pearls in our hands just for this purpose. Unfortunately, to complicate matters even further, Adam had developed the hiccups. Whenever we tried to position the pearls on his tummy, he would hiccup, and they'd all roll off. Eventually, as you can see, everything turned out well in the end.

After the babies had gone home, we took secret pictures of ourselves lying in the pearls, but I won't show them here; if I did, I'd be in big trouble with the Paspaleys.

Even today, many years later, we still talk about this shoot and how amazing it was at the time. Recently, while talking to Nick Paspaley, I asked him what the real value of all the pearls in the image was. He shrugged and said it was probably around 29 million Australian dollars (23 million U.S. dollars).

Adam 1994

alexander *and* harry *as* angels

There was a six-month period during late 1994 and early 1995 when I was shooting an angel calendar. There were feathers everywhere— duck feathers, goose feathers, chicken feathers, every type of feather imaginable—and lots of them. Feathers can't be rushed, and they cling to everything!

At the same time as I was shooting the angel calendar, I was also shooting *The Twelve Days of Christmas,* so it was a very busy time indeed, particularly feather-wise. On page 93, I tell an amusing story, for those who aren't too squeamish, about how we acquired some of the feathers, and the interesting sense of humor of some particular chicken farmers on the North Island of New Zealand who I won't name here (but you know that I know who you are).

Alexander and Harry, the two babies in this image, are three-week-old twins. Their wings were made from foam and plaster, and were already in place in the feathers (see below) when we laid the babies down. You'd think it would be easy to get two newborn babies to sleep in a feather bed (certainly, you wouldn't have to ask me twice), but in fact it wasn't, as the feathers kept tickling their feet, their ears, you name it!

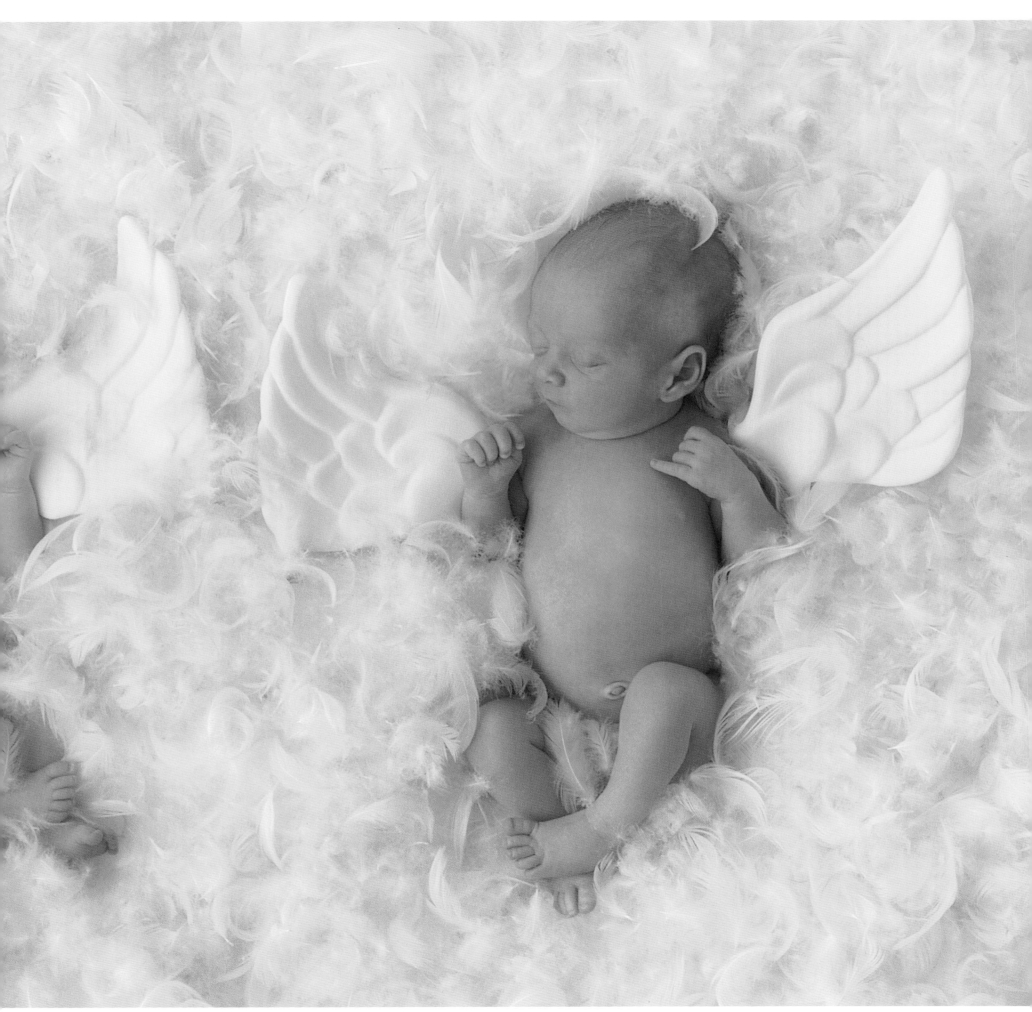

Alexander *and* Harry 1995

This image was taken in San Francisco in 1995. Alexus and Armani are twins, and at the time were nine and a half weeks old. It was fortunate that we managed to get them both to sleep at the same time, as they are much older than most of my sleeping newborns. Into the bargain, it was far more difficult than I had imagined to get them to sleep, as they didn't seem to enjoy the feel of cotton wool. I have since discovered that many people apparently do not like the feel of cotton wool on their skin. So, eventually we moved all of the cotton wool from under them and had them just lying directly on a soft blanket, which seemed to do the trick. They are almost mirror images of each other, and have the most exquisite little bodies.

alexus *and* armani *as* angels

Antonie 1995

antonie *as* *an* angel

This shoot formed part of my feather phase, and was also done in San Francisco in 1995. When Antonie came to the studio on the day, I thought he looked perfect, but suspected he would be a little too large to fit in the dish on the scales. He was a big baby, and nearly six weeks old, possibly too old to be a good sleeper in a photographic studio. However, it was one of those special (and lucky) moments, and the only time in your life when you can have all those chubby rolls and people will think it's cute.

Jessica 1996

Jessica 1996

aunty biddy's face △   autumn leaf *fairies* ▷

This image was from a portrait sitting. Jessica, twelve months old, was just learning to stand on her own. She was a real character, and apparently thought of herself as the family comedian. This is her own personal version of her Aunty Biddy's face. I'm not sure how Aunty Biddy feels about this . . .

I had an idea that she would look very sweet as a fairy (top right) but Jessica obviously had other ideas about this, as you can see!

I know you're probably thinking that these autumn leaves are real, but that's not the case. Amazingly, they were all hand-crafted out of latex. They were huge, for purposes of scale, in order to make the babies look tiny. Of course, it would have been easier to computer-generate the babies onto real leaves, but that wouldn't have made for such a good story, and the richness of color in the leaves perfectly complements the delicate blue fairy wings.

Christiaan and Annaliese are twins, just over two weeks old. I love this shot because of their little round tummies.

Christiaan *and* Annaliese 1996

I had found this wonderful old concrete pillar in a garden shop near the studio, and it was so old, fragile, and heavy that I had to shoot on location as it couldn't be transported to the studio. Besides, I also happened to like the wall behind it.

Generally, I don't like to do location work with babies, as I prefer a more controlled, comfortable waiting area for babies on a shoot. Babies need quite a lot of room to spread out—in fact, they are prone to taking over whole studios quite easily—and, understandably, it can get a little noisy at times, so we did the shoot before the store opened.

Kieran and Abigail are Down syndrome babies, which of course is completely irrelevant to the photograph, but I wish parents of these little ones would send in their photographs or contact me as a matter of course, so I can include more of them in my images.

Kieran *and* Abigail 1996

aimee *as a* fairy ▷

I am often asked to name my favorite images and this would have to be one of them.

Aimee was seven days old at the time I photographed her. What I love about this image is its absolute simplicity, and the delicate detail of her brand-new baby hair. It makes me feel like caressing her soft little head. A newborn's hair feels so fine and downy. I love to do this; it's an instinctive gesture.

Aimee was photographed lying on the lap of my studio manager, Natalie, who happened to have a big wet patch on her jeans underneath the white cloth. I think she would be pleased to be acknowledged for this!

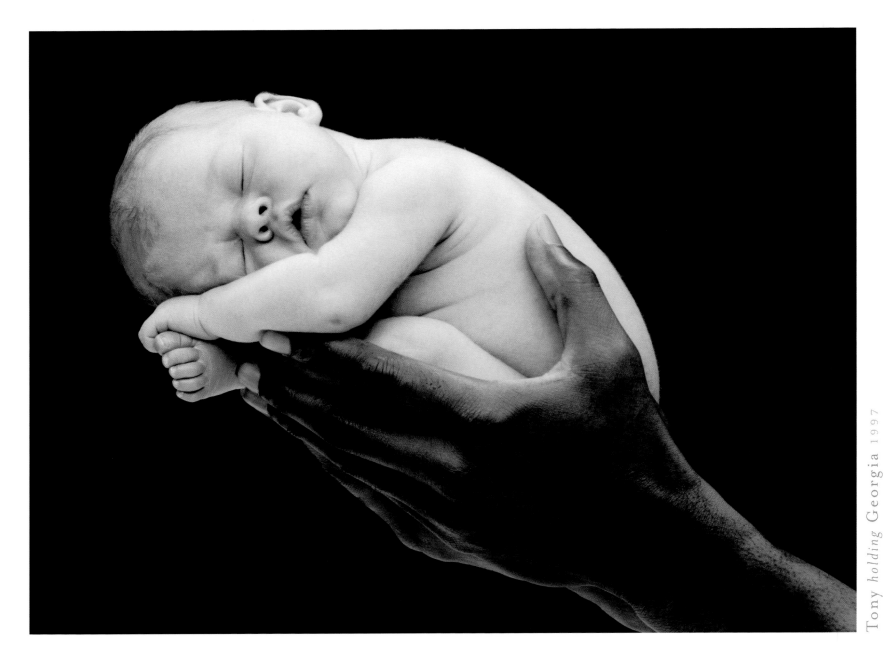

Tony *holding* Georgia 1997

tony *holding* georgia △

Georgia was only five days old, and had already been to the studio for another shoot the day before this image (above) was taken. She had been one of the forty-seven woodland fairies featured on page 188. She was very petite and perfect and I thought her face was exquisite. She also seemed to be a very good sleeper during the fairy shoot—and sleeping fairies are not always easy to find! I asked Georgia's mother if she would like to come back the next day to create this image, and she said she would love to.

I am always fascinated by the fact that newborn babies are so very flexible. This is most likely because they have been living in such cramped quarters for the previous nine months. For years I practiced yoga and was never able to achieve a pose like this. Tony, who is holding Georgia, played on a basketball team in Auckland. There is only a very small African American population living in New Zealand and so I have featured Tony regularly. He is always a really good sport, regardless of the number of times he has been christened in various ways by newborn babies!

Georgia 1997

gemma *and* amelia rose

Gemma is the baby who is asleep. Amelia Rose is the same baby who is lying on the country pumpkin (page 163). I was surprised when she opened her eyes and looked so directly at the camera.

Normally I photograph newborn babies asleep, because their eyes are still not focused properly, and tend to go in different directions! I think Amelia looks very wise; she almost seems to be smiling at me.

angel nursery

I photographed these newborn babies, with their different-colored feather wings, gradually over a period of a few weeks. Included are two sets of twins.

This image has been put together on computer, although more than once people have asked me what my secret is to getting so many babies asleep at the same time. Perhaps I should lay claim to being a miracle worker, but believe me, if I knew the key to getting even one baby to sleep on cue, I'd tell it to every new mother in the world!

As a matter of interest, the record number of babies I have actually photographed, together and asleep, at the same time, is thirteen. They are featured on page 291.

Angel Nursery 1995—96

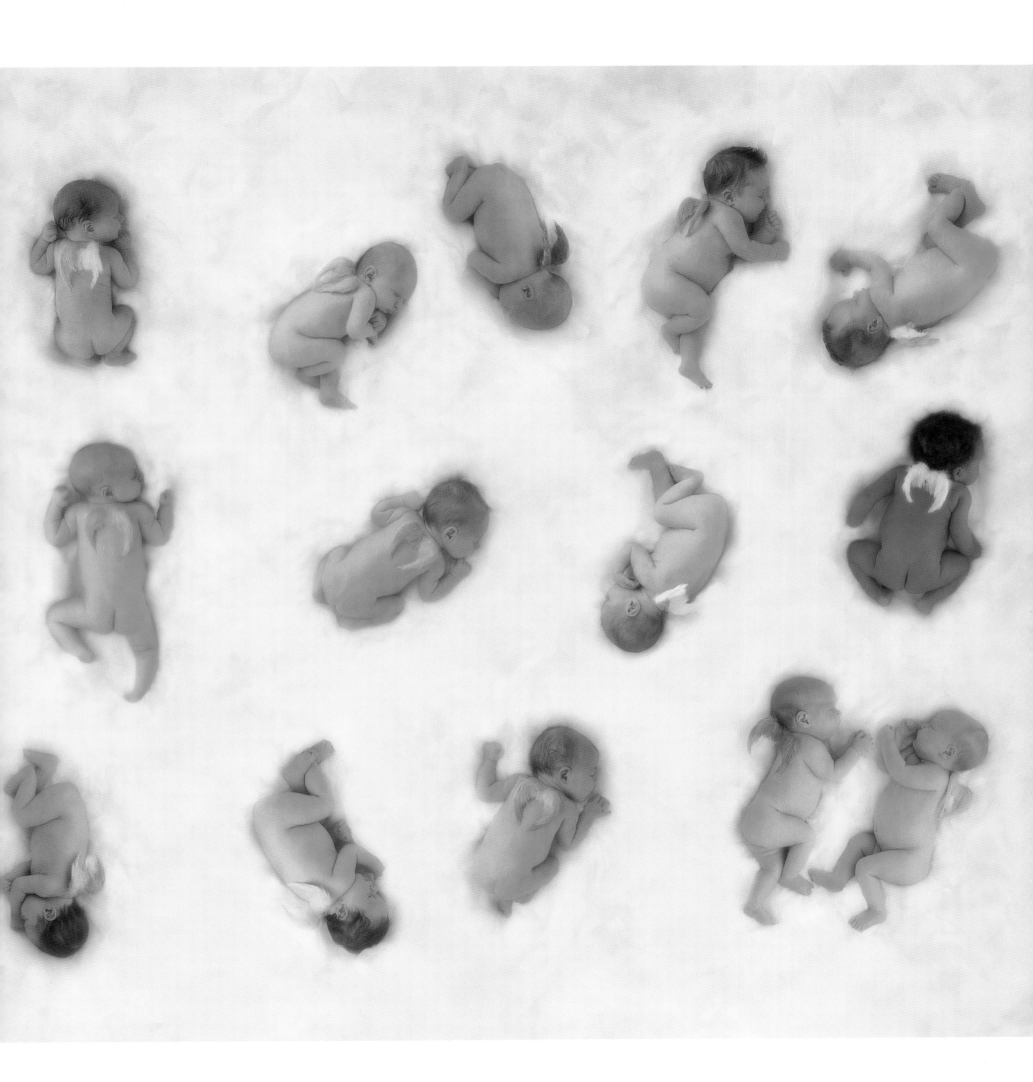

P U R E

A simple image can sometimes say a thousand words. This is the credo of the visual artist, but for all visual artists, myself included, it can take time to find the truth of simplicity.

Pure, my third coffee table book, is probably the one that is closest to my heart and closest to fulfilling my developing desire for simplicity and purity. Creatively, I was seeking a complete change from the more complicated props and styling of *Down in the Garden* and *Until Now,* and it was very liberating to find myself in free and open creative space where I was able to take on any new direction at will. If *Down in the Garden* provided me with a base on which to build my future career, *Until Now* had become the bridge I needed in order to completely leave heavy propping and flowerpots behind, to take on a more simple, ethereal style.

Over the years, the central theme in my imagery has always been pregnancy, the newborn, and the promise of new life. In *Pure,* I wanted to totally devote myself to this subject matter and examine the whole area more closely. Hence the overall theme of the book is a celebration of pregnancy and new life, the absolute natural, honest beauty of a pregnant woman, and the purity, innocences, and promise of a newborn baby.

The two smaller inset images which are included here are an example of how I use life-sized dolls to prepare for the shoot beforehand. Everything needs to be exactly right, lighting-wise, and totally rehearsed before the babies are on the scene.

I was fortunate in that *Pure* had no specific publishing deadlines, enabling me to take my time developing and experimenting with

concepts over the four years it took to complete the book. I pretty much lived and breathed *Pure* for the whole time, but I loved every minute. Images for *Pure* were shot in New York, Los Angeles, and at my studio in Auckland. In hindsight, I probably had enough images for the book after three years of shooting, but I wanted to extend another year before publishing because, well, to be perfectly honest, I am never really completely satisfied with my work.

My personal criteria for *Pure* were to keep the images simple, calm, elegant, and timeless. The catalyst for my creative direction in *Pure* came from a shoot I conducted in New York in 1997. I went to New York with very few preconceived ideas, just a few backgrounds, some fabric, and a couple of very simple props. Each day, I would go to the studio and try to create something fueled purely by the energy and beauty of the newborn babies who were there. And the images slowly evolved, every day, into something very simple and powerful. I remember thinking afterward that it was the most concentrated and nourishing creative time I had spent in many years. I often find that the experience of travel tends to free my mind creatively, and even though I find it more difficult shooting in studios that aren't my own, it's good to be out of your own comfort zone occasionally.

I specifically wanted the pregnancy images in *Pure* to give pregnant women everywhere a confidence that they are all, in their own special way, truly beautiful.

None of the pregnant women in *Pure* are professional models, nor had we ever met before. But all of them, without hesitation, even though they did not know me personally, were prepared—at such a vulnerable time in their lives—to embrace the project and be a part of the book. I felt privileged that these women placed so much trust in me.

The New York images were produced with a huge 20 x 24 inch Polaroid camera, and I found the process of creating such large and instant imagery in this way to be very stimulating and exciting. I came away from New York thinking that I now had a real direction for *Pure* in that I should discipline myself, not plan too much in advance; just let the images and ideas slowly develop.

Earlier, during the planning stages for the New York trip, I was puzzled that people said it may be difficult to find babies there and, in particular, newborns. When I asked why, the consensus seemed to be that New Yorkers might not be so friendly and forthcoming. Would they trust me enough to bring their newborn babies to a shoot? As far as I was concerned, mothers are the same everywhere, and I couldn't see why they would be any different in New York. Thankfully, my theory proved to be correct—people were open and friendly and came from everywhere with their babies.

Anyway, for those who are curious, when I am not shooting in my studio at home, here's how we go about finding babies in various cities.

Approximately one month out from the shoot, my studio manager makes contact with various groups and local organizations in that particular city who cater to the needs of newborn babies—for instance, midwives, multiple-birth associations, and twin clubs. Often this is all that is required. A week to ten days before the shoot, she travels to the city and establishes a base and phone number for people to make contact. As was the case in New York, gradually the

calls started to come in and, in no time at all, we had far more babies than we needed.

In New York, a local African American radio station was kind enough to interview me, which drew a great response from the African American community. We were even invited to a Sunday morning church service in Harlem, which to the uninitiated is not only deeply spiritual, but an amazingly vibrant and colorful experience, something we'll never forget. Kel and I were fortunate enough to be able to take our young daughters along and they still talk about it to this day.

We placed notices in local supermarkets and at one stage even received a phone call from a woman who said she didn't have a baby herself, but she had just seen our notice and there was a maternity hospital just down her street and she was heading there right away to put another copy on their noticeboard. You see, people are generally helpful and generous everywhere.

Mothers would bring newborn babies to meet me in the reception area of the hotel where we were staying. One mother arrived on the way home from the hospital with her newborn.

There was a wonderfully unique atmosphere and energy during that shoot in New York. It was very inspirational for me and the simplicity and strength of the imagery I was able to create during that time helped to guide my future direction for *Pure*.

I used two adult models for the whole duration of the shoot, Tuli and Emma, and neither had any prior experience working with babies, especially newborns. Both said afterward that they loved the whole experience, especially the close personal contact they were able to have with such brand-new life.

When I returned from New York, I spent a number of weeks reflecting on the meaning of the word "pure" in all its different forms. I have a large whiteboard in my office covering one whole wall, and on this I began to gradually build up a list of words or phrases to inspire thoughts on all sorts of imagery that related or linked in some way to the concept of purity. I invited my team to contribute, and each day I noticed the list getting longer and longer. My then thirteen-year-old daughter, Kelly, who was learning Spanish at the time, even contributed a few Spanish words. This list helped me delve deeper and was a reference guide during the process of shooting the book. In the end, I decided to include some of the words throughout the book—it seemed so appropriate and I had become very attached to them.

Thoughts relating to Pure ♡

Shells
breath
Silk

PURE
natural
bliss
Simple
unmixed
real
genuine
authentic
flawless
faultless
perfect
true
Simple
uncontaminated

defenceless
nurtured
dear
priceless
adored
marvelous
wonderful
halcyon
incomparable
Sublime
Glorious
Humbling

Delightful
Captivating
Gorgeous.
tranquil

wholesome
VIRTUOUS
Clean
unpolluted
unblemished
Untainted
innocent
Modest
blameless.
LOVE
Value.

joyful joyful
mellow
Velvaty
silken

WomB
DEWDROPS
EGGS
SOFT BREATH
RIPE
ADORABLE
PEARLS
First ripples

Uninhibited
White.
Water.
Air
Milk.

untouched
gentle
vulnerable.
fragile.

Caress
touch

recién nacido
inocente
leche
delicado

lustre
Shells
New life ♡
emerging
lillies
seeds
grass
flax
rain
Serene

Cotton
Lillies
Seed
fine
transparent
Beloved.
Treasured
protection / protected.

Snow
Primary colours
Nature
Baby/Newborn
Gold
Precious
Sinless
Pure light ie morning
Clear Skin
beautiful
Eggs

goosebumps
a special moment
LUCIOUS
EXTRAORDINARY

tender.
enchanting
unsurpassed
peaceful
Soothing

"PURE"

a simple image can sometimes say a thousand words

I am often asked how I go about planning my imagery, and here is a good example. Sometimes I begin with some very loose pencil sketches of body shapes and concepts, and I have used a few of them in this book to demonstrate what I mean. I am not, in any sense, a good sketcher, but it's surprising sometimes how much clearer an idea can become if it's loosely outlined on paper. My team is very used to my simplistic drawings of "sleeping newborn babies" and I am used to them gently mocking me about them. In fact, I recently gave my husband one of my sketches of a sleeping newborn, framed for his birthday. He looked pleased, so I must be doing something right—although he was in no position to be anything other than pleased!

I must say though that I regret a manic cleaning episode I conducted in my office a few years back where I threw away all of my original sketches from when I was planning *Down in the Garden.*

I don't sketch every image I create, but when I do, often if a simple sketch looks promising I know to proceed further. When I was planning this image of Emily holding Thompson (right) I sensed that if everything came together at the shoot, it would be a strong contender for the cover. I think a cover image on any book should, ideally, completely convey the meaning of the contents both visually and emotionally.

Emily was not a professional model; at the time, she was working for me as a darkroom assistant. I thought that with her delicate beauty, she had the perfect look and body language to carry off this image. I very rarely use professional adult models for my work; in fact, I rarely use adult models at all! We rehearsed with Emily the day before the shoot to get the lighting exactly right and experimented with one of the many dolls I keep in my studio specifically for this purpose (see images pages 214–15). Everything needs to be precisely prepared before the real baby comes to the studio, and I knew that once we had Thompson asleep with Emily, chances were that I would only have one opportunity to get it right.

Thompson was already naked and asleep after being fed by his mother. He was wrapped in one of our soft studio blankets, as is usually the case. When he was in a deep sleep, we placed a hidden absorbent cloth against Emily's tummy as a makeshift nappy (diaper) for Thompson and slowly curled him into Emily's waiting hands; then we carefully moved the fabric up and around them, and fastened it firmly out of sight behind Emily's back (had I also taken a back shot of Emily at the same time, it wouldn't have looked anywhere near as glamorous as the front—there were clips, fasteners, and tape everywhere). In this way, Thompson was gently supported by both Emily and the fabric. As we watched, Thompson stirred slightly, then snuggled into Emily and went back into a deep sleep. It was amazing to see him slowly resume a fetal position. I thought, "How pure is that!"

To create a book such as *Pure,* which contains 122 images, I guess I would have shot around 200 images in total. Naturally, the elimination process can be very traumatic.

jack *and the* triplets

In September 1999, three of the most delightful little girls were brought to my studio for what turned out to be a very special photo shoot. Charleē B, Susanna, and Jaclyn are identical triplets, which is quite rare. Their mother, Lisa, told me that the incidence of naturally conceived identical triplets is about one in 30,000. When I first saw them they were lying in their baby capsules, completely dwarfed by their clothing, with a tiny woollen hat on each head. Apart from Maneesha, they were the smallest babies I'd ever seen. In both Maneesha's image (page 157) and this one of the triplets, the beautiful big hands belong to Jack.

Jack had been so wonderful to work with previously, when he had held Maneesha, that I wanted to use him again. Unfortunately, by this time, he had left Auckland and moved further south to Christchurch, where he and his wife were to settle into a retirement home. I called Jack to ask if he would like to be a part of this image, and he said he would be delighted, so I flew him to Auckland especially for the shoot. Afterward his wife told me that he had felt like a movie star for the day, as we had made such a big fuss over him—which is as it should be. I hope he'll be very proud to see the background image (overleaf) that I've included in this book.

To hold a new baby in your arms is magical, but the experience intensifies to a whole new level when holding a premature or very tiny baby. There is a sense of exquisite fragility, a sense of a life that could so easily not have made it into the world, of a gift almost withheld. In this case, multiply the magic by three. The girls were just like tiny little birds that had been plucked from the nest—probably not the best description, but it's exactly what crossed my mind at the time.

Jack *and the* triplets 1999
Charleē B, Susanna, *and* Jaclyn

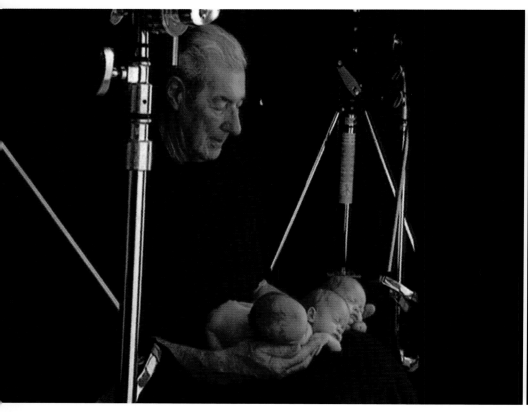

Jack and the triplets—behind the scenes

Charleē B, Susanna, *and* Jaclyn 2000
at 6 months

I'm sure that one of the reasons for the success of these images is that most people are rarely in close contact with a newborn baby in their daily lives, and I hope my work gives a feeling of what it is like. Newborns radiate a surprising amount of warmth—physical and emotional. I have noticed time and again that when a newborn is in the room, the whole dynamic seems to change. A newborn baby has an incredibly powerful presence, and I don't just mean at 3 o'clock in the morning!

I remember an occasion, a few years ago, that had a profound effect on me in terms of my realizing how my work could so positively affect others. I was photographing a week-old baby who was naked and fast asleep on a small foam shape we had crafted. I think the image may have been for the woodland fairy series but I can't specifically recall. The studio was very warm and quiet. The baby's mother stood just behind me and watched as my assistant gently lifted the wrap that covered her baby. Suddenly there was a soft gasp, and the mother whispered to herself, "Oh my God, look at my baby, isn't he beautiful?"

Through all of the excitement, hard work, and occasional chaos involved in bringing a brand-new baby home for the first time, sometimes it's easy to lose sight of the simple things. It suddenly dawned on me that rarely would new parents be able to stand back as that mother was right then—and experience the wonderful sight of

their newborn baby soundly sleeping, naked and absolutely perfect.

But back to the triplets. Sometimes magic happens unexpectedly and I knew the magic was happening when I photographed the girls in Jack's enormous hands. In this photograph (previous page), which is printed life-size, the girls are nearly two months old, although they look smaller. Triplet pregnancies often do not go full-term; therefore, newborn triplets can be petite at birth.

We filmed some background video that day, and as I looked back at the footage I remembered how I felt when we gradually got the first two babies asleep; the third baby was restless . . . then she went to sleep . . . and the first one woke . . . and so on. My hands shook as I operated the camera, a sure sign this image was going to be special.

When the girls were six months old (above right) they returned to the studio for a visit. I thought to myself, wouldn't it be amazing if they would all sleep together again in an image? Almost impossible odds, but they did. My luck ran out when they came back at twelve months—as you can see (right)—at this age it felt a bit like photographing an octopus. They were all over the place, arms and legs going everywhere—they simply didn't care to listen to me at all. I remember thinking, when I was photographing them, *Now I know why I gave up portraiture!*

right: Charleē B, Susanna *and* Jaclyn 2000
at 1 year

Here they are again at seven years of age (or, as they insisted I say, nearly eight!)

sheer magic,
combined with a lot of luck

The original concept for this shoot was to have just one tiny newborn sleeping suspended in the baby muslin. As normal, when I need one sleeping baby in an image, I have two or three babies in the studio at the time; I find the 3:1 ratio works best for everybody. Very new babies love to curl up, probably because toward the end of a pregnancy they lie like this in the womb and the sensation is very familiar and comforting to them.

My studio temperature is always very warm when I photograph naked newborn babies; therefore, the adults learn to dress lightly. India, the baby on the left, was the first to go to sleep, and we gently suspended her muslin pouch from the overhead pole mounted between two large supports. A unique problem I needed to overcome was that once the pouch was attached to the pole, it would very slowly start to rotate. At the top, out of frame of this image—apart from the very large knots—there are many safety pins and various pieces of string in place, to try to stop the rotation.

I had my planned shot. As I finished photographing India, Rebecca was already asleep in my studio manager's lap, with her baby muslin pouch gently gathered around her. However, she was only sleeping lightly, and whenever we moved her, even slightly, she would wake. Eventually, she went into a deep sleep and we were able to maneuver her into position next to India, who was still sleeping soundly. By this stage, I don't think any of the adults in the studio were breathing. Certainly it was very quiet, and it's always like this when we get a sense that magic could be in the air.

As Rebecca was bigger than India and therefore heavier, it was trial and error as to how low her pouch would hang once it was attached to the pole. Plus, whenever all hands were off the pouch she would

start slowly rotating. Once these issues were sorted, I had a lovely image of the two of them, a wonderful bonus.

On the day of this shoot, we filmed background video footage, and in hindsight, I wish I had done this with a lot more of my images. I was recently watching this video footage when I noted Natalie, my studio manager, whispering to me:
"Guess what? Isla's asleep."
"No, I don't think I can bear it," I replied.
"Yeah you can, come on, what's wrong with you, you're just scared."
"I am not scared."
"You are so."
We sounded like a couple of five-year-olds; although I must admit that I was scared—totally scared—of being disappointed. We were so close and yet the chances were that it might not happen. I knew I'd have to be pretty lucky to have three babies asleep at once.

We placed Isla into position, determined her correct height, and stopped her from rotating. Everyone in the studio held their breath. I was just about to take the first shot when India stirred and nearly woke . . . but she settled again. My hands shook as I changed my film backs. I was so relieved to get the first image down. I needn't have hurried, as they all stayed sound asleep for quite a while. On the video footage we can hear each of them snoring in unison—it was like a little chorus—with a couple of small puddles on the floor underneath as an added reward.

I've always thought over the years that I wish there was a way to give people a real sense of what my studio environment is like. Perhaps my description of this shoot gives at least some idea of the experience.

above: Natalie, my Studio Manager (in striped shirt) and Dawn, prop maker and stylist, handing me the Polaroid

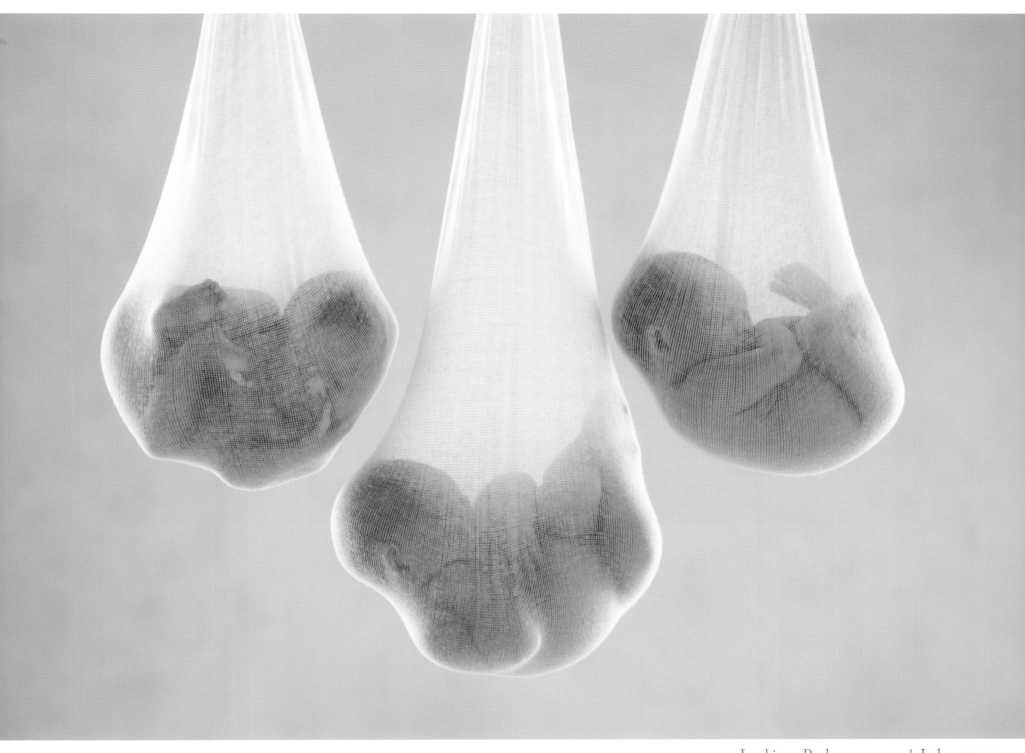

This image of India, Rebecca, and Isla is one of my favorites from *Pure*. They remind me of three little

plum puddings, and they are a perfect example of how unexpected magic happens, and why I continually

find my job so rewarding, but sometimes exhausting.

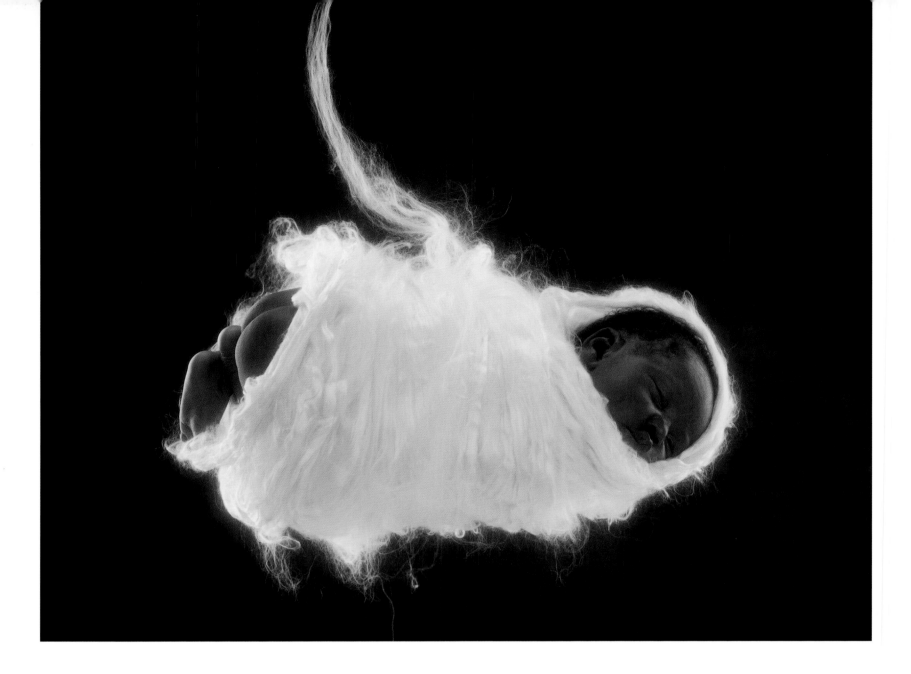

kwasi

Kwasi, pictured in these two images, modeled for me on a number of occasions when he was first born.

The texture of his skin was so beautiful and he had lips like round ripe berries. In the image (above) he is wrapped in soft raw silk and is lying in a soft dish, which is extended out on a pole through a canvas background. When I was shooting for *Pure* I went through a stage of loving raw silk, and used it in a number of images for the book. Raw silk can be quite tedious to work with and demands minimal handling, but the trouble is worthwhile. I wanted it to seem as if Kwasi was floating, so Dawn, whose job it was to achieve this effect, is gently blowing on the fine piece of silk in the top of the image. These days, of course, an image like this could possibly have been achieved using computer generation, but it wouldn't have been the same to me. Everything is totally real.

In his second image (right) with the butterfly on his back, Kwasi is lying on Natalie's lap, which is covered with black velvet. Underneath, for obvious reasons, is a waterproof covering. Again, I just love the texture of Kwasi's skin, and the lovely soft rolls of his body.

There are a few butterflies included in the *Pure* images, and I know you're wondering whether they were alive. Unfortunately, they were not, but of course they all died from natural causes. Generally, butterflies only live for twenty-four hours or a few days at most.

The reason I am explaining the life span of the average butterfly is to tell you that deceased butterflies are very fragile, and need careful handling, otherwise their antennae fall off—which happened quite a few times in the studio. Fortunately, we were able to glue them back on—very exacting and precise work!

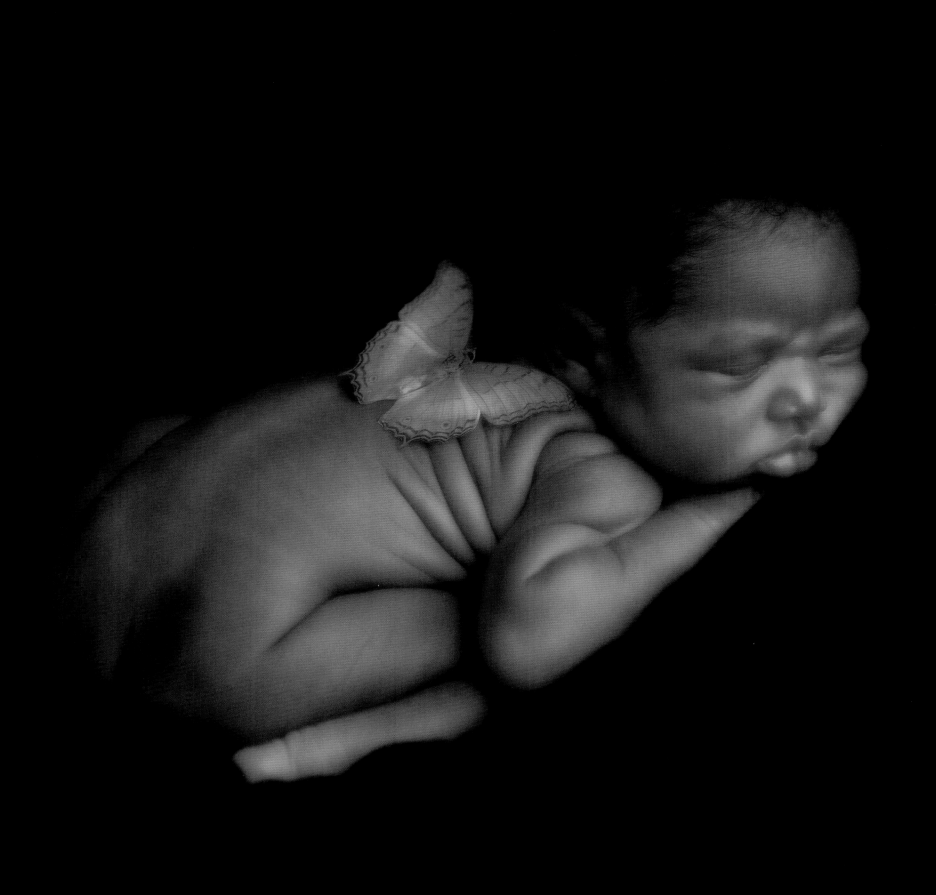

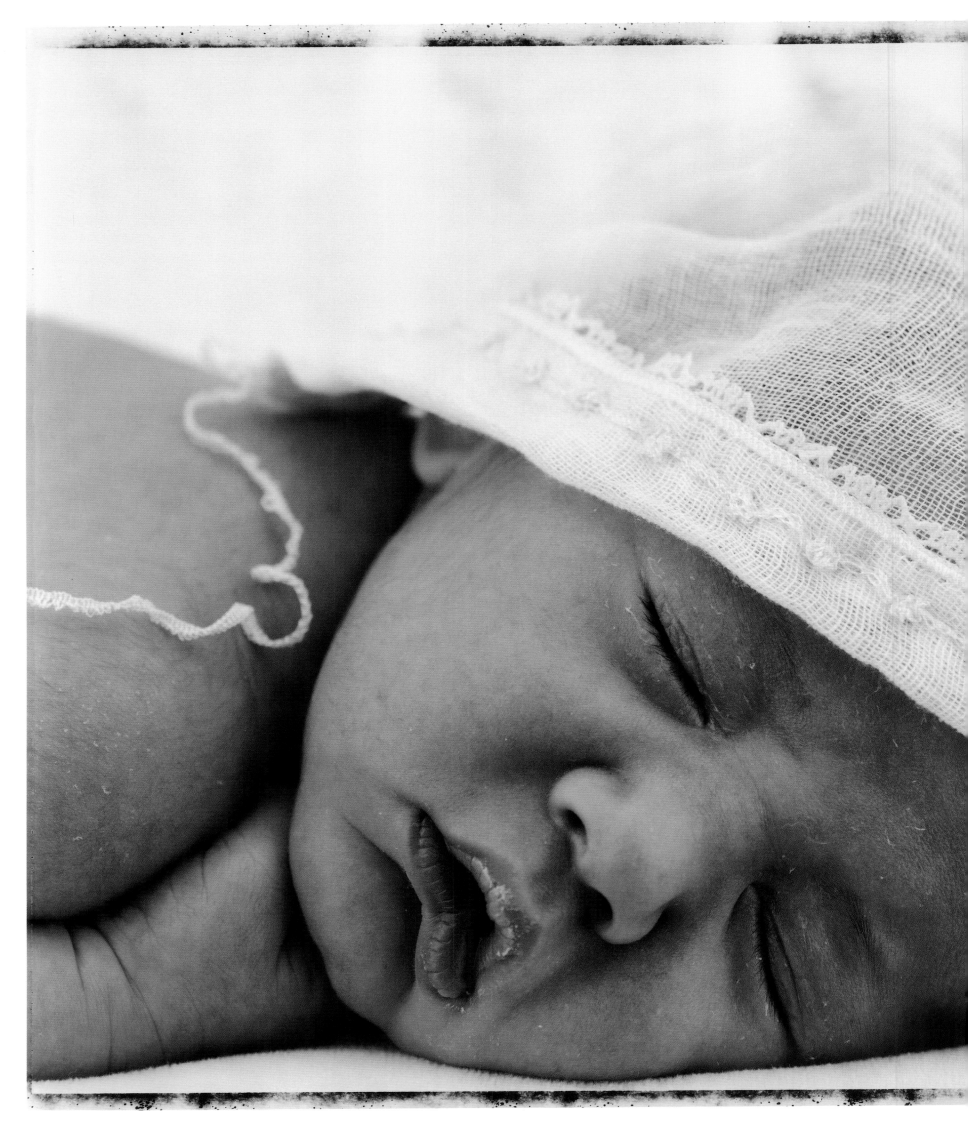

tungaroa

This image of Tungaroa again reminds me of how amazing it will be for the babies to look back on their images when they are grown, to see in such incredible detail the delicacy of their newborn skin, the detail in their lips and eyelashes, how perfect they were.

Tungaroa, who is Maori, was only nine days old when this image was taken. If you are wondering why it appears that his skin is peeling, this is very common and entirely normal for some newborn babies, and often occurs when they are overdue—it's a little bit like being slightly overcooked! This all disappears before too long. Some newborns also have a light downy covering of hair on their shoulders and backs, also very common and quite normal, which disappears quickly as well. Tungaroa was fast asleep, with a very full tummy. You may notice the remnants of milk on his top lip as evidence.

Tungaroa 1999

samuel *and* ryan ▷

If I were to create a short list of my favorite images—this one of Samuel and Ryan would have to be included. They were five weeks old at the time, and very tiny, as they are twins and often twins can be slightly smaller at birth than an average-sized single-birth baby.

As usual, before the shoot, I had a rough plan as to what I wanted to achieve, but I didn't imagine it would come together so beautifully.

Babies are not only individual beings, they are intrinsically connected to other human beings—and indeed to all of life. The connection between twins is one of the deepest and most mysterious and it was this mystery I was hoping to convey.

The boys, who had very full tummies, were fast asleep on my studio manager Natalie's lap. We gradually maneuvered them closer and closer together, and yet still in a sitting position, and then softly wrapped a cloth around them for support, followed by a piece of wool wadding combined with raw silk to complete the effect. Then we carefully carried them to the table, as they are here, fast asleep and enclosed together. I ran upstairs to my vantage point on the purpose-built overhead balcony and, looking down, couldn't believe how wonderful they both looked. It was a perfect yin and yang composition. Their heads are almost mirror images of each other, and I just love the detail in their tiny ears and their soft downy baby hair. All of the vulnerable, soft, subtle features of newborns are very apparent here.

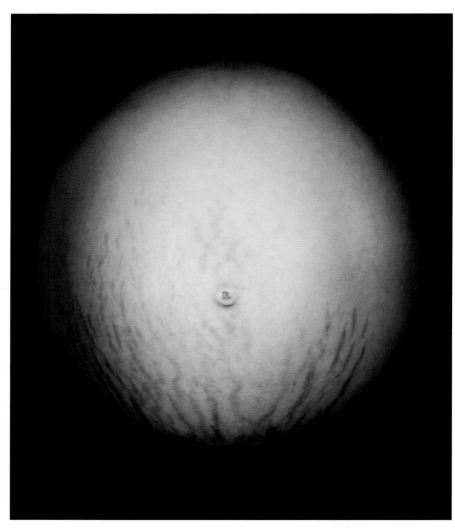

◁ rachel

I first met Rachel at the beginning of her pregnancy, shortly after she discovered she was expecting triplets. She was very excited and nervous at the same time, which is perfectly understandable. Triplet pregnancies rarely go to full term (forty weeks) and I was anxious to photograph Rachel's tummy at the very last minute. Of course, none of us knew when that would be, so it was a week-by-week wait for the perfect time.

On the day of the shoot, Rachel, who looked radiant, was telling me how relieved she was that she didn't have any stretch marks. I didn't quite know how to tell her. Obviously she didn't have a full-length mirror at home! And anyway, for me, the stretch marks made the photograph a celebration of round ripeness—it always reminds me of a lovely, big, ripe watermelon. The girls, Jade, Aimee, and Hannah, were born shortly afterward at thirty weeks' gestation. In the image (if you can visualize) one of the girls is lying across the inside at the top, and the other two right and left respectively.

Rachel *pregnant with triplets*
Jade, Aimee, *and* Hannah *at 30 weeks* 2001

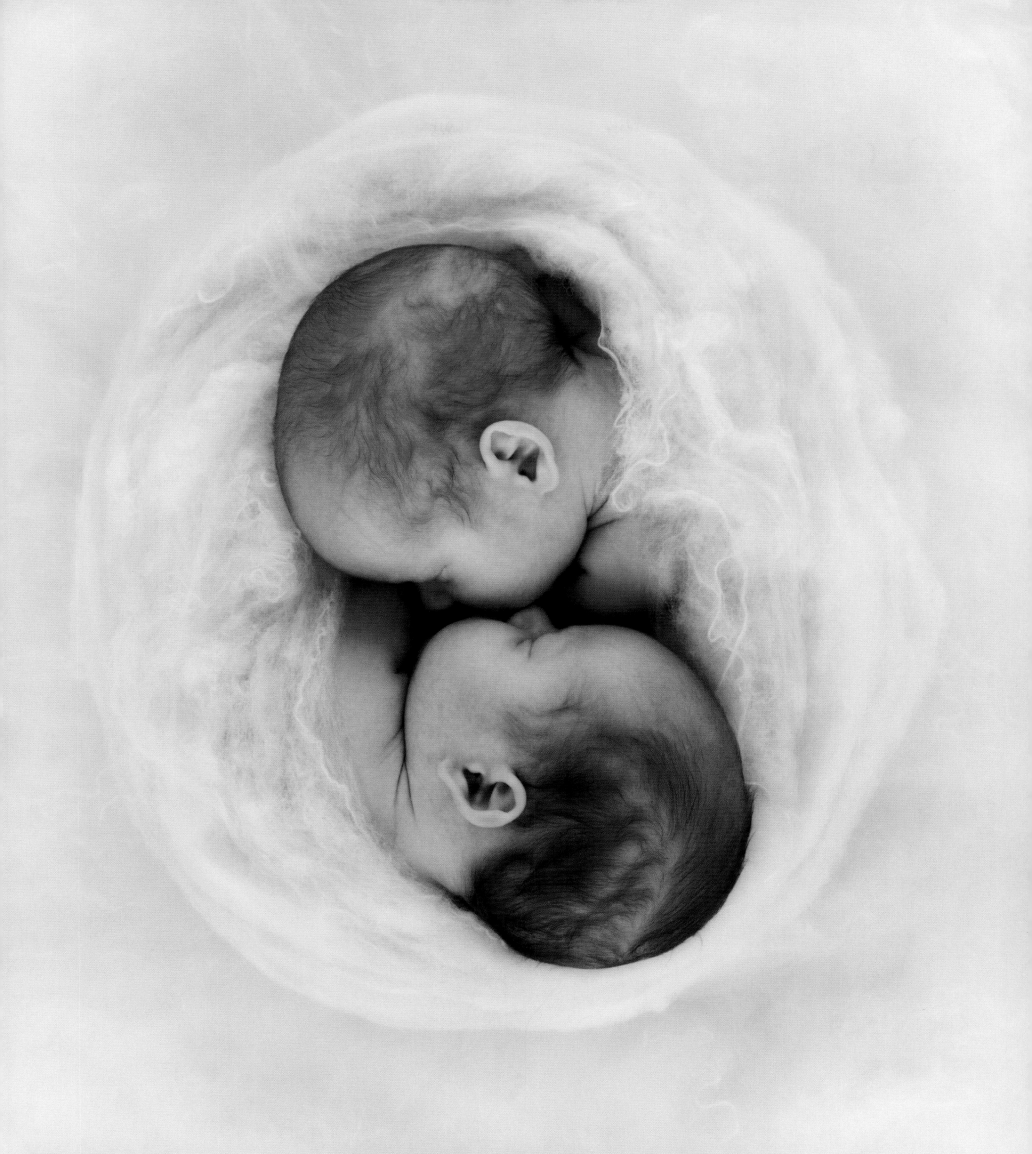

stephanie *and* kelly

These two images (opposite) are of my daughters, Stephanie and Kelly. I think they are beautiful, but then as their mother, I may be very biased! At the time these images were done, Stephanie was sixteen years old and Kelly had just turned thirteen. These particular ages to me are significant milestones in a young girl's life as Kelly had just become a teenager and Stephanie was blossoming into a young woman. Had I not been shooting for *Pure* I would have created them anyway, just for the girls to have. I also arranged for both of their shoots to be recorded on video for them to look back on.

I know that every parent must feel the same way, but when I look at these images now, they remind me of how fleeting childhood is, and how important it is to photograph your children as often as you can, through all of the different stages of their development. My own daughters, however, may disagree on this point—they joke that there has been a camera pointed at them for their whole lives, and that what they most remember is my saying, "Wait, just one more. . . ."

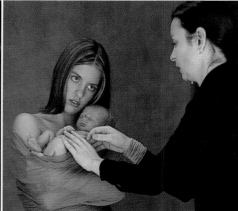

video stills from Stephanie's and Kelly's shoot for "Pure," 2000, with Natalie and Dawn assisting

Stephanie 2000

Kelly *holding* Madeleine 2000

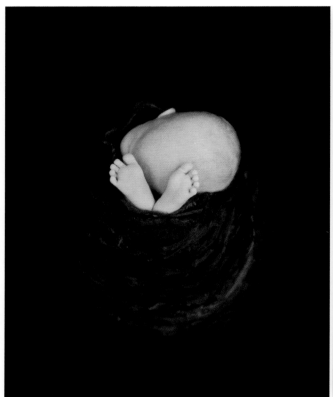

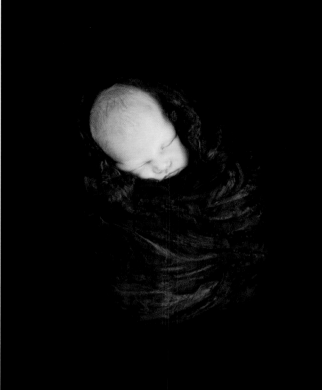

Ryan 2001   Lucy 2001   Aiden 2001

black silk
series

There is something so incredibly soft and beautiful about raw silk (although it can be difficult to work with in combination with babies, as it requires very minimal handling). Mind you, I guess that applies to both raw silk *and* sleeping babies. In fact, the babies in these images are enclosed in a combination of wool and raw silk. The images were all shot in one morning, after I decided to have six newborns in the studio, wrap them cozily, and then see what unfolded. My thoughts were to convey a sense of the complete trust and abandonment of sleep, and a subdued "womb-like" environment, both ongoing themes while I was shooting for *Pure*.

Natalie is holding the babies from behind a black velvet cloth which became the background. She is also wearing dark gloves to help disguise her hands. Whenever I look at these images I'm reminded of how peaceful that morning seemed, but then I guess if somebody wrapped me in something like that I'd be drifting off to sleep as well!

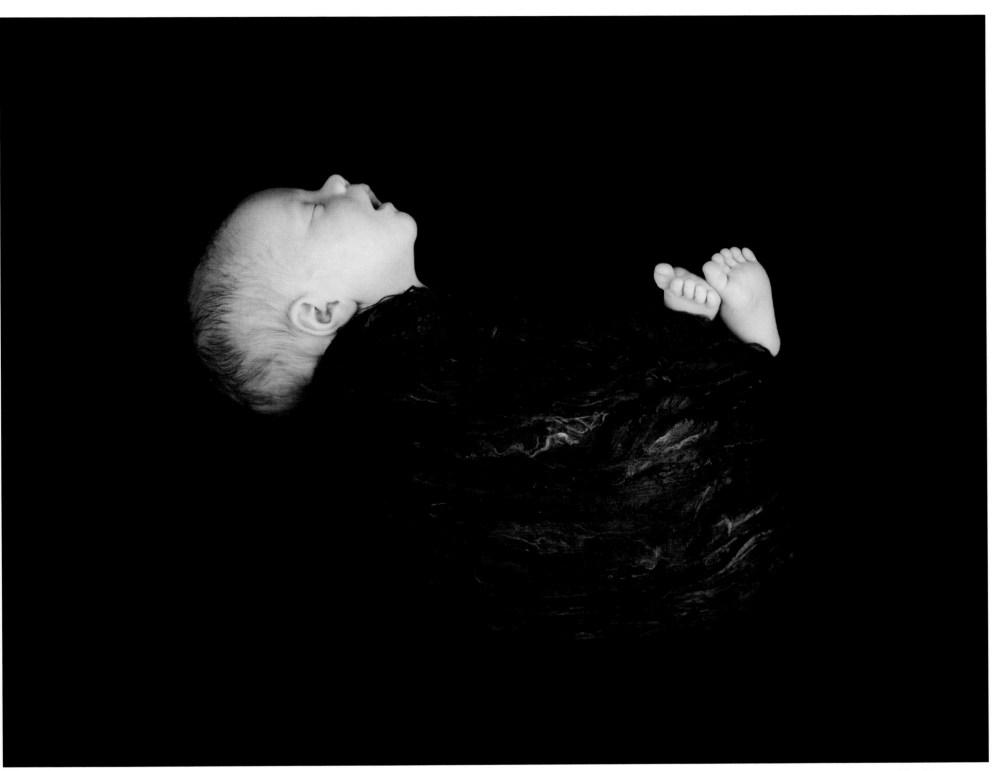

Holly 2001

ashleigh ▷

This image of Ashleigh was created just before the launch of my baby clothing range. I was photographing six-month-old babies wearing the new clothing, which is the reason Ashleigh was at the studio. In fact, there were quite a few six-month-old babies in the studio at the time, and when they are all gathered together the atmosphere always seems to be incredibly happy and positive.

I remember Ashleigh, sitting among all of the babies, looking around at everybody in her own quiet way, no doubt wondering what on earth was going on and what all the fuss was about. I fell in love with her little round head and the perfect shape of her ears—especially from the back. I just couldn't stop looking at her.

There's something incredibly blissful about caressing a baby's beautiful round and slightly bald head. A young baby's hair is so soft and silky and, often, they have a slightly bald patch at the back, from spending so much time lying down. It's a natural instinct to cup and stroke the curved shape—you see people doing it constantly,

particularly with babies of this age. Next time you see somebody caressing a baby's head, you'll also notice that they have a smile on their face. Little babies naturally draw us out of ourselves to talk to them, even in situations where to us they are complete strangers . . . but now I have drifted off on a tangent!

Eventually, I asked Ashleigh's mother if she would mind staying after everyone had left, so that I could try a classic black-and-white image of the back of her beautiful head.

Ashleigh is simply sitting on a box, with her back to the camera, and Natalie is sitting on the floor behind the box talking to her and distracting her with all manner of toys from our studio toy box.

I had to stay very quiet at the camera, as every time I said anything Ashleigh would turn around to look at me. Perhaps the sheer simplicity of the image speaks volumes for the delicate vulnerability of small children.

◁ ilham

Never plan to specifically photograph a baby yawning—because they'll never do it for you on cue, or so I thought until I photographed Ilham.

We all know that the act of yawning is catching. However, I wondered whether this applied to newborns. They always look so charming when they are yawning, but yawns are so fleeting and it's difficult in a studio situation to catch them at it. Are you still with me? Because if you think this is useless information, feel free to move on.

I put the theory to the test with Ilham, pretending to yawn myself, and I can now attest to the fact that it works, seriously, because this is exactly how we were able to persuade her to yawn on cue. I'm not kidding—it actually worked. Or, maybe, Ilham is just a super-intelligent baby—her mother would no doubt agree with me.

Ilham 2000

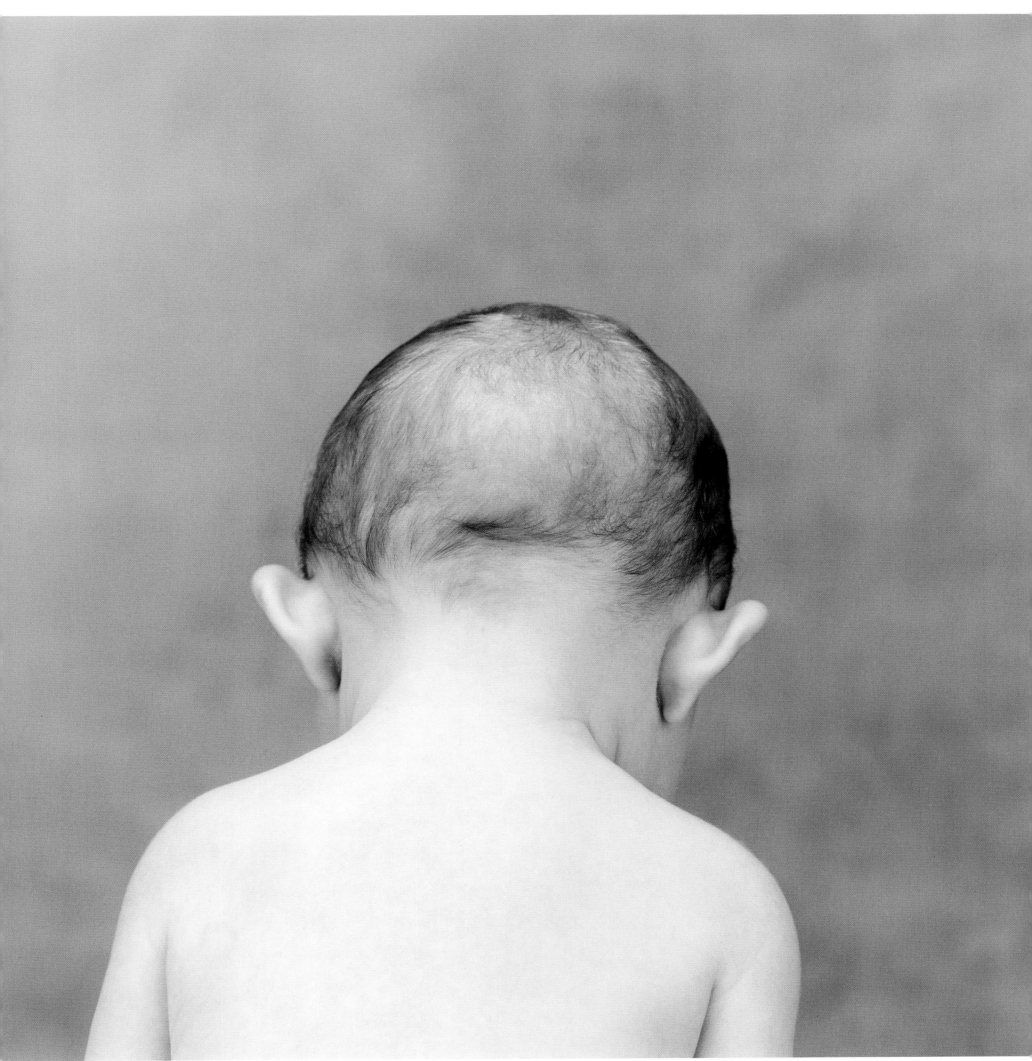

Ashleigh 2001

tuli *holding* nyla ▷

This image of Tuli holding Nyla is one of my favorites from *Pure,* partly because of the circumstances surrounding it.

It was late in the afternoon of what had been a very hot New York day, and I was thinking we would have to finish. Little Nyla had been at the studio for most of the day, along with other newborns who were coming and going with their mothers as we were photographing.

She was four weeks old and quite an alert baby for her age, so beautiful, with lovely round rolls and a gorgeous little face, but she was very determined not to sleep, and I was determined that she would. Often the only thing to do in these circumstances is play the waiting game, and as Nyla seemed to be very comfortable with this, that's exactly what I did. She was wide awake the whole time and taking in everything that was going on around her—she seemed to be having a wonderful time. Knowing that her mother

had traveled quite a long distance to join us for the day, I was also anxious not to disappoint her by not taking a photograph of Nyla.

I looked at Nyla and in return she stared back at me, wide-eyed, her dummy (pacifier) in full operational mode. I thought to myself, "Surely this can't go on for much longer," and wondered if I just had Tuli hold her closely for a while, she might doze off. Her mother agreed there was nothing to lose, so I placed her in Tuli's arms and, for ten minutes or so, Tuli quietly rocked her and whispered in her ear. We could hear Tuli making all sorts of rash promises to Nyla that there was gold at the end of the rainbow and she would come at any time to cuddle her in the middle of the night if she would just go to sleep right now . . . and the next minute she did.

So time and time again it's proven to me that sometimes the images that are hardest to achieve turn out to have the most power. Isn't she a delicious baby? I love the extra roll on her ankle.

Tuli *with* Jahad 1997

◁ tuli *with* jahad

Tuli had the most amazingly long legs. I had envisaged this image long before we traveled to New York for the shoot in the Polaroid Studio and I knew that it might be difficult to find a model who could comfortably rest her head on her knees in this way. Tuli hadn't worked with babies before, and loved being there in the studio with newborns all around her.

Jahad, who was two weeks old, was very much attached to his dummy (pacifier), which was gently removed after he'd fallen into a deep sleep, just before this image was taken. This is why his little mouth is so rounded and slightly open. He was obviously dreaming that the dummy was still in place, as his tiny tongue was still going back and forth inside his mouth.

Tuli *holding* Nyla 1997

pregnancy

Every woman will always remember precisely when she first discovered that she was pregnant. For most it is a transcendent moment . . . our own personal miracle.

Throughout the past twenty-five years, I have continued to explore photographically the subject of pregnancy, and here are some of my favorite images.

I hope they give women everywhere a confidence that at any stage of pregnancy they are all, in their own special way, absolutely beautiful. In a world that is deluged by a manufactured perception of beauty, it gives me a great deal of pleasure to be able to photograph what actually is "real" beauty. Pregnant women seem to have an intense aura about them and I am continually fascinated by the concept of the natural creation of a brand-new life and of being able to share your body as another human grows and develops right inside you.

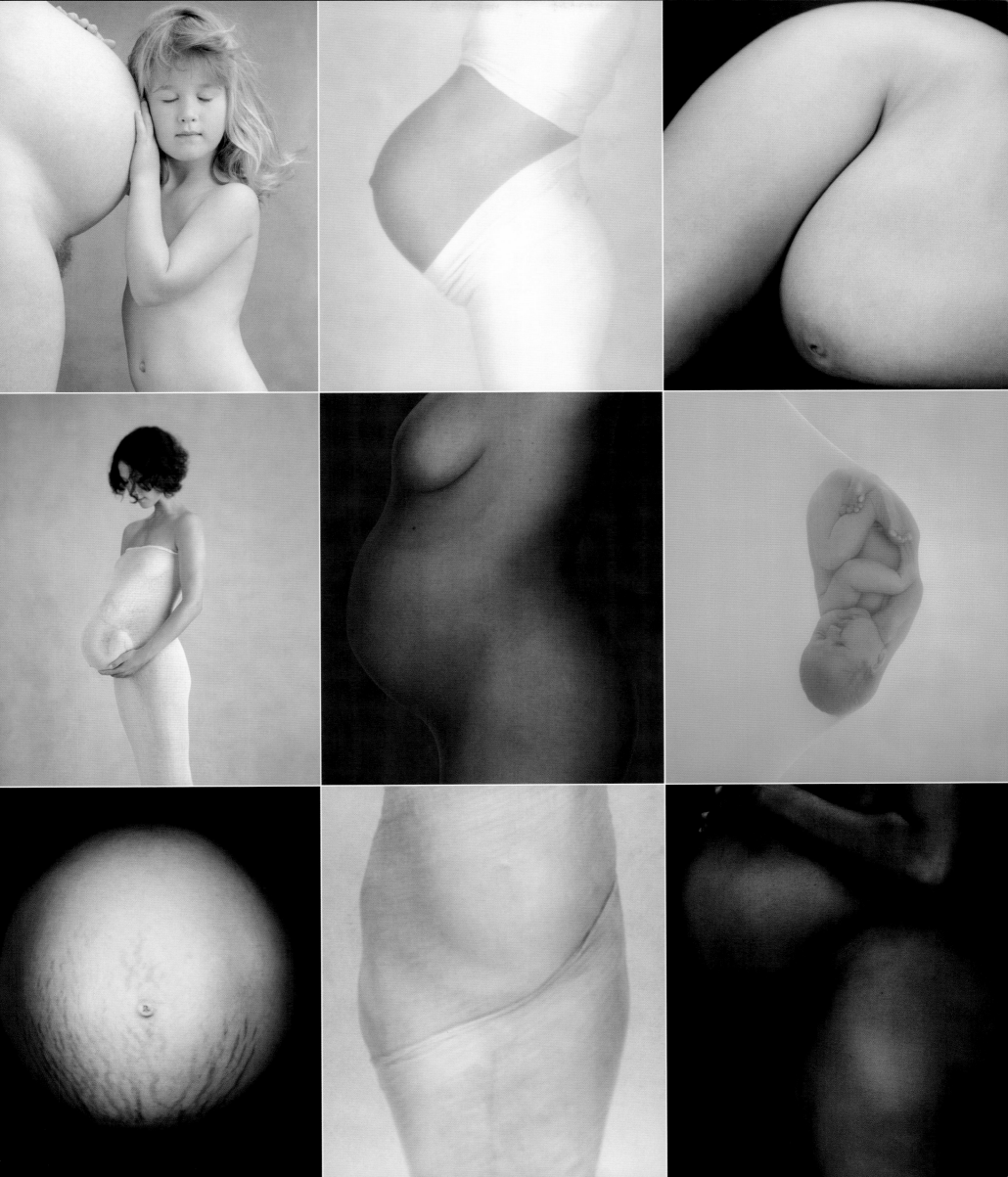

corinne *pregnant*

with charlie

Corinne is one of the stars of *Pure*. She is a dancer and I think this helped enormously in her images as she had an easy and quite serene presence in front of the camera. I used Corinne in a number of images for *Pure*, both when she was pregnant with her baby Charlie, and after he was born.

She is one of seven pregnant women featured in the book, none of whom were professional models. They were all beautiful, proud, and courageous, and prepared—at such a vulnerable time in their lives—to share their unique beauty with the world.

I think she looks magnificent. Corinne gave birth to Charlie shortly after these images were taken.

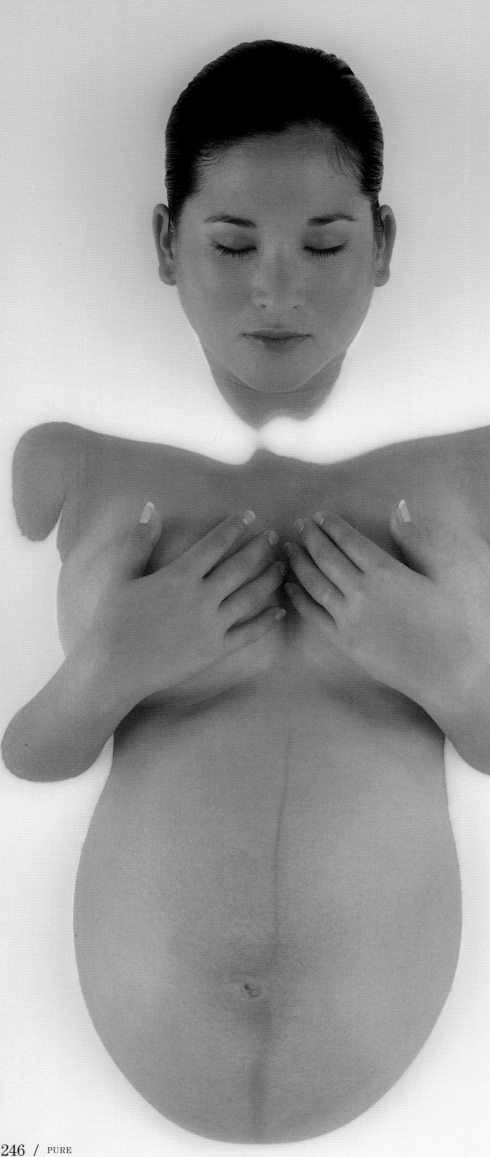

corinne *in milk*

When I was planning this image, I contacted my doctor to check whether it would be perfectly safe for Corinne to lie in the milk—he laughed and said, "Absolutely, what could be more natural?". When Corinne arrived for the shoot, she said she was beginning to have slight contractions and we tried to bundle her off to the hospital, but she would have none of it. As it turned out, Charlie wasn't born until a few days later. I know that water births are quite common nowadays, but I have my doubts about milk births.

There was much hilarity while we were shooting this image, and Corinne was a real trouper. We were all laughing so much it was hard for Corinne to keep still in order to have the surface of the milk completely smooth. To support her back and head and to keep her level when she was lying in the bath, we lowered some studio sandbags into the milk to prop her up slightly. A few days later the smell of sour milk began to permeate the studio and I found that unfortunately the sandbags were not in fact watertight and had absorbed some of the milk—needless to say, they were disposed of immediately.

The bathtub was situated underneath the overhead balcony in my studio, which I have previously mentioned I use if I wish to shoot downward. To fill the bath required 160 liters (or just over 42 U.S. gallons) of full-cream milk. Our local supermarket was a little curious as to where it was all going to be used. The milk had been gently heated to a comfortable temperature for Corinne, but not warm enough to form a "skin" on the surface (milk photography isn't as straightforward as you might think).

You will notice a dark vertical line on Corinne's tummy—it's called a negra line, which can often appear during late pregnancy and usually fades after the baby is born.

Two weeks after Charlie was born, Corinne brought him to the studio to meet everybody, and I created this image (right) of the two of them. Very often when a woman is breast-feeding the veins in her breasts become quite distinctive, as you can see here with Corinne.

left: Corinne 2001
right: Corinne *holding* Charlie 2001

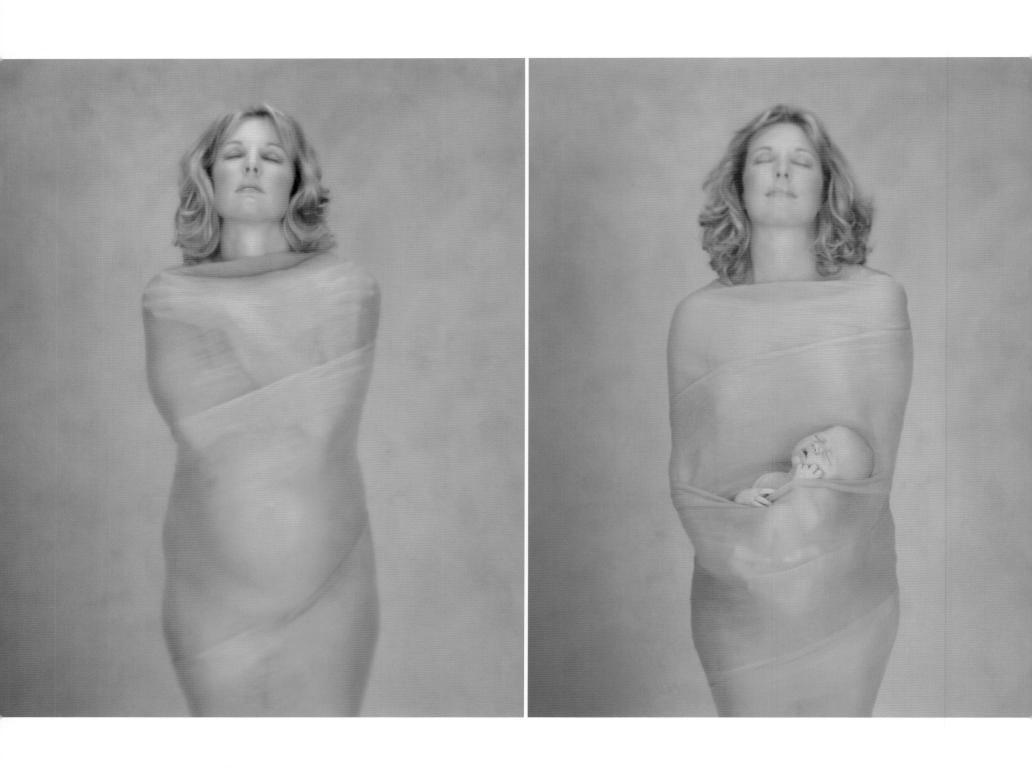

nicky *and* riley

Nicky is a (rather glamorous) policewoman who lives in Auckland and Riley is her firstborn. Just before Riley arrived, Nicky came to the studio to pose for the image (above left) at thirty-nine weeks. Then she returned to the studio with Riley, when he was two weeks old (above right), to pose again in exactly the same position, and the images were overlayed.

fisheye images

Long before I ever became a photographer myself, in fact when I was ten years old, I remember being fascinated by the images of scientific photographer Lennart Nilsson, which were first published in Life magazine in 1965. They were the world's first images of a living human embryo.

On some level I'm sure that this sense of wonder never left me. When I was shooting for *Pure* and exploring the subject of pregnancy at a deeper level, I kept remembering those images from so long ago, and drew inspiration from them.

Of course, the babies in my images are not still in the womb. These images from *Pure* were created in the studio using a fisheye lens. The babies are lying in what can only be described as a sort of "upside-down fish bowl," which is lined with soft wool wadding and strands of raw silk. The image has been lit from below in order to create the ethereal effect. Ruby and Bella are newborn twins.

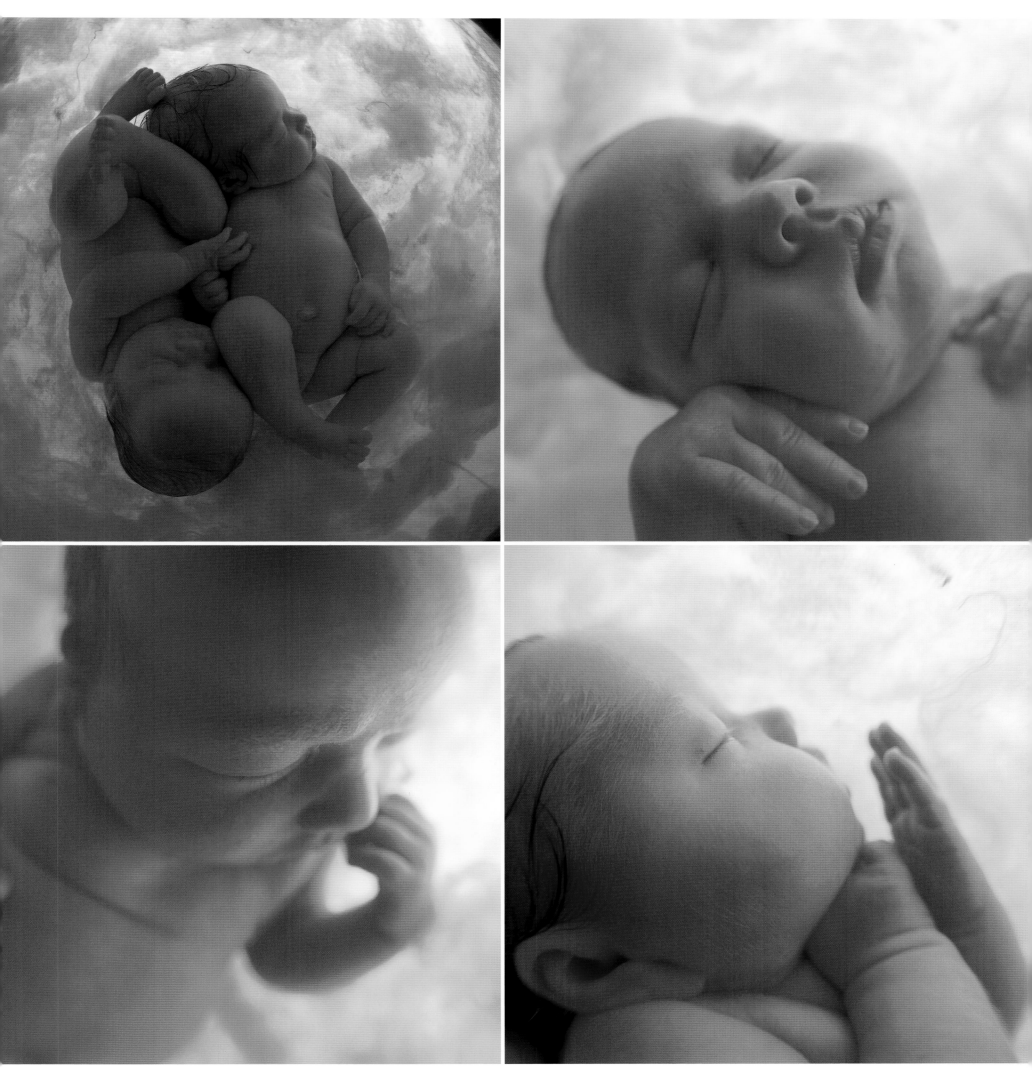

Ruby *and* Bella 2001

emma *holding* neville

Every time I look at this image, I think of little Neville, who weighed nine pounds at birth—hence we all christened him *"Nine-pound Neville."* I suppose I can also identify with him because my two girls were around the same weight when they were born. He had lovely padding in all the right places, including those rolls on his small ankles.

In case you're thinking that Emma was rather brave to be holding a baby like this without a nappy (diaper), underneath Neville (out of sight in the image) is a thick layer of absorbent fabric, always a necessity when photographing naked babies!

Emma *holding* Neville 1997

sally pearl

Sally Pearl, lying here peacefully asleep when she was twelve days old, eventually became one of the signature babies for my clothing range designs. Her parents, Rachel and Gerard, had both worked with me many times for different projects, so we were able to share in their excitement over Rachel's pregnancy, and observe her growing waistline over the following nine months. Naturally, I was keen to include Sally Pearl in *Pure*, which I was shooting for at the time she was born.

The simplicity and perfection of her pose made a simple line drawing of her almost impossible to resist. When we were photographing her, my studio manager, Natalie, commented that this was a classic "Anne Geddes" pose, and I guess it is, although I know that it's a pose I'd never be able to achieve myself! Newborns are so supple, and Sally probably would have been in a similar position to this during her last weeks in the womb, when space is usually at a premium.

She is curled in a small dish partially made from soft foam, built around a solid steel base. The dish is at the end of a pole which is hidden behind her, and has been poked through the backdrop. What a perfect little human being she is, with her soft silky skin; I especially love the wrinkles her toes have created on her head. She reminds me of a cat who is curled up contentedly.

Shortly after the shoot, which was right before Christmas of that year, Gerard sent us an e-mail to express his thoughts about the image. I found his message very touching, and would like to share it with you here.

Incoming Message	hohoho	Page 1 of 1

```
Subject:     hohoho
Date:        03/01/2001 1:56 pm
Received:    11/01/2001 12:25 pm
From:        gerard
To:          natalie


Happy two zeros and a one.

I need to tell you and Anne how much pleasure I get from the two prints
you have given us. They are photos of a treasure, and something to
treasure in the future. When photography captures the essence and spirit
of its subject it becomes magical; a whole new dimension is created
which goes way beyond the image itself. I look at those images and i
melt.

i see now why guys do what you do with so much passion. Thank-you.

see Ya'll

Big(sentimental old what???????)Boy
```

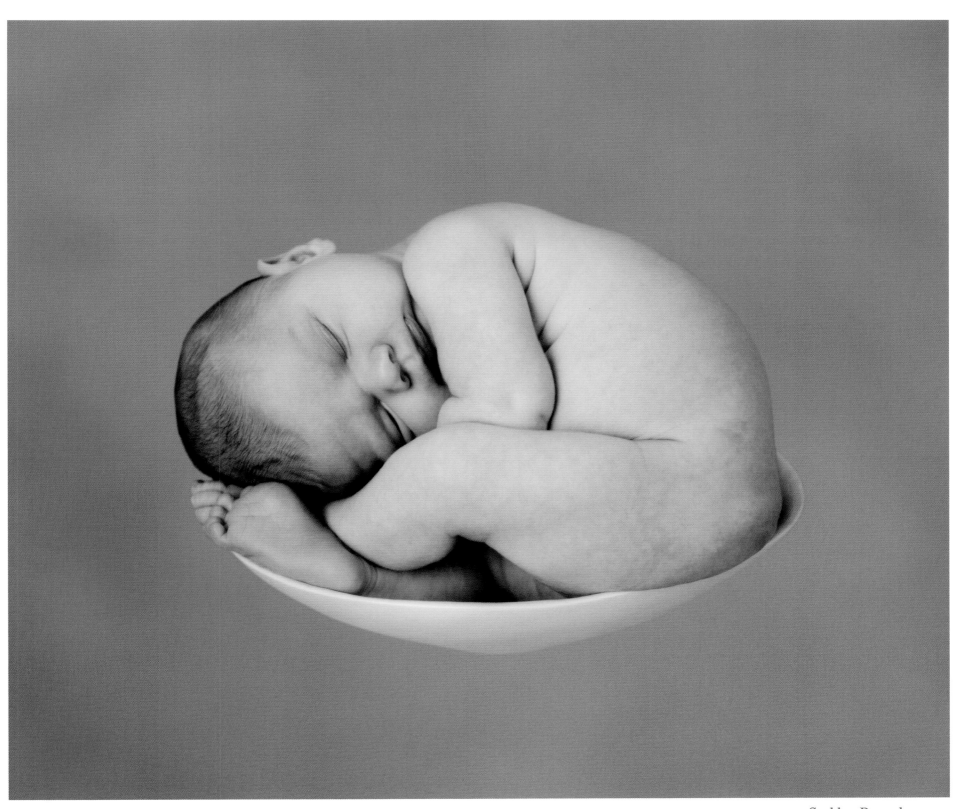

Sally Pearl 2000

womb babies

These babies have been photographed through a very thin layer of soft latex that has been stretched across a large wooden frame, which in turn is mounted vertically between two large stands. Dawn spent weeks perfecting the art of creating these very thin sheets of latex, which she mixed and spread thinly onto a flat surface and allowed to dry and cure overnight.

The process is very unpredictable—each time the latex dries, it can look totally different and react in a different way. Every morning she would come to work, unsure as to what she would find. I was wanting to photograph through a smooth and relatively unmarked sheet, and to achieve one perfect sheet would involve a dozen or so others that didn't quite work out. Often, bubbles had formed or bits of dust had been trapped, and these imperfect sheets would have to be discarded and the whole process would begin again.

Eventually, we had enough sheets to do the shoot, but as soon as

the baby's skin touched the latex it would leave a mark; the latex is very porous. To remedy this, as we were shooting, Dawn would gently dust the latex with baby talcum powder to try to remove the marks.

Natalie is standing behind the latex sheet and holding the sleeping baby, who is partly wrapped in soft polar fleece fabric, which has been dyed a similar tone to the latex. She is also wearing a gown and gloves made from the same fabric, in order for the background to blend, especially her hands, which of course are around the baby. This very glamorous outfit (I am joking) was similar to those awful hospital gowns we all know and dislike, and we were joking to Natalie that she might like to pose on her own later—an offer she politely declined!

Various parts of the babies' bodies were gently placed against the latex sheet as I photographed from the other side—it was as simple as that.

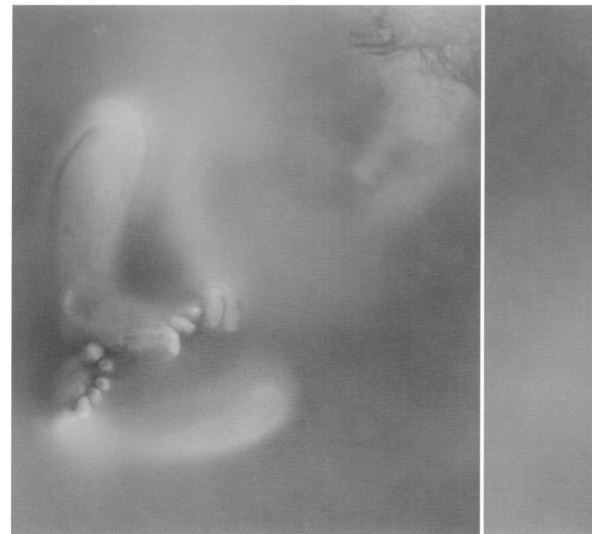 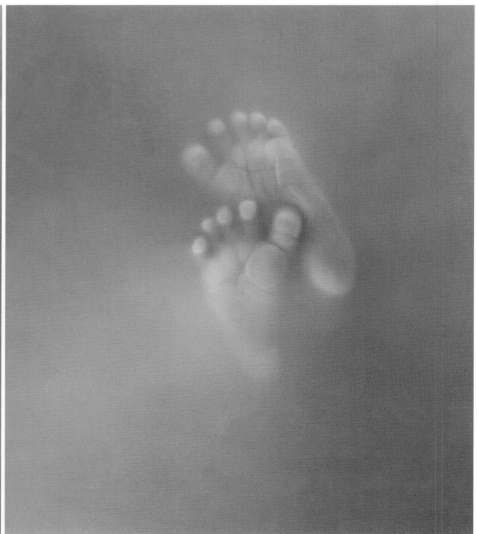

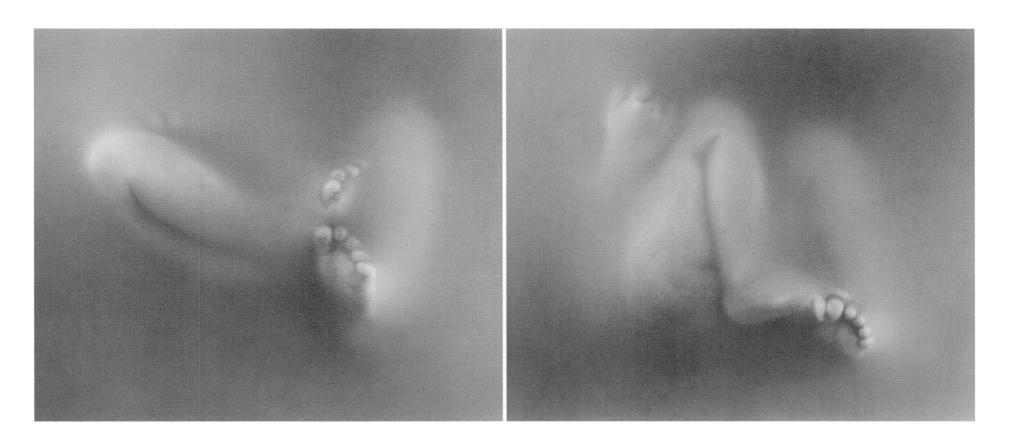

Some images are relatively simple to shoot, but require much planning and preparation beforehand, and this

series from *Pure* is a good example.

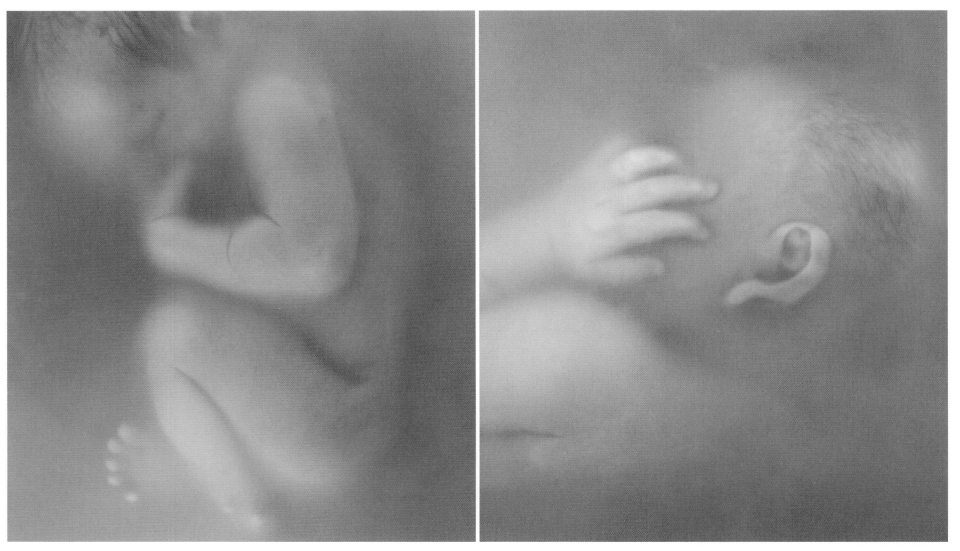

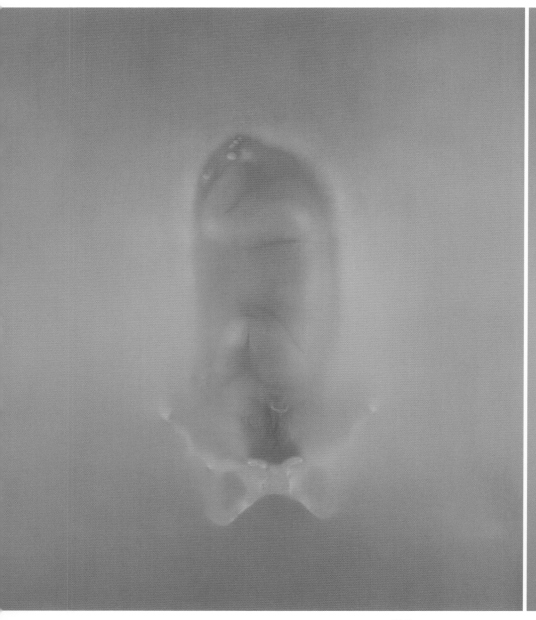

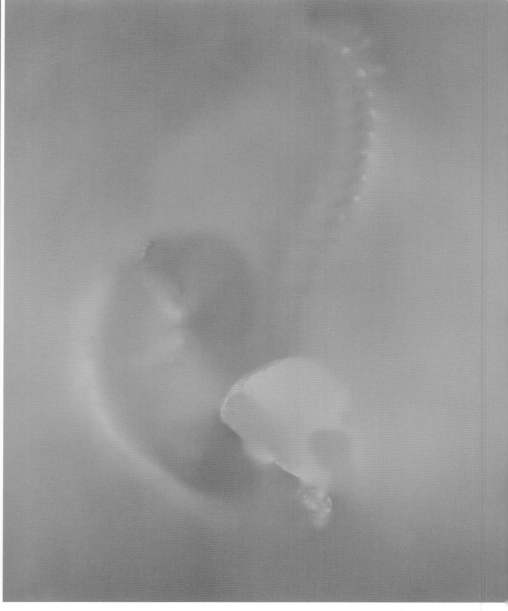

Olivia 2001

Arnaé 2001

olivia *and* arnaé

Unless you are a midwife or work in the medical profession, it can be a little unnerving to order a pelvis and a spine over the telephone, for delivery by post. But this is exactly what we had to do. Of course, they are only plastic and these particular models are used for medical training, particularly in the midwifery profession. We found them in an advertisement in a "medical monthly" newsletter—just goes to show that we all need to get out of our comfort zones sometimes!

The babies are curled and fast asleep in soft shapes especially created in a regular foam mattress. The surface of the mattress and the interior of the shapes the babies are lying in is lined with soft wool wadding which had been dyed a warm golden color. The image has been taken through a very thin layer of latex, the same as was used for the previous black-and-white series of images. A number of the images in *Pure* were photographed through this latex.

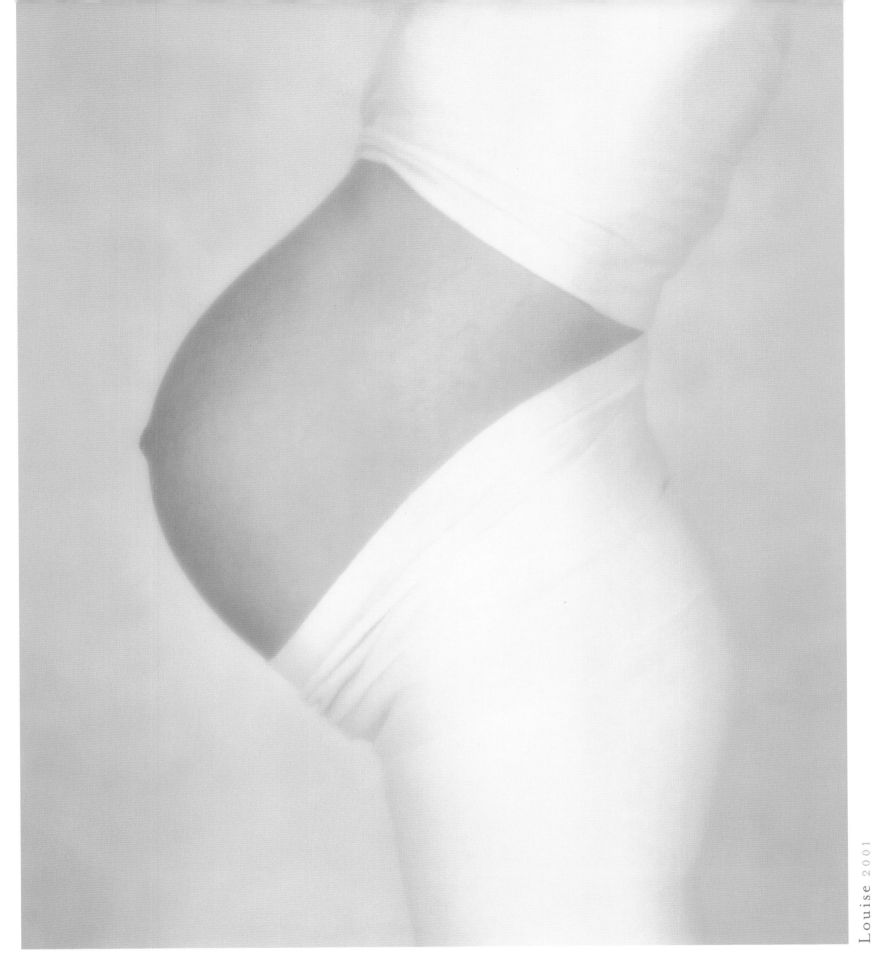

Louise 2001

louise

Louise was thirty-nine weeks pregnant and gave birth to her daughter, Charlotte, shortly afterward. She was lucky to still be so slender, at nine months, and yet with a big bump out front!

Whenever I look at this image, I think of a Thanksgiving turkey with the little indicator that pops out when the turkey is ready to come out of the oven. That's exactly what's happening here, I suppose.

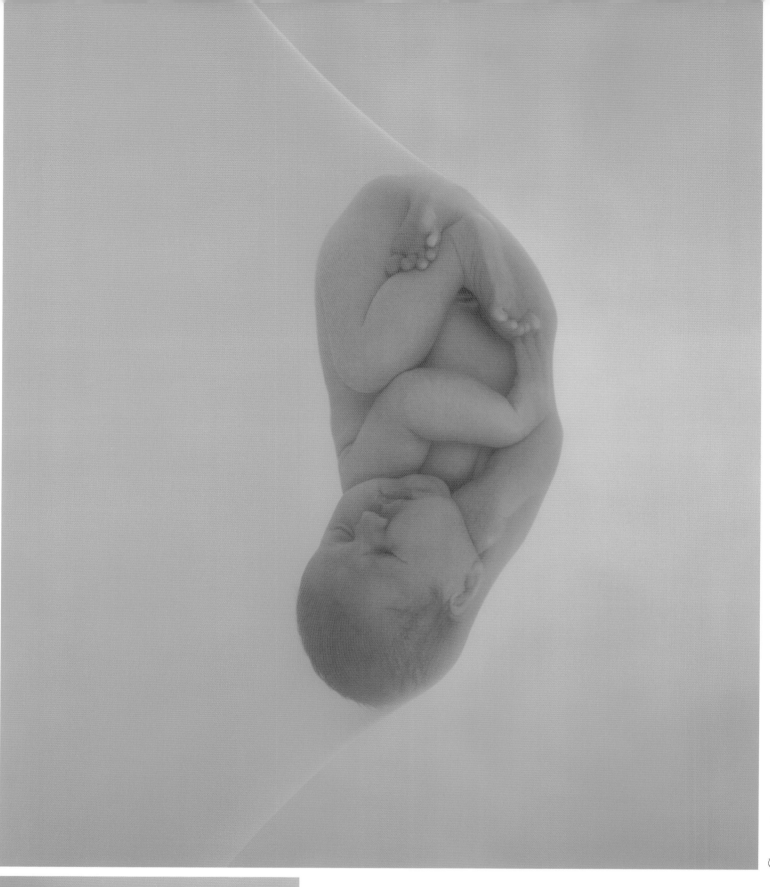

Courtney 2002

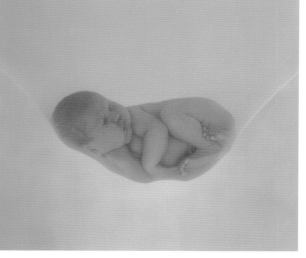

courtney

This image wasn't originally intended to represent a pregnancy, but as I was photographing, it became obvious that if the image was rotated it took on the shape in profile of a full-term pregnant tummy. Courtney would have looked exactly like that ten days earlier. No wonder she appears so contented.

Bee-be 1998

bee-be

I love the sense of absolute strength in this image of Bee-be, who, at the time, was thirty-nine weeks pregnant with twins Jasmine and Ulysses.

The gently rounded curves of her body and the formal balance of shapes remind me of a Henry Moore sculpture, and her hands resting above her pregnant belly lend a nurturing, feminine, and vulnerable human essence to the image.

In late 2003, I commenced work on the *Miracle* project with Celine Dion. Prior to this, I had wanted to take a year off to consolidate and reflect following the success of *Pure*, which had taken its toll. I shoot. I was creatively exhausted, and for relaxation had begun photographing flowers on my new digital camera. Every weekend I would spend at least a day by a particular window that had wonderful natural light, and work in a leisurely fashion by myself, simply photographing I came across. I felt very comfortable and even liberated just photographing quietly the pressure of a team of people or, for instance, having to worry about whether a Kel suggested that I should think about producing a book of flower images, but I my flower photography into work, so to speak, thereby adding pressure. Still, my f become the inspiration for my contribution to *Miracle*.

behind-the-scenes images from the "Miracle" shoot in Las Vegas, 2004

a miracle in the making…

Here is the story of how Celine and I met. A few years earlier, shortly before Christmas 1998, when I was shooting *Until Now,* somebody pointed out a magazine article to me. It was one of those stories we all see each year around the festive season, where celebrities are asked to list their favorite Christmas gifts. Celine had been invited to participate and she kindly said that one of her favorite gifts was my coffee table book *Down in the Garden.* What a lovely surprise, but then I thought nothing more about it.

I'm not sure if I believe in fate, but at the same time this happened, we were personally going through a very difficult and sad time, as a dear little friend of ours, Stacey (pictured on pages 194–95) was very ill with cancer. Stacey was only eight years old. She was also, I would have to say, probably the biggest Celine Dion fan ever, and would spend many hours in her hospital bed singing along to Celine's CDs. Her grandfather was attempting, via Celine's fan club, to have Celine relay a personal message to Stacey. Understandably, it's very difficult to organize these things from so far away, but I remembered that Celine loved my book, so I thought if anybody could organize something, perhaps I could.

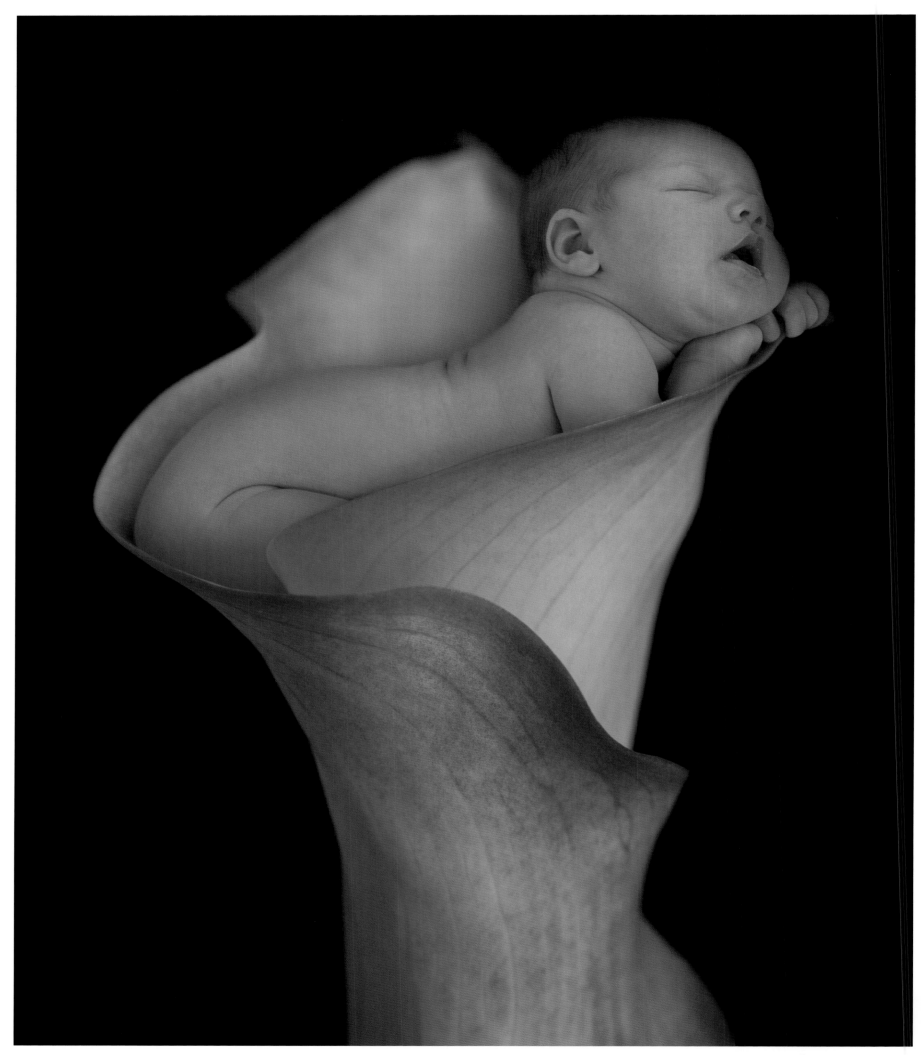

Camryn 2003

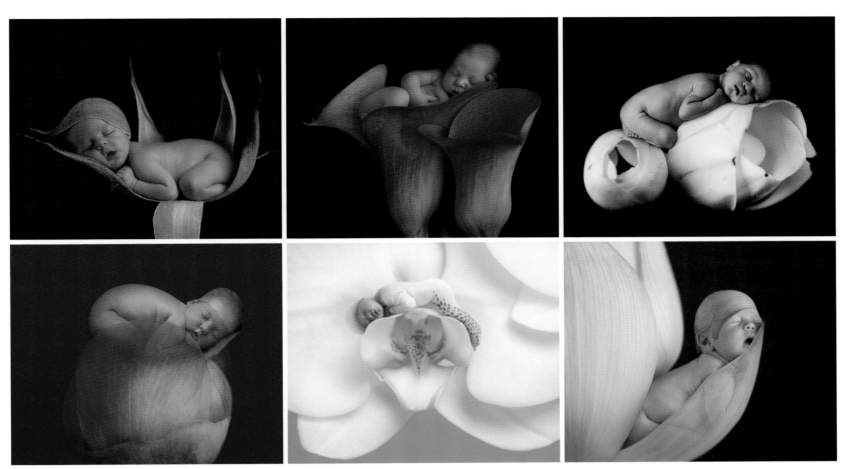

Travis, Jacob, Robert, Holly, Nakeeta, *and* Armen 2003—04

I managed to contact Celine's publicist and relayed Stacey's story. I said I was hoping that perhaps Celine could write a brief note to Stacey because it would mean so much to her. One Saturday morning, about ten days later, my telephone rang. It was Celine herself calling from New York to say that she had just telephoned Stacey and had had a long chat with her. As anybody would know who has tried to have telephone conversations with eight- or nine-year-old children they don't know personally, it's quite difficult sometimes to instinctively engage with them at their level, but Celine spoke to Stacey for over fifteen minutes. I remember saying to Celine, "You have no idea what a difference you've made to one little girl in a hospital bed on a Saturday morning in Auckland."

Celine and I maintained contact from then on, so I think I can safely say that little Stacey helped to bring the *Miracle* project together. When Celine became pregnant in 2000, even though I was no longer taking on private portraiture commissions, I offered to photograph her with her newborn son, René Charles, not necessarily to repay her kindness, but because I thought I would enjoy the opportunity to work with her. My team and I flew to Florida, where Celine was living at the time, and from then on Celine and I got to know each other well. We often talked about how much fun it would be to collaborate on a personal project together in the future—something that at the time had no definite shape—but we both agreed that it needed to be unique and meaningful to us both.

Celine mentioned that she had been given a song called "Miracle" as a gift when René Charles was born, by the songwriter Linda Thompson. What an extraordinary gift to be able to give someone. The first line of the song is "You're my life's one miracle," and as I believe that each new life is truly a miracle, it seemed perfectly natural to name our project *Miracle.* The song itself is very beautiful, encapsulating so well all of the feelings a mother has for her newborn child. We decided to make the song the basis for the project, and include other songs, some new and some classics, all of which can be interpreted as beautiful and meaningful love songs to the newborn. After all, the love affair between a mother and her newborn baby is incredibly powerful and all-encompassing.

I have a terrible singing voice, and as a joke to my then teenage daughters, I suggested that I was going to do the singing for *Miracle* and Celine was doing the photography. They looked at me in horror, and not because of Celine's photography skills, I'm sure!

Not knowing at this stage what form the project would take, my husband, Kel, reminded me again about my own collection of flower photography. It was perfect; both Celine and I would each be contributing something personal and meaningful to the project. For the two of us, our *Miracle* collaboration indeed came straight from our hearts.

The aim of the project was to create a beautiful coffee table book of images, which would also include a CD. The CD would also be sold as a separate entity. I decided to highlight six of the songs from the *Miracle* CD in the book, each song represented by a different flower with newborn babies nestling inside. As a link between the two, Celine would also be included in some of the images. It seemed like the perfect combination. The dilemma for me was how to incorporate Celine in the most meaningful way. After all, I thought it wouldn't be easy for her to compete with what turned out to be sixty-nine newborn babies. We decided that Celine would represent each of the six flowers depicted in the book and I set about designing the beautiful gowns and outfits she would wear for her part in the shoot.

It wasn't easy to decide which flowers to include in the imagery, but roses, being Celine's favorite flower, were a first and obvious choice. I then chose magnolias, lotus, moth orchids, calla lilies, and peonies. Of course, the choice is endless, but the flowers for this project also had to be able to accommodate a little something extra, newborn babies.

Thirty-nine of the babies who are featured in *Miracle* were photographed in my studio in Auckland and thirty babies in the United States. All of the flowers, with the exception of the lotus, were photographed in New Zealand. I often find that whenever I come up with an idea involving a particular flower, invariably it is either the very end of the season or they are not in season at all. True to form, lotus had just finished flowering in Auckland and the nearest place where they were still fairly abundant was in the warm tropical climate of Brisbane in Queensland, Australia. My team and I

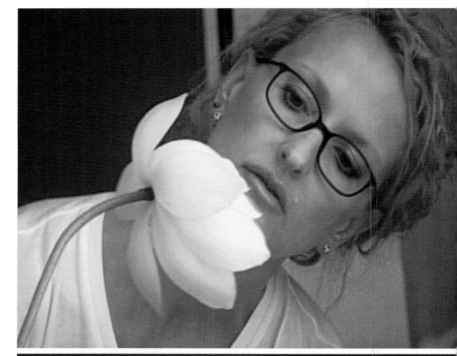

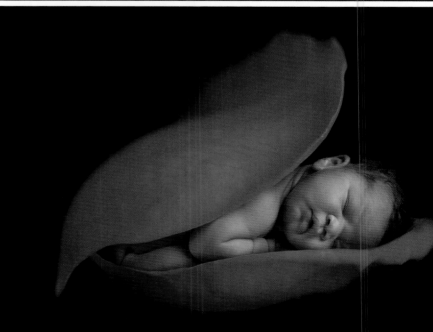

traveled there for a few days specifically to photograph the beautiful blooms. It was terribly hot in Brisbane at the time, and the studio we had hired had no air-conditioning. Finding that it was going to be impossible for the flowers to cope with the heat, I had to hire a huge portable air-conditioning unit, which was so noisy we could hardly hear ourselves think. It seemed like a lot of trouble to go to for the fragile lotus that a few weeks prior were abundant in Auckland!

The strongest images in *Miracle* for me turned out to be the calla lilies, which are the "accidental" flowers in the book. I had not intended using callas, but one day I was walking past a local flower store and was immediately captivated by their display of hundreds of these richly colored flowers. They looked amazing and I immediately knew they would be perfect for the project, especially because, once they were enlarged, their shape meant the babies could fit into them so easily and elegantly. The store owner was, I'm sure, very surprised when I bought nearly all of their display. Photographing flowers takes many hours of patience, and can include a lot of waste.

By the time I began shooting for *Miracle,* Celine had commenced her show in Las Vegas, which meant her availability was limited and travel would be difficult for her. We had little choice but to shoot in Las Vegas, so I planned to shoot the images in which she was included during a two-week break in the show's schedule.

As is always the case when I am shooting in a foreign location, it was necessary to research possible suitable venues. Our criteria is that there always needs to be adequate parking, comfortable and spacious facilities to accommodate the special needs of newborns and their parents, and there must be adequate temperature control, as the babies are generally photographed naked, and newborns cannot control their body temperature as adults can.

Obvious choices in Las Vegas were the huge ballrooms at the various hotel casinos, but access to these ballrooms is invariably via the gambling floor, clearly the main attraction of a casino. I felt very uncomfortable with the prospect of new parents having to walk newborn babies through areas such as this, not just because of the nature of the casinos, but the atmosphere is often full of stale smells and cigarette smoke.

Those few photographic studios available for hire locally were also not equipped for our special needs. Finally, the Lake Las Vegas Country Club and Restaurant kindly offered their premises. The location was ideal, with space to spread out and relative privacy and security. It took a day or so to black out all the windows from the bright Las Vegas sun, and convert the restaurant area into a makeshift photographic studio, which is where the behind-the-scenes images (pages 264–65) were taken. I'm sure the employees had never seen anything like it—there were newborn babies everywhere.

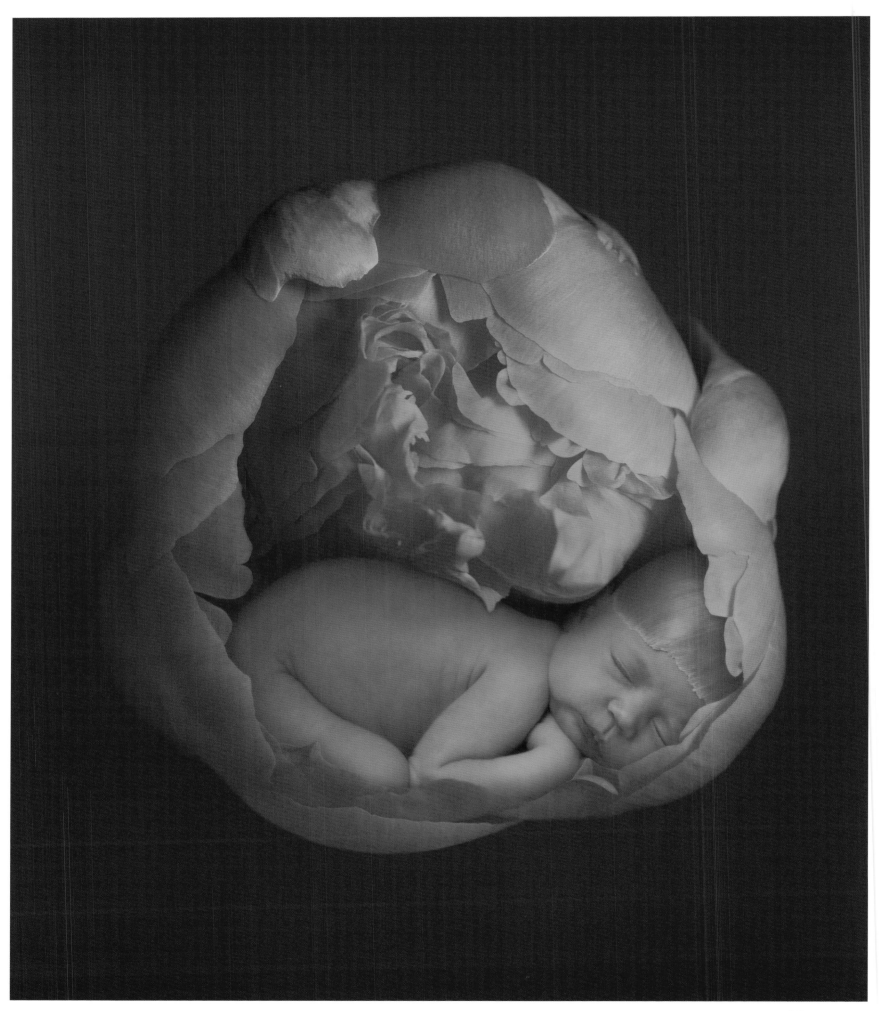

One unique problem at the shoot was that my very sensitive digital camera system began malfunctioning, in a strange way. By day three it had taken on a life of its own, and would indiscriminately fire itself whenever anybody was close by. In a panic, we had to consult the experts to diagnose the problem—their opinion was that it was static, caused by a combination of the dry air in Las Vegas, the temperature-controlled building, and the carpeted floor. From then on everybody in the studio had to remove their shoes and walk around in bare feet, which seemed to solve the problem.

There were many times when Celine was posing with a newborn and a little trickle began running down her arm; on numerous occasions, it was a lot more than a trickle! Celine was wonderful with the babies and didn't mind at all. She often joked that she wanted to take them all home with her afterward. Not so for me—much as I adore babies, I always say I have the best job in the world in that I have lots of contact with beautiful babies, lots of cuddles and kisses, then they go home to sleep at someone else's house while I have eight hours' blissful sleep each night!

A lot of people ask me how I create the images of babies in flowers. In fact, in the early days when I was promoting my first book,

Down in the Garden, I was actually asked during a couple of interviews, "Where do you get such big flowers?" I joked, "We always grow big flowers 'Down Under,'" to some very astonished looks.

By the time I was shooting *Miracle,* computer-generated imagery had become much more sophisticated and very different. When I compare the two books, which were published about eight years apart, I can really appreciate the unique qualities in each of them.

Down in the Garden is very real in the sense that all of the props and costuming were largely done by hand. I think this gives the book a very simple and distinct character that computer-generation cannot provide. *Miracle,* on the other hand, has a more otherworldly quality, a twenty-first-century take on fantasy. Of course, the babies and the flowers are real, but it's quite clear they have been combined on a computer. The computer is a wonderful tool, but I only like to use that kind of manipulation when it is completely obvious. I feel slightly uneasy at some of the deception that goes on these days; it's very hard to know what's real anymore.

After the shooting was completed, the task of putting babies and flowers together involved six months of full-time computer work.

I did not personally do this work (computer generation is a separate art form in itself), but for the whole time I sat by the screen, directing the process. I tried to keep the computer work for each image uncomplicated and minimal.

Generally for *Miracle,* I photographed the flowers before I photographed the babies. From studying each flower image, I determined the best place within the flower for the baby to nestle. A soft foam shape was then constructed which exactly mirrored that of the petal or the part of the flower that would integrate with the baby. We even determined the exact color of the fabric the baby would be photographed lying on, which would match the particular flower being used. This resulted in the color of the shadows on the baby being as accurate as they could be, appearing as if they were reflections from the actual flower itself. In the behind-the-scenes image on the bottom right of page 265 you can see a round pink shape being held over the baby who is being photographed. Amaya (previous page) was eventually lying on roses in the book, and the pink reflector threw a lovely rose-colored shadow onto her back. For me, the image came together perfectly, involving a minimal amount of computer work.

For those who are technically minded, most of the flowers and nearly all of the babies were photographed on a 4 x 5 inch film camera, the old-fashioned way. All of the images that include Celine with the babies, and the babies we photographed in Las Vegas without Celine, were photographed digitally. The reason for this was that I had very limited time to shoot in Las Vegas and I needed to see each image instantly, in order to be confident that I had achieved what I wanted; then we could move forward to the next shot. You can see us in one of the behind-the-scenes shots (pages 264–65) checking an image that had been taken just moments before. It was also a wonderful experience for the parents, who crowded around the computer screen at the end of each shoot to see their beautiful babies. While it all seemed perfectly normal to me, it occurred to me later that some of the parents must have thought the baby poses unusual at the time, as they were specifically planned for flowers they hadn't seen. Some of them would surely have been thinking, "I wonder what on earth she's up to?" However, as everyone agreed, it all came together in the end.

Miracle was released in October 2004.

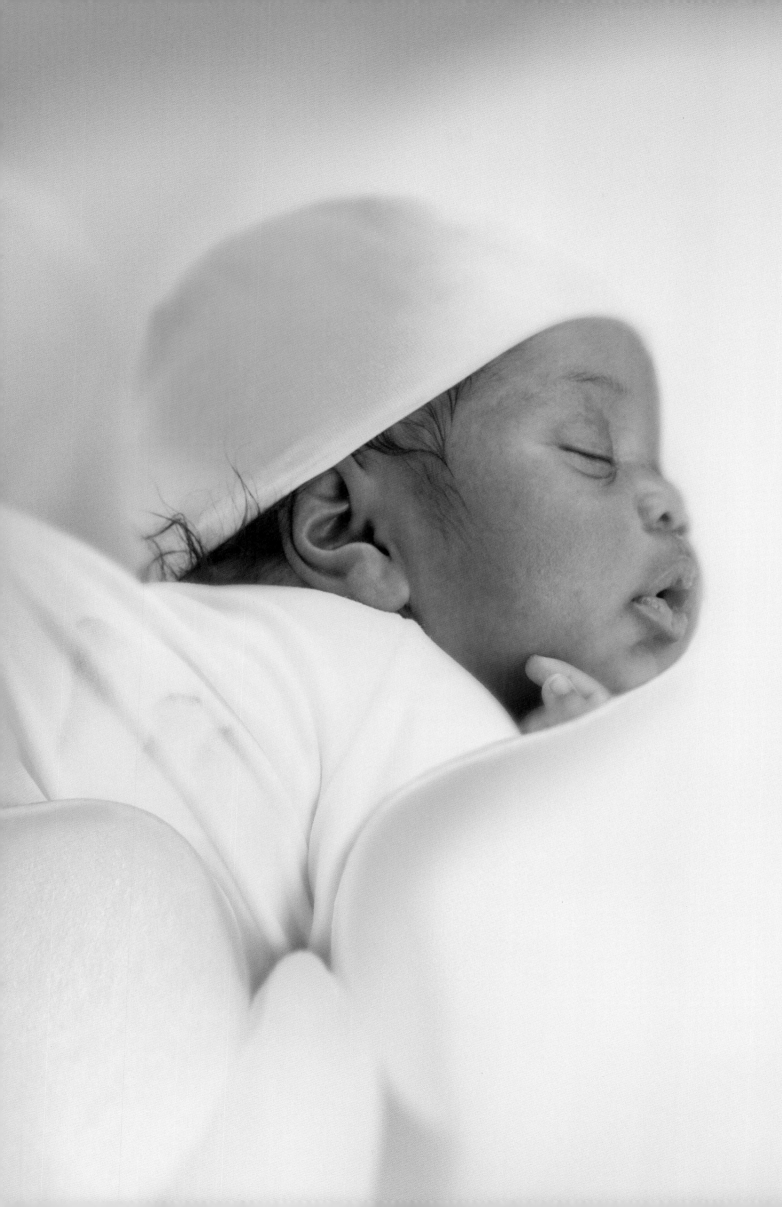

Telayiah 2004

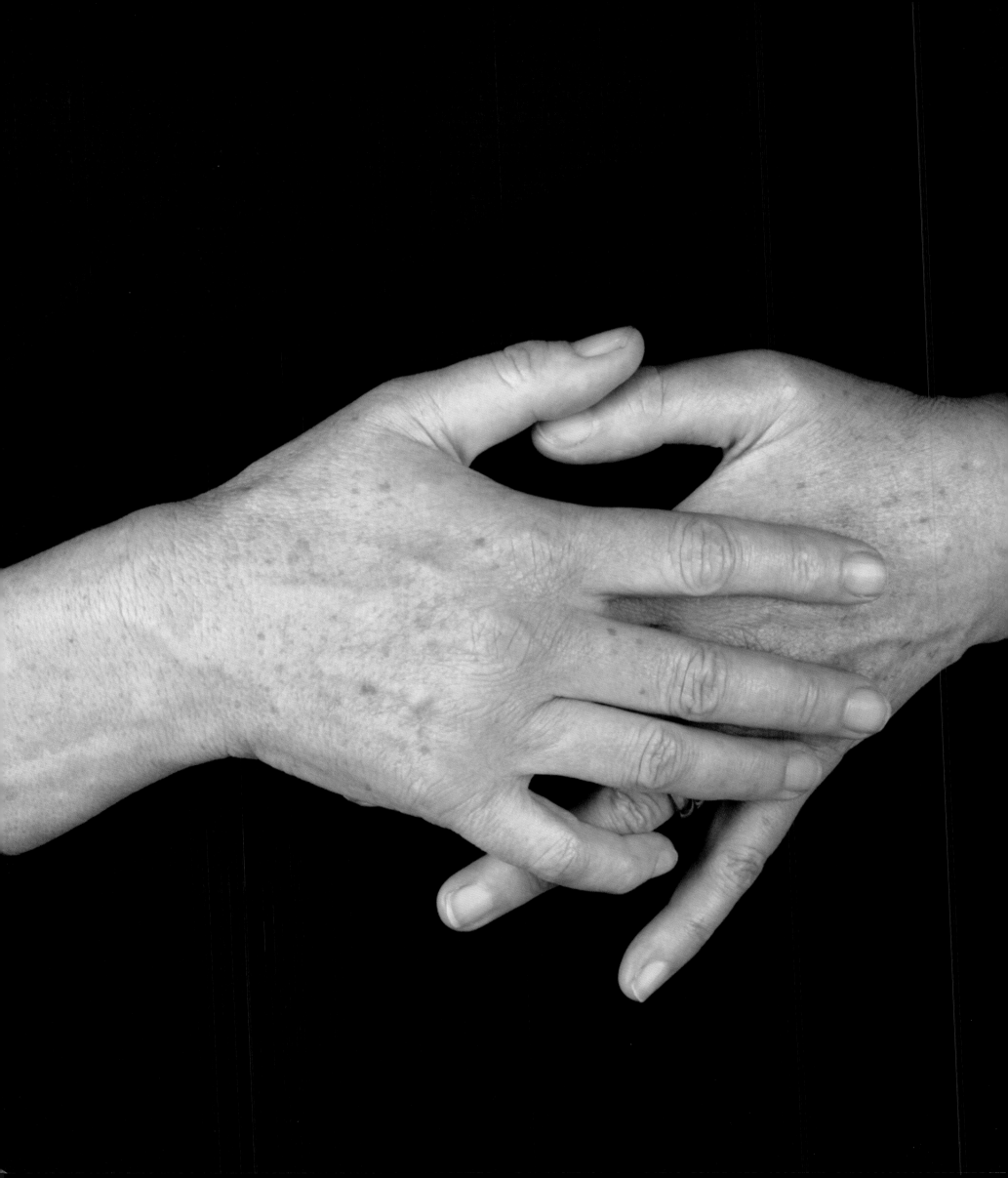

courage

This is a story of one woman's incredible courage. Sometimes, as a photographer, requests of a very personal nature can be made of you that can be somewhat daunting, but which you feel you cannot turn down. Often there is much to be gained by such experiences on a far deeper level for everybody concerned. This happened for me in November 1991, quite early in my photographic career.

Lee wrote to me when she was almost thirty weeks pregnant with twin boys. She planned to name them Hugh and Lloyd. At the time, she was living overseas, and also had three other young children. She explained to me that unfortunately the lungs of one of her twins were not developing normally in the womb, and even though both babies were progressing well in every other way, once they were born and had to breathe on their own, one twin, Lloyd, would not survive.

Lee explained that it was important for her to have photographs of both of her babies together. She wanted her surviving twin, Hugh, to feel a sense of connection to the brother he would never know. She asked me to be with her on the day, to photograph the cesarean birth of her babies and, if possible, the two baby boys together, however briefly. Her husband was not to be with her at the birth.

I was very moved by her circumstances and contacted her to ask if we could meet, as I felt that if I was to be present with her in a situation that was so profoundly personal and inevitably very sad, it would benefit us both if we were more than casual acquaintances. So we spent as much time as possible together, before the day the babies were to be born.

On the actual morning, I was naturally very nervous and emotional, not just because of the circumstances, but also because I had never before witnessed a cesarean birth, let alone photographed one. I felt a huge sense of responsibility to capture everything; not just well, but in a compassionate way. I was very conscious of the fact that, as a photographer, I was "out of place" in an operating theater, and was anxious to blend in with the proceedings in the most sensitive way possible. Most importantly, I didn't want to get in anybody's way—no easy task considering the surroundings and the occasion. The medical staff were very understanding and accommodating. I photographed the birth from my vantage point on a chair at the end of the operating table, and remember looking down at one stage to see a nurse stationed right next to me—she probably thought I would faint and cause chaos in the theater but I felt one step removed from the proceedings once I was looking through my camera—and probably just as well.

I had my assistant standing by with a second camera, and we planned to each photograph a baby, once they had been born. It was not clear before the birth as to which baby would be born first and once they were born everything moved very quickly. Nobody was certain at the time as to how long little Lloyd would survive, and as his situation was so acute, he was being monitored constantly; therefore it was very difficult to have the opportunity to photograph the two babies together. We did, however, take a number of pictures of them individually.

Knowing that there was nothing more I could do at the time, I left the hospital in the early afternoon and attended a Christmas play of my then seven-year-old daughter, Stephanie, at her school. Everything seemed surreal, and whenever I look at video from that afternoon of Steph and her little friends, holding hands and dancing around in a circle in the school hall, my thoughts revert to the small child who didn't survive, and the subsequent anguish of his family.

That evening, I received the anticipated telephone call from Lee to say that Lloyd had passed away. She asked if I would be able to return to the hospital and photograph her twins together now that all of the medical equipment was no longer required. It was one of the most difficult things I have ever had to do.

When I arrived back at the hospital, there were other family members present in the room, and I could sense that some of them were disapproving of my presence. But Lee was incredibly strong and very dignified. She sat in bed and cradled her two babies while I photographed the three of them together; then I gently laid the twins side by side for a photograph that I hoped one little boy would treasure forever.

I have not included any of the images taken on that day in this book, for obvious reasons, and while this has been an emotional story to tell, I also find it extremely uplifting. It is a tribute to one mother's love, insight, and courage in the face of such extreme sadness.

Many times over the following years, I wondered about Lee and Hugh and the impact of the photographs for them both, indeed for their whole family. Fifteen years after we had shared such a sad, moving, and emotional day, as I began writing their story for this book, I decided to try to find Lee again. After finally locating her (she had moved back to New Zealand) I telephoned and a young man with a deep voice answered the phone—it was Hugh. The last time I'd seen him, he was less than a day old. When Lee came to the phone I felt quite emotional. I explained that I was writing my life story and wanted her to be a part of it, and she said that she would be delighted and honored to have their story included. After the phone call I felt an incredible sense of joy and lightness. It was at that point when I thought how amazing it would be to include an image of Lee and Hugh as they are today.

We had a wonderful reunion at the studio on the day of the shoot, and Lee looked exactly as I remembered her. She had recently remarried and brought her new husband, Dennis, to meet us. Hugh, who is now a very handsome fifteen-year-old, towered even over me, and that doesn't happen very often, I have to say. He is just over six feet tall. Hugh wasn't too sure whether it was very cool to have his mum hugging him in a photograph, but otherwise, I think he was quietly excited about being in the book.

I couldn't take my eyes off him. It is difficult to explain, but to me there is something magical and awe-inspiring about the reach across time, from holding and photographing a tiny newborn and then embracing them again many years later, with very little or often no contact at all in between. I wonder if it's because I always hold them in my heart as newborns. Apart from a natural sense of curiosity as to what they look like now, I also feel a unique connection to them, as if I have been privileged to be a part of their lives in such a fulfilling way.

At the shoot, Lee told me how important the images have been to her family over the years and of how they all regularly revisited them to remember Lloyd. She said that, as time passes, if at all possible, their significance continues to increase. In a sense the images help to complete the family circle—Lloyd is always with them. But I especially hope that, for Hugh, the images from that day will always be a source of comfort and companionship throughout his life.

In telling Lee's story, the significance of the whole experience greatly intensified for me. I don't know about you, but I think that Lee's great gift to her son showed incredible foresight and courage. I consider myself fortunate to have had many moments in my career that have been incredibly rewarding, but my experiences and memories from that day will stay with me forever.

When I am photographing babies, I am photographing not just a symbol of new life, but also a vulnerable human being who, as in Lloyd's case, sadly may not continue to live. The shadow side of life is always the possibility of its loss. It would be naïve to ignore that, for many reasons, including illness, starvation, and war, babies have lost their lives. It has been an honor for me to work with parents who have had to face this loss.

I know that life is not perfect, and that, for many, there is a great deal of suffering, but I have faith in our ability to transform ourselves. Fortunately, most of my work deals with the joyfulness of new life. The continual promise that I see in the eyes of a new human being gives me hope, calmness, and strength—and I know that is why I continue to photograph babies. Babies give me, I think give most of us, something we need; the inspiration and the opportunity to change ourselves and our world.

I am frequently asked…

Q: You must be a very patient person—what's it like in the studio during one of your shoots?

Perhaps you'd have to ask my daughters if I am truly such a patient person! A lot of people say to me they imagine the studio atmosphere to be very noisy and chaotic, but it's not like that at all. On the contrary, it's usually very calm and quiet, particularly when I am photographing newborns, which is what I mainly do these days. It seems that the older I get, the younger my subject matter becomes. Perhaps it's also because I don't have the energy to chase two-year-olds anymore.

I like to play soft classical music in the studio, especially when I'm working, but it's more for me than the babies. I'm a big fan of Mozart. I find many of his compositions very calming, and I have a special music file that I am continually updating and always play as I shoot . . . the music puts me in a more relaxed and creative state of mind.

In fact, I so love Mozart that I spent a month in an editing suite earlier this year, preparing a combination of some of my images to one of his pieces. I find the blend of images and music quite captivating. The music seems to gently bring the images to life in a very emotional way. The images and the music become as one, and the result can be quite intense, as both music and images work on a subconscious level.

I know from personal experience that the first few weeks at home with a newborn are not only exciting, but also quite challenging and demanding. Therefore, in the studio, it's great for new mothers to be able to relax, socialize, and share common experiences with other women in exactly the same situation. It gives the mothers a chance to be open and honest about their feelings of inadequacy, rather than having to keep up a front of coping all the time. Sometimes, just a bit of adult conversation goes a long way to easing the stress and isolation of suddenly being at home and responsible for a brand-new baby twenty-four hours a day. I know it was for me when my girls were first born.

I have a comfortable "mothers' room" right next to the studio, more like a home lounge room, but fully equipped with a baby-changing area. There is also another lounge area in the actual studio, so mothers can be close to their babies while I am shooting, and feel that they, too, are part of the process.

Of course, babies in a studio situation need to be handled very carefully and skillfully. I work with a very small team of people whom I completely trust; we have been together for many years. They are very responsible and experienced with babies of all ages. I have my own basic, but strict, rules for my staff when handling babies. For instance, every baby has a separate changing area, with fresh

typical behind-the-scenes images from a shoot for "Miracle" (2003). The image far right shows the purpose-built balcony from where I am able to shoot directly downward through a large hole in the middle of the floor.

coverings at all times. Our hands are always thoroughly washed between handling of different babies. Whenever we are holding a baby, we always remain in eyesight of their mother and keep the mother informed at all times as to what is happening. Hot drinks are never served in the studio during shoots. The organization and care that goes on in the background is unnoticeable to anybody else, and that is part of being a professional team. I like to make everything look easy, seamless, and fun, but we are always conscious and respectful of the huge responsibilities involved with photographing such young children.

Another very strict rule is that older siblings, in particular toddlers, are never allowed in the studio when I am photographing small babies. There are obvious safety issues with photographic equipment, and toddlers running around a studio are not only distracting for all concerned, they can cause quite a lot of chaos.

These hard-and-fast rules have been established over many years, when I have learned that you have to have eyes in the back of your head and be attuned to everything going on in the room when a shoot is in progress.

I am often asked during media interviews to speak about how chaotic

it must be in the studio when I am shooting. I understand that people imagine this to be the case, but in my experience, nothing could be further from the truth. One of the reasons I very rarely allow film crews in the studio when I am shooting is that I know that they are invariably looking for footage of a crying baby to justify their preconceived agenda. I don't mean to sound oversensitive, but I don't believe my work practices should be misrepresented for the benefit of a thirty-second "grab." Of course babies cry in my studio sometimes, but not as often as people think, and a crying baby doesn't necessarily mean that the environment is chaotic.

In fact, it's always gratifying to receive letters from parents who have brought babies to my shoots, who invariably say how welcome they felt, how interesting it was to see how we worked, and what a wonderful time they had.

Q: How do you get the babies to sleep?

I'd love to say that I have a magic remedy for helping babies to settle and sleep, but that's definitely not the case. However, the sleeping babies in my images are almost all newborns, under four weeks of age. At this early stage babies will generally sleep for most of the time if they are warm, comfortable, and have been well fed. Very new babies also tend to be far less aware of their surroundings, and will sleep almost anywhere, as opposed to older babies who are more alert and interested in everything that is going on around them.

Of course, there is always an element of luck involved, but I've found over the years that the most effective way to get a baby to sleep is simply to pretend that you don't care either way. It's hard to be this nonchalant at 3 a.m., but generally it works for me in the studio. I also recommend that a good old-fashioned rocking chair be installed in the home of every newborn baby. I have one in my studio; in fact, Lucas and I are sitting in it in our photograph at the beginning of the book.

I try to photograph in the mornings, never the afternoons, because I have found that babies are usually more settled earlier in the day. This could be because mother's milk is richer in the mornings if they have managed some well-deserved sleep during the night.

I am always very organized prior to a shoot. Everything is prepared and rehearsed the day before, as once the babies arrive, everything needs to revolve around them. Adult models can always wait around while lighting is adjusted, but babies can't.

Mothers also need to feel welcome and relaxed. A relaxed mother generally means a relaxed baby. As soon as everyone is settled, and I have greeted everybody and explained the image I am wanting to achieve, we gently undress each baby and wrap them in one of my personally designed baby wraps. The skin of a newborn is very soft and sensitive, and I've found that when a naked newborn is wrapped for any length of time in a textured fabric, the pattern stays on their skin for a short while—which is the reason I use my own untextured baby wraps made from breathable cotton. The baby is then fed and generally they drift off to sleep. If a baby is to be naked in my image, it is important that they are undressed and wrapped before being fed, so I don't disturb them by having to undress them later.

Each baby is still wearing a nappy (diaper); however, it is not fastened at the sides. In this way, when the baby is asleep and ready to be photographed, the elastic on the sides of the disposable nappy has not left little pink marks on their skin. Marks such as this can be easily removed on a computer, but in the early days that wasn't so easy to achieve, and many times in early shoots I would have to wait for five to ten minutes until the marks disappeared naturally— quite stressful when I was also hoping that the baby wouldn't wake. Disposable nappies can also be very noisy to unfasten and I don't

want to disturb the sleeping baby just before I get them settled for the image.

A lot of mothers, when they are in the studio for shoots, are amazed that their babies settle so well, when, perhaps, they have been fussy at home the previous night. I'm convinced that newborns can smell their mother's milk, and sometimes when a baby has a full tummy and is still fussing, it's better to have somebody else cuddle and settle them. This is why new fathers need to also be up in the middle of the night sharing baby duties. (I'm not going to make myself popular with fathers by saying this!)

I'm also convinced that tiny babies are very instinctive, far more than we think, and will pick up on a mother's nervousness. I remember feeling initially nervous with my own baby daughter, and like many new mothers, it was unfamiliar to be handling a baby. Of course, now I know that this is entirely normal. I'm convinced that newborns have a built-in sense that you're confident and know what you're doing. Little babies are a lot more aware than we give them credit for.

Q: Do you stay in touch with the babies when they are older?
Yes, quite often I do and I love to receive letters and e-mails from some of the early babies that I photographed who are now teenagers and young adults. It's lovely to see how those beautiful chubby six-month-olds, for instance, have grown into tall gangly teens. In *A Labor of Love* I have photographed six of the babies who have featured in my early images, as they are now.

People sometimes ask me, and I myself have wondered over the years, how the babies I have photographed in the past now relate to the images of themselves as newborns. I hope that they are pleased and proud to have been involved, even though at the time they really had no say in the matter. I have not taken this huge responsibility lightly throughout my career, and to meet and reacquaint myself with some of the early babies for this book was an incredibly rewarding, and also surreal, experience for me.

In fact, we all enjoyed the experience so much that perhaps I may do a more comprehensive book sometime in the future showing many more of the babies as teenagers and young adults. Now, that would be a great project to work on. So, if you are one of the babies that I have photographed over the past twenty-five years and we have lost touch, please contact my Web site (www.annegeddes.com) if you feel that you may be interested in taking part.

above: after the completion of the "Miracle" project in October 2004, all of the babies who were photographed in my studio in Auckland
were invited to a morning tea get-together to celebrate. It was a beautiful day, and the roses in the Parnell Rose Gardens in Auckland were in full bloom.

Q: Did your photographic career begin when your own daughters were small babies and are they included in any of your images?

I am often asked this question, but in fact I had begun my career before our girls were born, although in a limited way. When they were first born and into their early school years, I was mainly concentrating on developing my private portraiture business.

Unfortunately, by the time I had begun to create my early imagery for calendars and greeting cards, they were no longer babies. However, I have many personal photographs of them both as babies, and thousands of images of them through their childhood years and into early adulthood. They are included in a few early greeting card and calendar images, and they are also featured in *Pure*. They have grown up with cameras and photography constantly in their lives, and since they were both very young I have always tried to involve them in my work in all sorts of different ways. They were often enlisted to help with shoots (see below) and in fact are now both quite accomplished photographers in their own right. Nowadays, they are very fond of turning the camera on me, perhaps as revenge for years of being in front of my camera!

Q: As a mother, how do you balance career and family commitments?

I have always tried to include our girls in whatever I was doing, which seemed perfectly natural to me as I don't consider my photographic career to be a regular job, so to speak. It's more a way of life. Ever since they were very small, we have integrated our work and home life, as we lived in the same building in which my studio is located, and during the times when I was shooting overseas we always tried to have them with us whenever logistics and their schooling schedules allowed. I have always emphasized to them that they should follow their own dreams. One of life's greatest gifts is to work in a profession that you are passionate about, and I hope I have been able to demonstrate this to them by example.

Q: This is the time of the digital revolution—has this brought a difference to your work?
Essentially no. A beautiful image speaks for itself, regardless of whether it was created on film or in a digital file, and they both have their own unique attributes. I use digital cameras pretty much exclusively for my personal photography. Particularly as I travel so frequently, I no longer have to worry about carrying exposed but undeveloped film, which can be easily damaged in X-ray machines at airports.

Q: In your professional life, is there one moment or achievement that stands out for you as having made you proud of what you do?

I'm incredibly proud of the fact that over the years I have been able to contribute significantly toward raising the level of awareness of the problems of child abuse and neglect. For personal reasons, as explained earlier, from the publication of my very first calendar in 1992, I have been proudly associated with this cause. My husband, Kel, and I, through the Geddes Philanthropic Trust, assist many charities around the world that are working in this important area. At the time of publication of *A Labor of Love* we have donated several million dollars to this cause, and that figure will continue to grow.

But in terms of one single moment, I think it would have to be the day, in January 2001, when we were able to offer a U.S. $1,000,000 donation to Childhelp USA to support their twenty-four-hour National Child Abuse Hotline (1-800-4-A-Child). Kel and I both felt that finally we had been able to make a solid commitment in one area that would clearly make a significant difference not just to abused children, but to the wonderful people who dedicate their lives to working in this area, often with serious funding issues.

Q: Was there a moment when you realized that your work was going to be a global success and how did you feel about that at the time?

I'm not sure if there was one specific moment, but certainly right after my first book, *Down in the Garden,* was published in 1996 and quickly climbed to number three on the *New York Times* bestseller list, I was astonished at the enthusiastic public response. Of course, it was hugely gratifying, as I had no idea at all that the book would be such a success. That whole time was very exciting, but also strange in a way; I felt very exposed.

At the same time, my calendars and greeting cards were also becoming successful, so everything was quite overwhelming for me. As anybody who has been in the public eye would know, once you put yourself and your work into the public domain, and particularly with such an emotive subject matter, you are open not just to praise, but also criticism; my own inexperience meant I wasn't prepared for that. Criticism can certainly rock a person's confidence, but it can also make them stronger and more determined.

I felt quite alone and vulnerable in that there was nobody else working exclusively in the area of baby photography—I was creating my own unique path, and at that early stage, I still wasn't quite sure of my future direction, and my own personal style was still maturing.

It was very frustrating for me in the early days not to be able to explain what it was really like for me when I was photographing in the studio, and the motivation, dedication, and level of commitment behind my work. I don't feel that I am a great verbal communicator at the best of times, and in those early days I was also far less experienced and confident at speaking about the personal meaning and passion behind my work. Everybody was looking for cute baby stories, which is perfectly understandable, but I became quite weary, and anxious about it all.

Writing for *A Labor of Love* has, in fact, been quite cathartic for me, as finally I've been able to put down my thoughts about not just the seriousness and the huge level of responsibility involved with what I do, but also my commitment to my photography and raising the level of awareness toward the issues of child abuse and neglect.

In the very early days, many had the distinct impression that *Down in the Garden* was a one-off publication. I don't think they understood the level of passion and commitment I had to making the photography of babies my life's mission. I felt that this attitude could only slowly change if I demonstrated by example that I was serious about the continued development of my work, and dedicated to being a voice for the babies.

There is no doubt, however, that the initial success of *Down in the Garden* gave me an enormous confidence boost to continue with my work. People around the world were incredibly generous and encouraging, and I was very touched by this. Even to this day, one of my greatest pleasures is having people show me photographs of their babies, and share their stories, their pride in their own children. I'm just so lucky to be working in an area in which, regardless of different cultures and nationalities, the emotion is exactly the same—everybody adores their babies.

Q: Where do you find the babies that you photograph?

This is one of the questions I am most frequently asked. The babies I feature in my photographs come from numerous sources. Many parents simply send their own photographs directly to the studio. Naturally, it is impossible to involve all of those babies in my photography, as I don't photograph on a regular basis unless I am working on a specific project. However, we still love to see the photographs that arrive daily. I have been located in the same studio in Auckland, New Zealand, for many years, so I therefore have a large number of local contacts in twin clubs, multiple birth associations and the like, and a strong network of midwives in the Auckland area who, for a long time, have been very supportive and helpful.

We often receive telephone calls from brand-new parents who are still at their hospital or birth-care center, to tell us the news of their new arrivals. In fact, I recall one very excited and proud new father phoning us half an hour after his baby was born!

Q: How old was the youngest baby you have ever photographed?

I have photographed a number of babies who were one or two days old, but the newborns in my images are generally over one week old before they come to the studio. At times, the studio visit is a baby's first outing since arriving home. One mother brought her baby to the studio on her way home from the birth-care center and went to sleep on our couch in the middle of the shoot. When I was photographing her baby, I turned to her to say, "Look how beautiful he is," but she was fast asleep. Poor thing, she was exhausted, but in those first few weeks, most mothers are.

Q: You have traveled the world talking about your work, as well as shooting on location. Do you find a difference in mothers in the various countries you have visited?

Not at all. I find that, regardless of nationality, the emotions are identical. The language of motherhood is universal. Of course, there are cultural differences in styles of parenting and upbringing between various countries, but that is to be celebrated. Everywhere I travel, I love the fact that people—flight attendants on planes, waiters in restaurants, people from all walks of life, in fact—show me photographs of their children. I think I'm so lucky to be able to share in their stories. After all, the babies in my images really could be any nationality at all.

I have traveled extensively through Europe on promotional tours for my books, and regardless of the language differences, the questions people ask me and their response to my imagery are essentially the same. I have photographed many times in the United States, and everybody is friendly, welcoming, and in love with their babies.

I have had the pleasure over the years of working with mothers from all walks of life. One of the most rewarding times for me was working with the Black Infant Health Program in California, during a number of my shoots there. This wonderful group of people provides support, care, and guidance for very young girls, some of them mothers at the tender age of fourteen or fifteen. After our shoots, it was gratifying to hear feedback from these young girls, who said that they had been made to feel valued and special and more confident in themselves as mothers. Some of them said that we helped them to view their babies in a different light.

Q: What do you think your images mean to other people?

I think one of the main reasons for the success of my imagery is that most people are not fortunate enough to have close personal contact with a newborn baby in their daily lives. Only when there is a newborn in the family, for instance, do we really have a chance to interact with, or hold in our arms, a brand-new baby.

In this "new world" in which we all now find ourselves, it has become even more important to reinforce our core values. Our lives have become fragmented and busy; a lot of people (including myself) are searching for a regular source of calm, comfort, and balance. The babies pictured in my images I hope, to some degree, provide this.

Many of the images of babies we see in the media today are not of newborns specifically, even though the babies are purported to be newborn. The mothers who bring their newborn babies to my studio are doing so not just because they completely trust me, but because they also believe in my message, which is to portray the absolute purity and promise of the newborn.

On many occasions, for instance, people have told me that they visit my Web site every morning, as a form of positive affirmation for the day. That speaks volumes for the energizing power of a newborn. My own desire is that my imagery will help to create a strong platform of hope and promise for humanity and the future. Babies speak a universal language. In any country in the world, the emotional connection between a mother and her newborn is equally powerful.

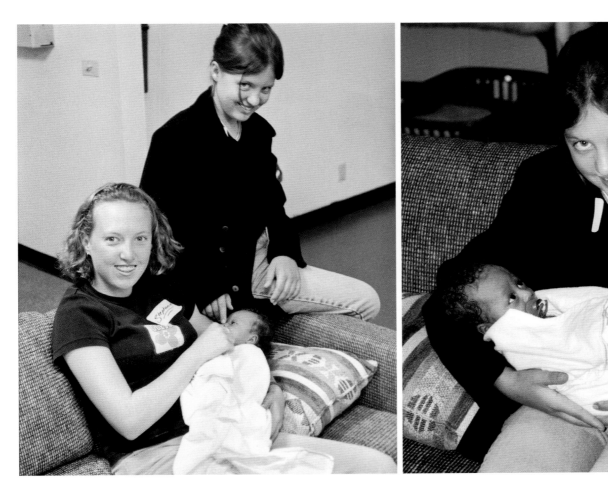

above: my daughters, Stephanie and Kelly, helping during the Los Angeles shoot, 1998

Q: Do you audition babies?

No, that would be impossible. However, there was one notable exception. In 1998, I was planning a very large shoot in Los Angeles. I was to be there for a month and for this particular project needed quite a few newborn babies, with a special emphasis on newborn African American babies, as it is very difficult for me to find African American babies where I live in New Zealand. A local Los Angeles radio station kindly volunteered to make an announcement on my behalf, and consequently over two thousand people responded. Of course, this created quite a dilemma for me. My team of helpers telephoned everybody to make sure their babies *really* were newborn. It often happens that people say they have a newborn and in fact the baby can be anything up to a year old; people often have different concepts of "newborn."

We were eventually able to reduce the number of people who were still keen and eligible to around six hundred. So I held an "audition" for six hundred beautiful babies. What else could I have done? The organization behind the scenes was incredible. I was anxious to not create the impression that I was choosing one baby over another, even though technically people knew they were coming to an audition. I wanted everyone to feel very welcome and appreciated. Any parent of a very young baby knows that they need to carry around a lot of baggage. It seems that the older the baby becomes, the less paraphernalia you have to take on an outing, but at the very beginning it can seem as if you are carrying your entire house with you.

First, I was concerned about the weather, so we had a wet-weather contingency plan, plenty of assistants available with umbrellas to greet people when they arrived and, of course, parking was arranged nearby. Then there were nappy (diaper) changing facilities, catering, and extra people to watch over accompanying older brothers and sisters. Even my two daughters (above) were recruited as willing helpers.

Despite the large number of people and the sheer logistics of making it work, it turned out to be a great day. I took a lot of care to try to meet everybody, and we took Polaroid photographs and contact details of all of the babies and their parents. Then, what else could I do but draw twenty-five babies' names out of a hat. I could not possibly choose!

So, apart from the exceptional circumstances I've described above, I honestly don't see any point in auditioning babies. I know it's a cliché, but I believe that all babies are equally beautiful. Each of them from birth has their own look and personality and I couldn't possibly choose one over the other. Almost all of the babies who are featured in my images come, sight unseen, to the studio, where we meet for the first time on the day of the shoot. Many years ago I volunteered to judge a charity baby competition at a local country fair. Afterward, I promised myself never to do it again; it was just too difficult. I was a terrible judge because I declared them all winners!

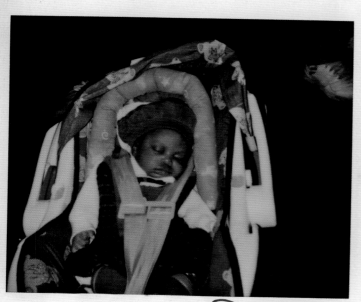

DonTré

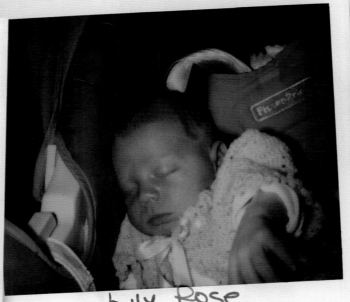

Lily Rose

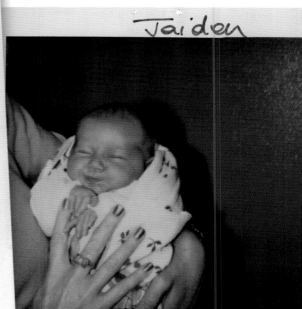

Jaiden

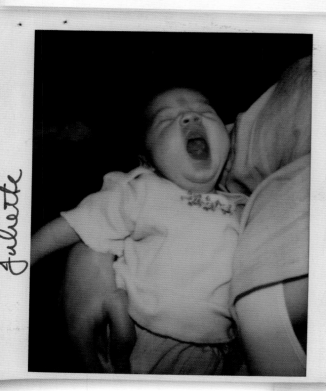

Juliette

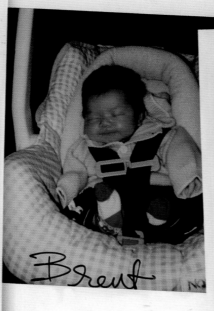

Brent

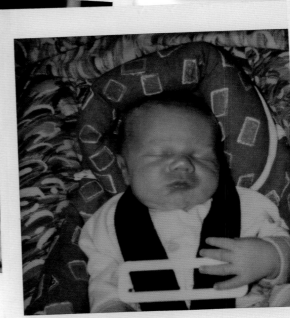

Hayden

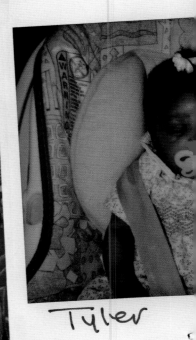

Tyler

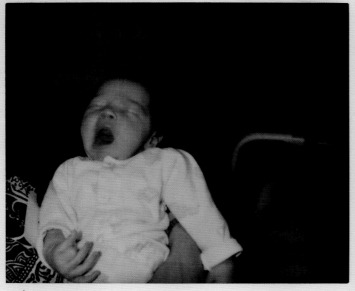

Lilyann

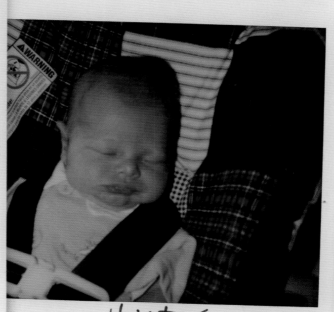

Hunter

Tsikai

4 lb
6 oz.

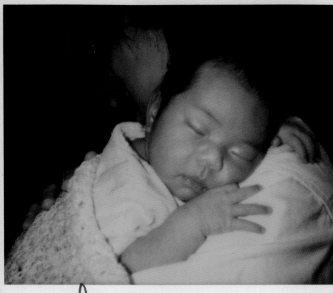

Lauren

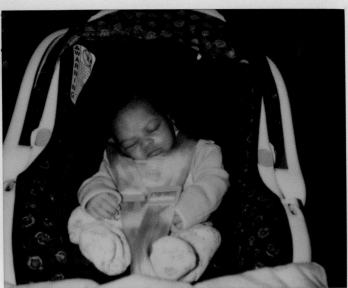

Kendall

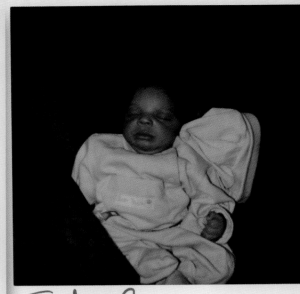

Caleel

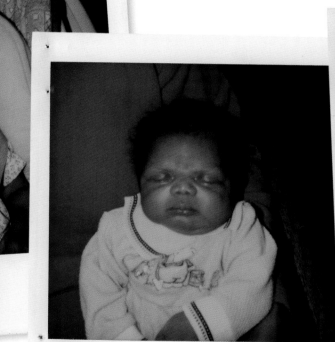

Justin

Graham + Dean

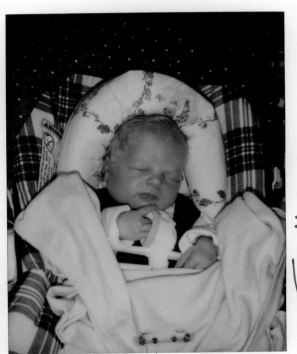

Timothy

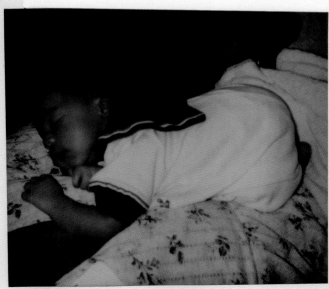

Garrison

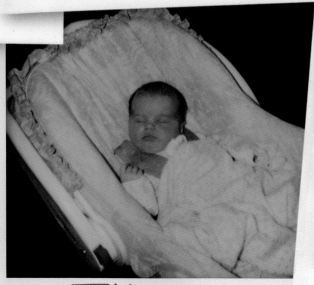

Julia

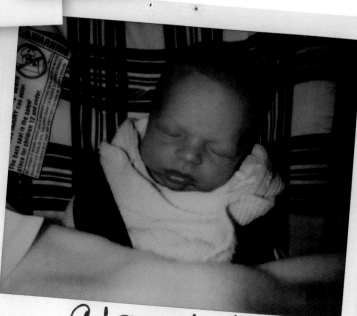

Alexander

Q: What are mothers like during shoots—do you encounter many "stage mothers"?

To be honest, in my experience, stage mothers of newborn babies are extremely rare. Over my twenty-five years of photographing babies, I have met many different types of mothers. Some are laid-back, some are nervous and unsure, some are anxious, some are relaxed and confident, and most have a great sense of humor. Almost all are suffering sleep deprivation.

I have met some very famous mothers, and mothers from different nationalities, cultures, and all walks of life, and I can honestly say that all mothers are the same in their concerns for their babies, especially in those first few weeks of life, when every experience is so new.

One of my favorite "mother" stories is about a wonderful feisty Jewish grandmother who came to one of my shoots in New York. The room was literally full of newborns and new mothers, and she was holding court with her brand-new grandbaby fast asleep on her shoulder. My husband, Kel, was there at the time and must have made what he thought to be a harmless comment and she turned to him and said, "If men had babies, there'd be no more babies." Everyone in the room just collapsed with laughter. I think Kel was a bit outnumbered on that occasion!

First-time mothers, in particular, are on a steep learning curve. But I think every one of these "mother types" is normal. In fact, I know that as a mother myself I have been all of these at one time or another, and continue to be, even though my girls have grown.

Q: Do you have any advice for new mothers?

Only to relax and be yourself. Trust your own built-in instincts, because, more often than not, they will be right. This invaluable piece of advice was given to me by a nurse on the day I left the hospital with my first baby, and it has proven to be true time after time. Most importantly, remember there is no absolute rule book for motherhood, and if there was, I wouldn't be rushing out to buy it. From my own experience with my girls, I've always tried to be

my own person, to maintain my own unique identity within the all-consuming and often overwhelming experience of mothering. It was important for me, even when the girls were small, to have them know me as myself, the unique person that I am—that we all are. I was determined not to become a "professional mother," whatever that might be. That notion never seemed like much fun to me.

These days there are increasing pressures on parents, and particularly mothers, to be superhuman. There is no way any of us can be perfect mothers, because the perfect mother doesn't exist. We're just human, after all. We are under pressure to ferry our children, constantly, from one activity to another—every spare second of their lives is filled with a schedule. We even provide them with televisions in cars. Well, I don't, but some people do. What on earth happened to conversation, and looking out the window? Why are we raising our children to not have a second to themselves—some breathing space?

Every child needs to have regular time to just do nothing at all, for daydreaming. But there doesn't seem to be any time left for children to just do nothing at all; to use their imaginations, enjoy their own company, dream a little, be still—not just physically, but mentally. I know for me, daydreaming is not self-indulgent, it's vital—it enriches me and calms me.

Daydreaming feeds the soul. When I was a child, my sisters and I would go and play in the yard for hours on end. I know for a fact that it nourished both my relationship with my sisters, and my imaginative life. If we agree, and most surely would, that the best things in life are simple, why are we making our children's lives so complicated?

Now, every mother is different and every mother unique, and that's cause for celebration in itself. Babies are also incredibly forgiving little people. So, if it doesn't take much to make them happy, why do we put so much pressure on ourselves? We all know that babies would rather play with the gift wrap than the gift. We wonder at the innocence and the guileless nature of babies, and yet we're in such a hurry to take all of this away from them as soon as we can. The wonderful thing about babies is that they are so completely *themselves*. And they allow us to be children again. In fact, they demand this of us—that we go back to the simple gestures in life—which are important for the soul. To me, two of life's greatest pleasures would have to be the sound of a baby laughing, which is delightful and incredibly captivating, and the delicious and unique scent of the back of a sleeping newborn's neck. In fact, everything about a newborn is a delight—that lovely combination of velvety rolls, soft downy hair, and brand-new life. To stroke the tiny, soft, and exquisite head of a brand-new baby is surely to take oneself back to the true essence of life and the reasons for our existence.

I don't know how many times over the years I've had normally strait-laced and reserved fathers on the floor of my studio, pretending to be all manner of animals, singing silly songs, just to win a smile from their baby. It's wonderful to see. One day in the studio, I was trying to coax a smile from a baby, and her dad, who had come from work in his suit and tie, to watch the shoot, whispered in my ear, "She loves it if you pretend you're a 'choo-choo train'" . . . Oh, really?

A newborn baby would be happy to sleep in a shoe box if that's all that was available—it's what's wonderful about them. One of my assistants told me that when she was a newborn she slept in the bureau drawer for her first few weeks as her parents couldn't afford anything more. Obviously, it was not a problem.

We need to be honest with ourselves as women and share our experiences more. During my shoots, I always love to have mothers chatting and communicating—sharing their stories—because I know from my own experience, particularly with a first baby, that motherhood can be daunting. Motherhood is also about guilt, from the day they are first born and throughout our whole lives.

To be honest, even now I still occasionally question whether I have been a good mother—and my girls are in their twenties. I know they'd laugh at this notion, but it's true. In fact, one afternoon as I was writing this book, my oldest daughter, Stephanie, telephoned to see how I was progressing. I said, "At the moment I'm dispensing mothering advice," and

she laughingly said, "Are you sure you're qualified for that?"

Dance with your children, be silly with them, make mistakes and allow yourself to be human occasionally. They'll love you for it.

When I had my first baby, in 1984, I had very little experience with newborns. I was totally unprepared for the fact that I would be responsible for the care of a small human being twenty-four hours a day, and for the rest of my life. The quote "The decision to have a child is to know that your heart will forever walk around outside of your body" is so true and, also, a little unnerving.

It's normal to be concerned that you won't hear them cry in the middle of the night (you always do), normal to sometimes find the responsibility overwhelming, normal to crave adult company (we can't all do baby talk twenty-four hours a day), normal to be so tired you could go to sleep leaning against the wall, normal to feel inadequate at times. Working mothers are normal, as are non-working mothers. Mothers come in all shapes and forms, and we are all normal. Tiny babies are a lot tougher than we think, and generally everything works out—which doesn't mean we don't need to learn and grow as mothers.

But for all the advice in the world, just when you think you've really got it all together as a mother, you've always got your kids to bring you down to earth. Here's a little note, below, that I received from my daughter Kelly (who has always been a prolific note writer) when she was about six years old.

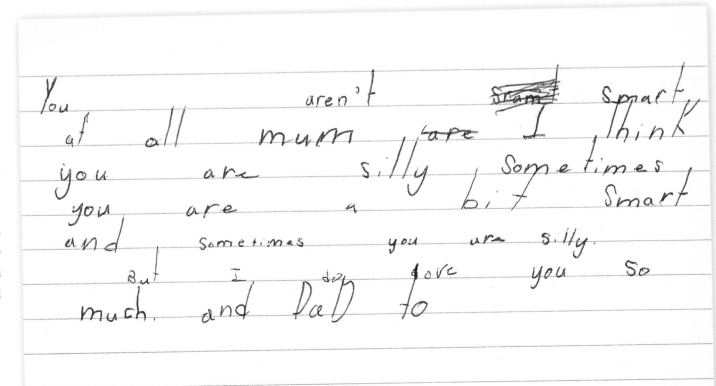

A pircot
Flowers
bunch
Danille

Room 10
Waimairi School
Tillman Ave
Christchurch 5

May 1998

Dear Anne Geddes

My family has just bought one of your
"books, Down in the Garden" and we love it. I
took the copy to school and showed the class.
My teacher, Mrs O'Connor liked the Earth Worms
page best! She thought it was incredible how
the Earth Worms stayed asleep. I've been
thinking do you remember a model named
Cassandra? She was my best friend at my old house
in Auckland. My mum wants to know what
the logs that the fairies stood on were made
of. My teacher gave her Mum a card with
Mother Nature on it and she wrote you never
know what you will find at the bottom of your
garden, so her mum went out to find what
Mrs O had hid. (Really she had not hid
anything) All she found was a dead RAT!
(Ha Ha)

Down in the Garden lover:
Caroline aged 11

water lily
Tyler

Dear An

takers, My
fans o
photograp
calender
year ag
is really

MY
my bab
Costume.
a picture
to copy
didn't.

I u
to you

m
take
I would
of
which
other
publishe
otos
nking

Kelley

sleepy santas 1993   baby bunny nest 2001

Q: What is the most number of babies you have had asleep in an image at the same time?

Over all my years of photographing sleeping babies, I have never consciously thought about creating a record for the greatest number of babies asleep in a single image. Some days, just one baby sleeping is a miracle! In 1993, when I was creating a Christmas image for the December page of my calendar, we had a number of newborns in the studio, dressed in some beautiful little Santa costumes.

I photographed them from my vantage point in the ceiling. As I began to photograph the first baby, then added the second and then the third, all of the babies in the studio seemed to go to sleep in unison. Eventually, all six were in the image, dozing away.

For many years this was the studio record, until the day I managed to capture thirteen newborns (above right), all asleep in the bunny suits which are a feature of my baby clothing range. Again, there was no

intention to have that many babies in the image, but as we kept adding them, more would be asleep, and eventually they were all included.

It is a lot easier to photograph sleeping babies who are fully clothed, because they require minimal handling. It also means that I don't have to worry about whether my hands are cold, which is often a problem when photographing naked newborns; sometimes I wear cotton gloves for this reason. Naked newborns are always wrapped in a blanket before they go to sleep, which then needs to be carefully removed without waking them before I photograph them.

Of course, in some of my other images where there are many sleeping babies, I have used computer generation; for example, the Woodland Fairies scene on pages 186–89, and Peggy's Worm Farm on pages 118–19. However, one little girl (see left) wrote to me after *Down in the Garden* was published, to ask how I managed to get all the worms asleep together at the same time.

Q: Why, as a photographer, have you branched out into baby clothes and other merchandise for babies?

Over the years I have had approaches from various clothing companies, to design and produce a range of baby clothing under my name. At first, I totally rejected the idea, as I just couldn't visualize the values contained within my imagery translating easily into clothing, a totally different product altogether. Gradually though, the idea of designing baby clothing became more and more intriguing to me, and of course, I always love the idea of being creative on multiple levels.

Even though some of the design proposals I had received were of a very high standard, to me there was something missing—they just didn't seem to capture a certain intangible charm and character. I always knew deep down that if it was going to work at all, and for me to be entirely happy and in control, I would have to design the range myself. Easier said than done, I must say. For somebody whose abilities in this area stretch to sewing on a button, it has been a very steep, but ultimately rewarding, learning curve.

I knew that my main challenge would be how to translate the character and energy of my photographic imagery onto fabric in some form, either directly or through illustration, and set about experimenting with endless combinations of both. Printing onto fabric, especially photographic imagery, is totally different from paper printing, and the interpretation of the imagery onto the clothing was my biggest obstacle. Adding to these difficulties was the fact that I was wanting to print onto cotton, a natural fiber, which is notoriously difficult when compared with printing on synthetic fabrics. I was also not, initally, a fan of photographs directly represented on fabric.

My initial concept for the clothing was to create a range that did not consist of costumes, which would have been too obvious and wasn't to my personal taste, but rather to reflect the subtle nuances that I see in babies and especially love about them. I also wanted to use soft, breathable cotton for the comfort of the babies, as I know from my many years of working closely with them that they feel most comfortable wearing breathable cotton.

Of course the styles needed to be cute, but also classic, hard-wearing, and easy to care for. I didn't want the styling to be too adult, as a lot of baby clothing can be, especially for boys. After all, babies have plenty of time to dress as adults for the rest of their lives.

In the clothing design process, it's been fun and inspiring to revisit some of my early imagery and interpret my feelings about babies in a totally different way. By working with a team of really talented people, who are able to take my ideas and translate them into other design forms, I'm exposing myself creatively to all sorts of new ideas.

From early beginnings and a basic range of items, as my confidence grew, I expanded on the baby clothing range, to also include other baby products such as soft baby wraps, tote bags, nursery and bed linen designs (including wallpapers). And we are adding new designs all the time as I grow more experienced in this new and exciting area of creativity.

I am very selective in terms of other merchandise that carries my name, simply because of my subject matter and my need to protect the babies in my imagery. For a while in the beginning, being so passionate about my work and seeing it quickly become so remarkably popular felt in a way as if it was being taken from me and placed into another realm. Sometimes, even today, I am startled by this concept, and surprised when I see it on the world stage, as it were. Sometimes I think to myself, "How did that happen? I started out being a photographer, and became Anne Geddes."

Q: What do you most enjoy about the photographic process— the concept, the creation, or the final product?

I enjoy every part of the process, and every shoot is different. As you can see from my stories in this book about various shoots, some involve quite complicated props, much preparation with long lead times; other images are created purely on the spur of the moment.

Prop making can be interesting and challenging in itself as, of course, safety elements are paramount, and the comfort of the babies my principal concern. However, regardless of whether the image is complicated or simple, each baby provides their own form of magic, and it's not until the babies are on the scene that the image comes together totally. Some of the best images for me are where something unexpected and spontaneous has happened, and I don't just mean a particular expression, but even perhaps simply the way a baby is lying, the energy they give out—every one of them is different in ways that can be so subtle, and yet unique.

Q: Why babies?

I absolutely adore babies, and everything they stand for. Not only do they represent our future, but to me they also represent absolute promise and potential, which should be the automatic right of every new human being from the moment of birth. Unfortunately, we all know that, for some babies, this isn't the case.

Babies to me represent hope. They are not only an incredibly beautiful and meaningful subject matter for me but, purely as an artist, I find them continually inspiring. They are all brand-new citizens of the world, with no notions of hatred, racial bias, political dogma, or religious intolerance. Since the moment I first picked up a camera, I never wanted to do anything else; it just felt completely natural to me. When I was beginning my career as a photographer, people would just assume that I was photographing babies because I was a woman. And other photographers would often say that they photographed babies themselves when they were just starting out, as if babies weren't a legitimate subject matter for an established artist. I was always puzzled by this attitude. Personally, I couldn't think of a more important, rewarding, or meaningful subject matter.

Q: Besides babies, are there other subjects you're passionate about and do you think you'll ever pursue them in your photographic work?

I always have my camera on hand, and I'm a passionate photographer of my family. I just love photography in general. But as I explain in my story about the *Miracle* project, for many years I have photographed flowers as a personal project and for relaxation. I don't see myself ever publishing them in their own right. The reason for this is that my flower photography involves no "performance pressure," so to speak, and I find that, generally speaking, flowers are far more cooperative than babies!

Q: Do you ever use modeling agencies to find babies?

No, I never use modeling agencies to find babies for my work for the sole reason that modeling agencies are where one goes to find professional models. I have used modeling agencies to find professional adult models, but personally I just don't feel that there is such a thing as a very young baby who is a professional model, or at least not to my knowledge. I once received a telephone call from a modeling agency when we were shooting in the United States to say they had a professional six-month-old model, which I thought absolutely hilarious.

I am often asked by parents whether I think they should register their young baby with a modeling agency and I always say that it is not something I would ever do. I have heard far too many stories about babies at commercial shoots, with photographers who are inexperienced or insensitive to the needs of very young children, and it's just not something I would like to put my child through. Now, with due respect to the many reputable modeling agencies that are operating and who care very much for the young models on their books, I am only referring to extremely young babies.

Q: Does photographing all these lovely babies make you long to have more children?

No, most definitely not. I have two daughters and two step-daughters, who have all grown into delightful and loving young women, and who have satisfied my desire to be a mother. They are all pictured below.

My job is, to me, the best in the world. I am in regular contact with beautiful babies, and then they go home to sleep in somebody else's house. I love to be around them, to cuddle them, and photograph them, but I also love my eight hours' sleep at night. Whenever I find myself thinking how wonderful it would be to have a baby in the house, I remember the 3 a.m. feeds and all of the hard work involved!

Q: Do you have any advice on photographing babies at home?

Please, don't try to replicate any of my imagery using your own baby at home. My images are created in a careful and professional environment, with a very experienced team of people, and some can be deceptive in terms of the degree of difficulty involved. However, in order to take great images of your babies and children at home, I can give you some basic guidelines which have worked with my own personal photography over the years.

Probably the best advice I can give is to have a camera handy at all times, so your children become used to being photographed and therefore more relaxed about the process. I have literally hundreds of photographs of our girls since they were first born, and I am still photographing them today even though they are now in their twenties. Our favorite gifts to each other these days are our own personal images.

From the moment a baby is born, and particularly in the first few months, they change so quickly. You might not think so at the time, but believe me, you'll soon forget how tiny they were as newborns. Of course, right at the time when you should be taking lots of photographs, your life has become more hectic than ever and photography probably takes a back seat to just getting through each day. Even though you are busy (a huge understatement if you

above: Kel's four favorite girls, all together in New York, Christmas, 1998.
(L–R) Stephanie, Renée, Michael (Renée's husband), Kelly, Trena, Murray (Trena's husband)

have a newborn in the house), it is so important to take as many photographs as you can. Particularly now that digital cameras are so affordable, it is inexpensive and fun to take as many photographs as you like, without the added expense of developing and printing of film. Here's what I'd recommend:

- Always have your camera on hand and your battery charged. If this sounds like obvious advice, sometimes I fall into the trap of a camera with a flat battery.

- Most of all, relax and have fun with your photography.

- Aim to keep your images as simple as possible. A simple image will invariably have the most impact.

- Be aware of your light source. The best times to photograph outside in natural light are early morning and late afternoon, when the light is softer and more flattering.

- Try to use elements of scale in the image, such as hands or everyday objects. Newborn babies grow very quickly and within even a few weeks can look quite different.

- Don't use flash unless it is absolutely necessary (and by that I mean that you are surrounded by complete darkness. Even then, try to go without). I virtually never use the flash on the camera that I carry with me everywhere. On-camera flash in the wrong hands can be a creative crime and some people are addicted. Last year, Kel and I were on vacation at a beach resort. Every afternoon I would sit on the beach to watch (and photograph) the sunset. Mother Nature puts on the most spectacular free shows every evening at this time; her color combinations are sometimes unexpected but always astounding—sunsets should be a "flash-free" environment. A young couple had just been married and were having wedding photographs taken at the water's edge. Behold, the beautiful young bride in a gorgeous flowing lace gown, her long wavy hair cascading around her shoulders, and the most subtle and flattering golden light was everywhere around them. (I feel a poem coming on . . .) The two wedding photographers they had hired for the occasion proceeded to pose them in every cheesy traditional wedding pose imaginable and every image was taken with full-on camera flash, which would have totally obliterated any semblance of the beautiful natural light. I was so tempted to just run down there and say, "Excuse me, but can I have five minutes with my camera . . ." but of course I didn't.

- Always be aware of what is happening in the background of your photograph when you are composing your image. The background is often overlooked, resulting in trees or poles growing out of heads—one of the most common problems associated with amateur photography. Try to keep your background as simple as possible.

- Avoid asking your children to pose for photographs, or that's exactly what they'll do. Just let them be themselves and you'll love the image even more.

- Don't be too precious with your camera. Buy one that's easy to use and relatively inexpensive, and let your children become familiar with photography by taking photographs of each other. It's far simpler now with the advent of digital photography—you can easily delete the less than successful ones.

- Most of us use digital cameras these days, so beware of deleting images too soon after you have shot them—give yourself a few days and then revisit them. If you still feel the same way, then go ahead and delete. But you may change your mind about something that you thought was insignificant at the time . . . I know I have.

- Try not to use cell phones to record your children's lives, or anyone's lives for that matter. Call me old-fashioned, but cell phones are for making telephone calls. The file sizes at the moment are far too small to reproduce or enlarge to any extent. Better to invest in a relatively inexpensive, small digital camera.

- When photographing babies and small children, try to get down to their eye level. It will help you to see from their perspective.

- The simple little everyday moments are the most precious of all. Don't just bring out the camera for special occasions.

- You can never, ever take too many photographs of your children. Try to surround yourself with small, framed images of family and friends. I have hundreds of images, on every surface of my home, and I love revisiting them constantly.

- Try to include yourself as often as possible in images with your children, because when they are older they'll also be very interested in how you looked at the time. This, of course, will leave you wide open to ridicule for your fashion sense when they were small. There is no protection against this; it's inevitable.

Barring unforeseen circumstances, your children will know you for longer as adults than they did as children, and vice versa. You only have one chance to record your lives together when they were small, and you will never regret any photograph that you take, whether it has significant artistic merit or not.

my personal world

This photograph, which is one of my all-time favorite images, is, I think, a great example of the need to have your camera on hand at all times.

It was taken in April 1999, when my daughters, Stephanie and Kelly, were in their early teens, as were their two close friends Morgan and Danica, who are with them in the image. It was summer and we were all vacationing together at a beach in the north of Australia. The four girls were all very excited to have pocket money to spend and decided that they would each invest in a set of fairy wings from a local craft store. My first thought when they all returned from the store was that this was possibly the last time they would ever want to invest their hard-earned money in this way, so I grabbed my camera just as they all rushed out into the garden to try out their wings. Priceless.

When I think of the thousands of photographs I have created since the day I opened my first tiny studio, by far the ones which have given me the most pleasure are my own private images of ordinary everyday family life.

To me, even after all these years, there is still something miraculous about the capture of a feeling and a moment that will last for the rest of time. When these images are of our loved ones, their meaning becomes even more cherished and powerful. The images on the following pages are not in any way special artistically, but they are so very special to me. They are a selection from some of my favorites that are displayed around our home, on every available surface. In the rare times when I find myself alone, I invariably start pottering around and looking at them all—they give me not just a quiet sense of how incredibly lucky I am to have such a wonderful family, but constantly refresh my memories of all of the little, ordinary moments that make up a lifetime. I suppose, by including them here, they are my way of inviting you into my personal world.

Left: (L–R) Kelly, Morgan, Stephanie, and Danica, Port Douglas, April 1999

Steph & Kelly, Fiji 1989

I'm 10!

Steph's 10th birthday invitation — April '

I Love all of you!

LOVE from Kelly

Kel + Kelly - beach - N.Z. 1990

Kelly's feet (2 yea

Steph, Kelly + I - Auckland 1995

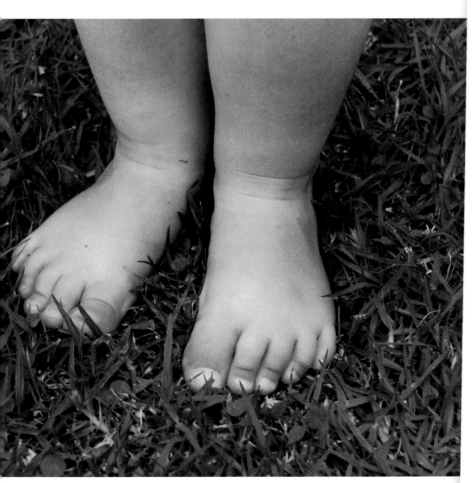

1988

Stephanie, Port Douglas - 1997

Steph's braces! 1997

Kelly having breakfast - Sydney - 1999

Steph reading, Port Douglas 1999

Baseball game - Xmas 2000

So typical! Fiji 1999

Steph + Kelly, Tutukaka, N.Z. '89

Steph + Kelly, Fiji 1989

Hopskotch on the beach, Port Douglas 2000

I Love both of you.

I are very nice perants.

1994

Kel + Steph - boating trip - Port D. 1997

Kelly in Peggy's front room, Sydney 1999

Kelly + Danica, Port D. 1999

Kelly, Port Douglas 2000

Kerry + I starting work on 'a Lab...

me in sunflower field, France 1996

Angel? Kelly

Rosee, Hunter Valley, March 2006

Cafe in Paris, Steph + Kelly, 1998

Sydney 1999

Kelly's favorite photo with Kel, Port D. 2000

Kel + I on vacation, Port Douglas 2000

Kelly watching Television New York, Christmas 1998

Steph + I, New York 1996

Kelly in the bath, France 1996

Steph running, Port Douglas 1997

Me, Lake Como, Sept 2006

Steph -17- before her School Ball, 2001

Little Poppy, smiling, N.Z. 1999

Kel, myself + Kerry — my 50th — Lake Como — Sept 2006

Kelly # braces — beautiful! 1999

Kelly reading Harry Potter, Port D. 2000

Steph & I, Arizona, 2002

Stephanie, Frankfurt, 2000

Renee + Steph, restaurant in Sydney 2005

Kelly + S, Auckland 2001

By the pool, Port D. 1997

Steph, Kelly, Kel + S — the day I received my
N.Z. Order of Merit, M.N.Z.M. Wellington NZ 2004

Kel & Trena, Xmas dinner, N.Y. 1998

Murray + Trena, N.Y. Xmas Day 1998

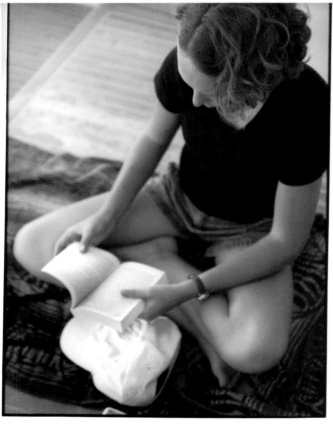

Steph on boat, P.D. 1997

Renee + S, Sydney 2005

Steph + Kerry, Sydney 2005

Steph + Kelly - cafe in Sydney the day before we left for Morocco 2005

Christmas Day, N.Y. (it's snowing outside!)
L-R: Steph, Renée, myself + Kelly, 2000

Stephanie — as I know her

Kelly, Central Park, N.Y. 2001

Steph + I, before her 21st birthday party, Sydn

2000

PHOTO BY SCOTT BRINEGAR

Opening day — our store at Downtown Disney, October 2005

April 2005

Kel + I, Sydney 2005

Steph + Kelly, Port Douglas 2000

Lake Como, Italy, Sept 2006

PHOTO BY FAY LOONEY

Kel + I on a rainy Dublin day, 1999

Kelly + I, Xmas 2005

"terrible two!" Kelly + Ruby, P.D. 2001

Steph, New York, 2002

Kelly, P.D. 2000

Kerry + I celebrating Thanksgiving, Auck 1999

Steph, Auckland 2002

my favorite photo of Kel♡ - Sydney 2005

Kelly, Port Douglas 2000

Stephanie -16- Auckland 2000

Two of my favorite images - "self portraits"
by my daughters, Stephanie + Kelly.

Self-portrait, by Stephanie Geddes, 2006

Self-portrait, by Kelly Geddes, 2004

a final word... I think of the child who rode her horse in the solitude of the Australian bush, discovering the beginnings of a lifetime of fantasy and dreaming, and of the girl with her many sisters, playing and arguing, and of the young woman who first innocently picked up a camera—and I know they all still live within me. I am made of my past, as everyone is. I have no memory and hardly any images of the baby I was, but I have become a recorder of images of babies from all over the world.

I have traveled in many countries with my work and I often observe babies and how people respond to them. Babies speak such a universal language—they transcend all of humanity's self-imposed boundaries of culture, class, religion, and nationality. Babies effortlessly communicate to everyone, and we would do well to reflect on the reason why. We might not have any words in common with the parents, but the smile or tears of a baby are understood everywhere. Even, or perhaps most of all, babies communicate when they are peacefully, silently asleep. Their rhythmic breathing, their air of utter trust, speak of a deep tranquility that could be ours if only we, too, could similarly let go of our anxieties.

At the beginning of our lives we are all more or less the same; we all originate with the same potential. Some are born in more fortunate circumstances, but each baby contains a new and unbroken spirit. The underlying message through my work is the absolute promise of every newborn to reach their full potential. As a photographer, I am able to see babies as not only aesthetically appealing and incredibly beautiful, but, in fact, to see them as a compelling and persuasive symbol of human hope and the transforming power of unconditional love.

As Mother Teresa once said, "We can do no great things, only small things with great love."

If my images of babies are *love made visible,* then I can ask for nothing more.

Anne

the geddes philanthropic trust

The mission of the Geddes Philanthropic Trust is threefold:

- To raise worldwide awareness regarding issues of the prevention of child abuse and neglect.

- To provide funds to selected institutions or groups that can make a direct difference.

- To fund selected fellowships around the world, as incentive for doctors and other medical professionals to train and continue to work in this very important area.

A major reason why many child abuse cases go undetected is because normal, everyday good people have trouble believing that a child could possibly be suffering in this way. Or, they know it is happening, but feel it is not their place to become involved. According to a recent survey conducted in the United States by Childhelp, although the majority of people polled believe that everyone should play a role in stopping child abuse, many people also admit to witnessing child abuse and doing nothing about it.

The reasons for not reporting abuse very often include not knowing where to call to find help, or misconceptions regarding what will happen once a report of known or suspected abuse is made to the police or a child protective services agency. Many people believe, incorrectly, that by law, abused children must be removed from their homes immediately. In fact, this is the least likely outcome. Child abuse can be reported anonymously, and in most cases, the person reported for abuse is not entitled to know who made the report.

As a very positive trend, in numerous countries around the world, specialized child abuse hotlines are now being established, which are totally dedicated to the prevention of child abuse. Many of these hotlines are listed on our Anne Geddes official Web site, and are being continually updated. As an example, in the United States the Childhelp National Child Abuse Hotline, 1-800-4-A-CHILD, has received close to three and a half million calls since its inception twenty-five years ago, offering a lifeline to countless victims, families, and those who suffer from the trauma of abuse.

These calls come from children at risk of abuse, distressed parents seeking crisis intervention, and concerned individuals who suspect that child abuse may be occurring.

In addition to hotlines, many groups and charities specifically working in the area of the prevention of child abuse, struggle to exist with little or no government funding. They are totally reliant upon support from generous contributions of concerned organizations, foundations and individuals. The Geddes Philanthropic Trust has made a commitment to regular ongoing funding to a number of organizations around the world that are run by committed, dedicated people, many of whom freely donate their time in an endeavor to make a difference.

Long may these groups continue to be a part of the solution, for as the saying goes, "If you are not part of the solution, then you are part of the problem."

The Geddes Fellowship program was established alongside the trust's regular ongoing commitments, in 1998. The first fellowship was awarded at the children's hospital at Westmead, in Sydney. In principle, the Geddes Philanthropic Trust funds a salary (over individual twelve-month periods) for a nominated doctor or medical professional to train and conduct specific research within the area of the prevention of child abuse and neglect. Essentially, the fund was initiated as an incentive for people within the medical profession to make a conscious choice to specialize in this very important area.

The success of the inaugural Geddes Fellowship in Sydney provided encouragement for us to investigate the possibility of expanding the program to other countries. A particular requirement for the establishment of each additional fellowship is the instigation of an active exchange program between the various institutions. This exchange initiative is funded by the trust in the form of travel and accommodation expenses, and aims to encourage communication and the sharing of ideas and vital information between teams of specialists from other countries and cultures.

PHOTO BY GARY SPECTOR

In 2006, the trust established the second Geddes Fellowship at the Children's Hospital of Orange County (CHOC) in the United States. Shortly afterward, a third fellowship was established in the multi-agency center Puawaitahi, at the Starship Hospital in Auckland, New Zealand. The ongoing development of this Fellowship program around the world will be one of the trust's main goals for the future.

The Geddes Philanthropic Trust has to date donated (in different currencies around the world) the equivalent of US$4 million to the charities and institutions listed below, which are all working in the area of the prevention of child abuse and neglect.

USA
- The Henry Kempe Centre
- Childhelp®
- Children's Hospital of Orange County (CHOC) (fellowship)
- A donation of clothing from the Anne Geddes baby clothing range, for Hurricane Katrina relief, made through the organization Feed the Children.
- The Family Support Center of Southwestern Utah

ASIA
- Donation to UNICEF for the 2004 Asian Tsunami relief fund, to care for children affected.

UNITED KINGDOM
- National Society for the Prevention of Cruelty to Children (NSPCC)

AUSTRALIA
- National Association for the Prevention of Child Abuse and Neglect (NAPCAN)
- The children's hospital at Westmead, Sydney (fellowship)

NEW ZEALAND
- Doctors for Sexual Abuse Care (DSAC)
- Puawaitahi multi-agency center, Starship Hospital, Auckland (fellowship)

thank you

When I first sat down in front of a blank computer screen to begin writing this book, I found the prospect terrifying. Initially, I had assumed that the best approach would be to employ a ghost writer and simply talk my way through my life (possibly into some sort of recording device), believing that I could speak more effectively purely through my imagery. But I soon realized that some of my stories were so personal, they really needed to come directly from me. And I knew that I needed help, in the form of writing assistance and moral support.

In early 2006, I nervously telephoned my dearest friend, Kerry Wapshott, with whom I have corresponded daily for the past ten years, to ask her whether she would accompany me on my year-long writing journey—thankfully she said yes. She has sat with me, through many hours of soul-searching and general chatter about all aspects of my life, always managing to look interested, steer me in the right direction, be sympathetic at the right times, and reassure me that I was on track. Before we began working together, we spoke at length about our mutual concerns that our friendship could be jeopardized by taking on this project, and working so closely over such a long period. Fortunately, it has only made it richer.

And then, of course, there is my darling husband, Kel. He, too, has borne the brunt of many hours of heartfelt and emotional conversations, and has provided me with the quiet courage to tell my story truthfully and yet with grace. We have been together constantly for the past twenty-seven years, and never seem to run out of things to say, or tire of each other's company. Our girls recently said, "What on earth do you talk about when you are out for dinner together, after all this time?" Lots of things! Without your love, support, and encouragement (not to mention great cooking skills), I would never be where I am today. Thank you so much.

Left: Kerry and me, on my 50th-birthday trip to Italy, September 2006

credits

Writing Associate
Kerry Wapshott

Writing Mentor and Advisor
Patti Miller/Life Stories Workshop

Copy Editor
Shelley Kenigsberg

Design
Lisa Waldren

Mac Operator
Terry Small

Production/Printing and Color Management
Relda Frogley

Digital Systems Supervisor
Relda Frogley

Anne's Studio Team
Natalie Torrens, Dawn McGowan

Photographic Assistant
Rebecca Swan

Black-and-White Printing
Marie Shannon, Rebecca Swan

Photoshop/Retouching Artist
Joanne Gray

Special thanks
Epson/Dan Steinhardt

Additional Photography
Nick Tresidder

Copublishing
Anne Geddes Publishing
Kevin Chapman, Kent Bowyer-Sidwell,
Gerry Matthee, Karen McMillan

Produced by
Kel Geddes

**The rest of the Geddes Group and
Kel Geddes Management team globally**
Terry McGrath (CEO)
Gary Brown (COO)

(in alphabetical order)
Carl Anderson, Stephanie Baker,
Richard Barclay, Nicki Brown,
Katherine Calvert, Rebecca Douglas,
Jane Gadd, Bryan Harris, Tonya Jenne,
Betty Leiataua, Peter Maney,
Warren Mattmann, Elspeth McDonald,
Dervla McKenna, Kirsten Mitchell,
Angela Mobberley, Matt Morrison,
Estelle Murray, Alison Newton,
Carla Pawley, Renée Polomski,
Vanessa Read, Claire Robertson,
Victor Shi, Melanie Strand, Ron Talley,
Claire Tegg, Natasha Webb, Sue Wright

- Quotation page 9: *"They can cut all the flowers, but they can't stop the spring"* – Pablo Neruda.

- Quotation page 16 & 17: *"There is always one moment in childhood when the door opens and lets the future in"* – Graham Greene.

- Quotation page 36: *"The more you rely on good tools, the more boring your sculpture will be"* – Auguste Renoir.

- Quotation page 46: *"Babies are always more trouble than you thought – and more wonderful"* – Charles Osgood.

- Quotation page 62: *"There are two things in life for which we are never truly prepared – twins"* – Josh Billings.

- Quotation page 72: *"All that is necessary for evil to triumph is for good men to do nothing"* – Edmund Burke.

- Quotation page 106: *"Through the eyes of a child, all wonderful things seem possible"* – Author Unknown.

- Quotation page 118: *"Of all animals, few have contributed so much to the development of the world, as we know it, as earthworms"* – Charles Darwin.

- Quotation page 289: *"The decision to have a child is to know that your heart will forever walk around outside of your body"* – Katharine Hadley.

- Quotation page 314: *"We can do no great things, only small things with great love"* – Mother Teresa.

- Quotation page 314: *"... love made visible"* – Kahlil Gibran (Syrian poet, novelist, essayist and artist, 1883–1931).

- Quotation page 316: *"If you are not part of the solution, then you are part of the problem"* – Author Unknown.

www.annegeddes.com

© 2007 Anne Geddes

The right of Anne Geddes to be identified as the Author of the Work has been asserted by her in accordance with the Copyright, Designs and Patents Act 1988

First published in 2007 by Anne Geddes Publishing (a division of Hachette Livre NZ Ltd), 4 Whetu Place, Mairangi Bay, Auckland, New Zealand

This edition published in 2007 by Andrews McMeel Publishing, LLC, an Andrews McMeel Universal company, 4520 Main Street, Kansas City, Missouri 64111.

Designed by Lisa Waldren
Produced by Kel Geddes
Printed in China by 1010 Printing International Limited, Hong Kong

ISBN-13: 978-0-7407-6562-9

ISBN-10: 0-7407-6562-0

www.andrewsmcmeel.com